Contents

"Innovation distinguishes between a leader and a follower."

— Steve Jobs

1. Understanding the Terrain: Charting the Course through the Linux Kernel Ecosystem

In the ever-evolving landscape of technology, the Linux kernel stands as a towering edifice that has revolutionized the way we think about computing. This book, "Kernel Kong's Climb: Maneuvering the Linux Kernel Ecosystem," is a journey through this formidable yet intricate domain. Designed for both seasoned professionals and eager learners, it demystifies the complexities of the Linux kernel by providing a structured path to understanding, navigating, and ultimately mastering this pivotal component of the open-source movement.

As the backbone of countless systems ranging from smartphones to supercomputers, the Linux kernel's importance cannot be overstated. Yet, for many, its intricacies remain daunting. This book aims to illuminate these complexities by exploring the architecture, development processes, and the vast ecosystem that surrounds it. Through an analytical yet accessible approach, we will uncover the historical context, the core technical foundations, and the modern innovations driving this open-source powerhouse.

Join us on this expedition as we climb the towering structure of the Linux kernel, step by step, demystifying crucial concepts, exploring best practices, and unveiling the potential that lies within. Embark with an open mind and a readiness to transform your understanding of the technology that shapes our digital world.

2. The Foundation of Linux: A Historical Perspective

2.1. Origins and Evolution of the Linux Kernel

The Linux kernel owes its inception to the convergence of several factors that blended to create a robust open-source operating system, ultimately transforming the technological landscape. The narrative begins in 1991 when Linus Torvalds, a Finnish computer science student, sought to create a free alternative to the MINIX operating system, which was widely used in academic settings. Frustrated with MINIX's limitations, Torvalds began developing the kernel from scratch, leveraging his academic background and passion for programming.

As Torvalds wrote and released the very first version of the Linux kernel, labeled '0.01', he did so under the GNU General Public License (GPL), which allowed users to freely view, modify, and distribute the code. This critical choice set the stage for the collaborative development model that would come to characterize the Linux ecosystem. Torvalds's candid communication about his project and his willingness to invite contributions sparked interest among programmers worldwide.

The early years of the Linux kernel were marked by a rapidly growing community of developers and enthusiasts who played a vital role in its evolution. This collaborative spirit, cultivated through online forums and mailing lists, led to significant improvements in code quality, feature enhancements, and performance optimizations. With Torvalds at the helm, the kernel evolved through various versions, each often surpassing its predecessor in functionality and stability. The introduction of version 1.0 in 1994 marked a pivotal moment, signaling that Linux had matured enough to be considered a viable alternative to proprietary operating systems.

As Linux grew in popularity, it began to attract attention from corporate entities willing to invest resources into its development. Companies such as Red Hat, SuSE, and later IBM recognized the potential of Linux as a foundation for enterprise solutions, further driving its evolution through investment in infrastructure and human resources. This paradigm shift also influenced the direction of kernel development, necessitating better scalability, security, and support for a wider array of hardware platforms.

Concurrent with these developments was the rise of the open-source movement. The philosophy behind open-source software, championed by advocates like Richard Stallman, emphasized collaboration, transparency, and freedom from vendor lock-in. The Linux kernel became emblematic of this movement, as it demonstrated how collective contributions could yield a powerful, cohesive, and flexible system that rivaled proprietary offerings. The success of Linux underscored the idea that software development could be a communal endeavor rather than solely the domain of large corporations.

Throughout its evolution, the Linux kernel has undergone numerous architectural transformations, both to improve performance and to integrate emerging technologies. This adaptability has allowed it to remain relevant amid evolving hardware capabilities and software requirements. Features such as modularity, where components of the kernel can be loaded and unloaded dynamically, enabled the system to remain lean and efficient, adapting to the specific needs of different environments—from embedded systems to high-performance computing setups.

Moreover, the Linux kernel has been influenced by its need to support an increasingly diverse array of devices and applications. From the early days of simple personal computers, it has expanded its reach to encompass everything from smartphones and tablets to network routers and mainframe computers. This evolution was driven by the community's responsiveness to the demands of users and developers alike, all pushing for enhancements to support the broadening use cases of Linux.

The role of maintainers also emerged as a critical aspect of the evolution of the Linux kernel. A hierarchical structure developed, with

Torvalds as the ultimate authority overseeing the entire project, while a cadre of maintainers managed their respective subsystems. With this decentralized approach, the kernel could evolve more rapidly, as different experts focused on specific areas of development, introducing innovations while ensuring stability.

Beyond technical evolution, the underlying culture of Linux development has also played a significant role in its rise. The formation of conferences, such as LinuxCon, and the establishment of various working groups within the Linux Foundation have created spaces for developers to exchange ideas, promote inclusivity, and share best practices. This vibrant community culture promotes not just technical excellence, but also mentorship, fostering the next generation of developers who carry the torch of Linux into the future.

As we look to the future, it is clear that the Linux kernel will continue its trajectory of innovation. The principles of collective development and open-source collaboration that defined its origins will remain central to its evolution. The kernel stands poised to integrate emerging technologies, such as artificial intelligence, machine learning, and enhanced networking capabilities, solidifying its place at the core of the computing ecosystem for years to come.

This intricate tapestry of history, community, and technical growth gives rise to the rich ecosystem surrounding the Linux kernel. Understanding its origins allows us to appreciate its current state and offers insight into the future developments that await as we navigate the vast landscape of this open-source marvel.

2.2. Key Visionaries and Developers

The landscape of Linux kernel development is rich with the contributions of various visionaries and developers who have shaped its past, present, and future. This subchapter aims to shed light on some of the key figures whose ingenuity, tenacity, and collaboration have propelled the Linux kernel into becoming a cornerstone of modern computing.

Linus Torvalds, the figurehead behind the Linux kernel, initiated this journey in 1991. He not only penned the first lines of code but also established a collaborative model that would define the future of software development. Torvalds's leadership style, characterized by open communication and a hands-on approach to code review, set a tone that encouraged contributions from programmers across the globe. His commitment to meritocracy—where good ideas and code were prioritized over hierarchy—was fundamental in fostering a vibrant, engaged community.

Prominent figures have emerged alongside Torvalds, each bringing unique perspectives and innovations to the project. One such developer is Andrew Morton, who has played a pivotal role in the kernel development community for many years. Initially the maintainer of the Linux kernel's "-mm" series, Morton was instrumental in integrating many experimental features and patch sets into the mainline tree. His sharp focus on performance improvements and debugging techniques has led to significant advancements in the kernel, contributing to its scalability and efficiency.

Another significant contributor is Greg Kroah-Hartman, who has become synonymous with Linux kernel development, particularly in the realm of device drivers and stable kernel releases. As the lead maintainer of the stable branch of the Linux kernel, Kroah-Hartman has been pivotal in ensuring that the kernel remains reliable for users. His advocacy for the inclusion of robust testing processes prior to releasing stable versions exemplifies his dedication to quality and security—principles that are essential given the widespread usage of Linux in critical applications.

On the international stage, numerous developers from diverse backgrounds have lent their expertise to the kernel project. One such notable figure is Ingo Molnar, known for his work on real-time processing and scheduler improvements in the Linux kernel. Molnar's contributions not only advanced the performance of the kernel in handling time-sensitive tasks but also expanded Linux's capabilities in environments requiring high precision, such as telecommunications and industrial automation.

Furthermore, the contributions of developers like Sarah Sharp have significantly amplified the focus on inclusivity and diversity within the kernel community. Sharp has been a vocal advocate for improving the culture surrounding Linux kernel development, increasing awareness of the importance of a welcoming environment, particularly for underrepresented groups in tech. Her efforts, including the establishment of outreach programs and speaking engagements, have fostered a more inclusive community, ensuring diverse voices contribute to the ongoing evolution of the kernel.

The Linux kernel not only benefits from the expertise of individuals but also draws upon the collective strength of numerous organizations. Companies like Red Hat and Intel have dedicated resources and personnel towards advancing the kernel. This collaboration has enabled the integration of features that cater specifically to enterprise needs and innovations around hardware optimization. For instance, enhancements for multi-core processing systems have emerged as a direct result of collaboration between kernel developers and hardware manufacturers, ensuring that Linux remains competitive in the face of rapid technological advancement.

In parallel, the contributions from the broader open-source community have enriched the kernel's development. Numerous volunteer developers have their own areas of expertise, contributing to everything from security improve to support for new hardware. They enable Linux to remain a cutting-edge choice among operating systems, driven by a community that records contributions through patch submissions, reviews, and discussions on mailing lists.

Educational initiatives, such as the Linux Foundation's training and certification programs, have also played a pivotal role in cultivating new talent and nurturing the next generation of developers. These educational pathways empower individuals to engage with the kernel from the ground up, ensuring the continuity of knowledge and skill development.

As we examine the journey of these visionary individuals and the communities that form around the Linux kernel, it becomes clear that the kernel is much more than a collection of code; it is a living ecosystem fueled by collaboration, passion, and innovation. The continued evolution of the kernel depends not only on the technical contributions of skilled developers but also on fostering an inclusive, dynamic environment where new ideas and improvements can flourish.

In essence, "Key Visionaries and Developers" is not simply a recount of individuals; instead, it encapsulates the collaborative spirit that embodies the Linux kernel's ethos. As we advance through the complexities of Linux, we must acknowledge that behind every feature and enhancement is a dedicated group of individuals motivated by the principles of transparency and community empowerment, ensuring that the Linux kernel remains a formidable force in the landscape of technology.

2.3. Milestones in Kernel Development

In the progression of the Linux kernel, several milestones stand as testaments to its growth, resilience, and enduring influence in the computing world. These milestones are not merely chronological markers; rather, they reflect major shifts in development philosophy, features, adoption, and the surrounding ecosystem that have shaped the Linux kernel into the powerhouse it is today.

The journey of the Linux kernel officially began in 1991 when Linus Torvalds released the first version, '0.01'. This initial release targeted a niche audience of hobbyists and developers dissatisfied with existing operating systems. However, it was the version 1.0, launched in 1994, that signified a major turning point. This version included a more stable and complete feature set, marking Linux's evolution from a personal project to a viable alternative for users needing a reliable operating system. As the first milestone, version 1.0 laid the groundwork for the community-centric model that would define Linux development.

In rapid succession, various enhancements began to accumulate. By 1996, version 2.0 made its debut, introducing support for multi-processor systems, which expanded the kernel's potential significantly. This version showed a clear acknowledgment of the growing demand for performance and scalability and presented new architectural designs aimed at catering to diverse hardware environments. Each new version served as a testament to the kernel's increasingly sophisticated architecture. The introduction of the Modular Kernel and Loadable Kernel Modules further underscored the Linux kernel's flexibility, allowing for real-time performance improvements and more efficient resource allocation.

The late 1990s and early 2000s saw the kernel community grow exponentially, driven by the rise of the open-source movement. The release of the 2.4 version in 1999 represented a major stride in not only code quality and performance but also in hardware support, including USB devices. The 2.4 series solidly established Linux in the server market, making it a compelling choice for enterprises looking for stable, performance-oriented solutions.

In parallel, the acceptance of Linux in corporate environments was solidified by significant industry support. Companies such as Red Hat and SuSE began professionalizing Linux with robust distributions, contributing back to the kernel development process, and further entwining the growth of the kernel with enterprise needs. The establishment of formalized testing processes and certifications underscored a commitment to quality and reliability that resonates strongly within the community today. Here, a pivotal milestone was reached with the creation of the Linux Foundation in 2000, which provided a collaborative space for development and funding.

The transition into the 2000s continued with the release of Version 2.6 in 2003, a monumental version that brought enhancements in performance, scalability, and security features. This release marked a significant leap in adoption rates as it addressed the professional demands of a variety of sectors, enabling Linux to be implemented not just in personal computers but across data centers and embedded systems. The 2.6 kernel included improved support for large memory systems, advanced filesystems, and new security mechanisms (such as SELinux), which laid the foundation for Linux's reign in both enterprise and cloud environments.

Milestones continued with each subsequent version of the kernel. The introduction of 3.x in 2011 and later 4.x and 5.x series showcased continuous innovations in areas such as power management, virtualization, and networking capabilities. For example, the work done on Containers and cgroups (control groups) in version 3.0 revolutionized how applications were deployed and managed, enabling resource isolation and limiting resource consumption effectively. This response to emerging needs in virtualization set the stage for the widespread popularity of container platforms like Docker and Kubernetes, which subsequently became critical components in modern application development cycles.

As the Linux kernel climbed into its 5.x series in 2019, it showcased efforts beyond simply accommodating new hardware features; it also reflected a robust strategy aimed at improving developer experience and safety. Features such as memory management enhancements, built-in support for new hardware architectures (such as RISC-V), and the introduction of BPF (Berkeley Packet Filter) for networking and security demonstrate the kernel's adaptive nature.

Another critical evolution in kernel development was the introduction of the "long-term support" (LTS) strategy, ensuring that certain versions of the kernel would receive dedicated maintenance for extended periods. This decision recognized the necessity for stability within enterprise environments, acknowledging that while innovation is essential, many users require a reliable platform that minimizes disruption due to updates or changes.

The pivotal role of community and innovation around the Linux kernel cannot be understated when considering these milestones. The evolution of patch submission processes, the Linux kernel mailing lists, and the formalized roles of maintainers has created a collective structure that facilitates contributions from both individuals and corporations alike. The emergence of collaborative development practices has democratized contributions, allowing developers from diverse backgrounds to engage actively in kernel evolution. In an important milestone, during 2018, Helen Beal, among others, emphasized how this collaborative structure not only encourages diversity of thought but also pushes back against technical debt, a critical aspect of maintaining such a vast codebase.

In summary, the milestones in kernel development reflect much more than simple version upgrades; they encapsulate a collective journey characterized by community-driven innovation, gradual adaptation to technological advancements, and proactive engagement with industry needs. Each milestone represents a stepping stone in the evolution of an ecosystem that is ever-expanding, adaptable, and above all, resilient. As we look forward, the evolution of the Linux kernel continues to promise exciting developments that will further solidify its relevance in the global technology landscape. This rich tapestry of milestones serves not only as historical markers but as guiding points for the future challenges and innovations that lie ahead.

2.4. Open Source Movement and its Impact

The open source movement stands as a revolutionary force in the landscape of software development, and its impact is profoundly embodied in the evolution and growth of the Linux kernel. This kernel not only serves as the foundation for thousands of systems worldwide but also acts as a beacon for principles that define open source: collaboration, transparency, and community-led development.

At its core, the open-source movement emerged from a growing discontent with proprietary software models, which often placed restrictions on users, limiting their ability to modify, share, and build upon existing code. The movement began gaining traction in the

1980s, spearheaded by figures like Richard Stallman, who championed the idea that software should be freely available for anyone to use and improve. The Free Software Foundation was established in 1985 to promote the philosophy of free software, emphasizing the ethical dimensions of sharing and collaboration.

The unique birth of the Linux kernel is intrinsically linked to this open source ethos. Linus Torvalds' decision to release the initial version of the Linux kernel under the GNU General Public License (GPL) in 1991 initiated a new form of software development that invited contributors from around the world to take part in a shared project. This decision was monumental, as it reinforced the belief that the collective contributions of passionate individuals could result in a product that rivals proprietary software in terms of quality, functionality, and performance.

As Linux began to gain momentum, it became a central element of the burgeoning open-source community. The kernel's rapid development was fueled by programmers across the globe, who shared a mutual interest in enhancing its functionality and stability. Online forums and mailing lists became crucial conduits for communication, allowing developers to share codes, propose changes, and discuss improvements, thereby creating a vibrant ecosystem where collaboration thrived. This model fundamentally shifted the cultural norms around software development, fostering an environment where merit, innovation, and shared goals were prioritized over corporate hierarchy.

The impact of the open-source movement on the Linux kernel has been multi-dimensional. Firstly, it has enriched the kernel's feature set substantially. High-quality contributions from skilled developers allowed the kernel to evolve quickly to meet changing technology landscapes and demands. This adaptability was exemplified in its capacity to support a wide range of devices—from embedded systems and smartphones to enterprise-level servers—and respond to emerging needs like cloud computing and containerization technologies.

Moreover, the communal approach offered by open-source sparked a wave of educational initiatives, nurturing the next generation of programmers and software engineers. Organizations like the Linux Foundation have invested in training and certification programs, equipping individuals with the skills required to engage to the fullest with kernel development. This focus on education ensured that the Linux kernel would not only benefit from immediate contributions but also maintain a pipeline of enthusiastic new developers ready to push the envelope of what is possible.

Importantly, the impact of the open-source movement also resonates beyond technical boundaries; it encompasses a cultural transformation within the software industry. The Linux kernel community has continuously evolved to emphasize values of inclusivity, diversity, and collaboration. Efforts to create space for underrepresented voices have been evident through outreach programs, conferences, and advocacy, helping to transition the environment from a traditional perspective of exclusivity to a more comprehensive approach where all are welcomed to contribute.

Another significant impact of the open-source movement is seen in the establishment of a sustainable ecosystem. Corporations have recognized the tremendous value embedded in the open-source philosophy and have actively participated, often contributing code back to the Linux kernel and supporting its ongoing maintenance. The relationship between community-driven development and industry engagement has proven mutually beneficial, as companies rely on the kernel for their technology solutions, while the community benefits from the resources and infrastructure provided by corporate sponsors.

Security is yet another area profoundly shaped by the open-source ethos. The transparent nature of open-source software means that vulnerabilities can be identified and rectified in real-time, allowing for quick response to potential issues. This contrasts sharply with proprietary models, where the time-lag between identifying and patching vulnerabilities can be considerable. The collaborative vigilance of the community surrounding the Linux kernel has cultivated an ecosystem responsive to security threats—an approach that continues to inspire best practices in software security paradigms globally.

The interplay between the Linux kernel and the open-source movement continues to evolve, particularly in the face of emerging technologies such as artificial intelligence, blockchain, and beyond. The kernel's adaptability and the collaborative spirit fostered by its open-source nature make it well-equipped to integrate with these technologies, further solidifying its place at the heart of modern computing.

As we reflect on the trajectory of the Linux kernel within the open-source movement, it is clear that its impact is indelible. The kernel is not only a technical achievement but also a case study in the possibilities that arise when people unite to share knowledge, skills, and passion for technology. Looking ahead, the continuous interplay between the Linux kernel and the open-source movement promises to profoundly shape the future of technology, underpinning innovation and instilling a sense of community-driven progress that will undoubtedly carry on for generations to come.

2.5. Challenges and Triumphs in Early Days

In the early days of Linux kernel development, a complex interplay of challenges and victories defined the nascent project's trajectory. Just as any monumental success is underpinned by hurdles, the journey to establish the Linux kernel was riddled with both technical obstacles and structural evolving dynamics that would profoundly shape its future.

At the outset, Linus Torvalds faced the daunting task of building a functional operating system from the ground up. The primary challenge stemmed from the very nature of the project: it was ambitious to create a free and open alternative to established systems like UNIX. Torvalds sought to develop a kernel that would be accessible to a community of developers rather than being a solitary endeavor; however, this openness also invited critique and input from developers with diverse motivations and varying levels of expertise. This situation required Torvalds to navigate the delicate balance of incorporating suggestions while maintaining a coherent vision.

Many early contributions arrived as a mixed bag of code quality and ideas. Torvalds quickly learned the importance of a rigorous review process, emphasizing quality over quantity to establish a stable codebase. He developed a decentralized model of contribution that would enable more skilled developers to take ownership of specific code areas, thus enhancing overall quality. This was a critical turning point; embracing collaboration positioned the kernel not just as a Linus Torvalds project, but as a community-centric collective that could adapt to the needs of its users more effectively.

As development progressed, the kernel faced technological hurdles, primarily related to hardware compatibility. In the early 1990s, the rapidly evolving hardware landscape presented a challenge; the kernel had to evolve to support a myriad of devices. The lack of a unified hardware standard necessitated intense research and development efforts to ensure the kernel remained adaptable. Through rapidly iterating kernel versions, the community learned to troubleshoot driver issues and compatibility problems collaboratively, demonstrating a resolve that would become a hallmark of the Linux community.

Moreover, the need for documentation arose as the community expanded. Early developers recognized the importance of sharing knowledge and clarifying the kernel's architecture to new contributors. This need fueled the creation of mailing lists and online forums, paving the way for collaborative problem-solving and shared learning. An essential milestone was the establishment of clear guidelines and documentation for contributing to the kernel, addressing the confusion surrounding the patch submission process and setting expectations for code reviews.

In parallel, the lack of resources posed a challenge during the kernel's formative years. Initially, contributions came through individuals motivated by a shared belief in free software rather than financial incentives. This model required developers to invest extensive volunteer hours, often juggling full-time jobs alongside their passion projects. Yet, this barrier also became a crucible for innovation, as developers brought real-world experiences from their professional work environments into their kernel contributions. Many contributors even formed relationships for collaborative projects that led to more formalized roles and eventual corporate support.

The evolution of the open-source movement played a pivotal role in transforming these challenges into triumphs. As the community grew, a wave of corporate backing emerged from companies recognizing Linux's potential. Early adopters, such as Red Hat and SUSE, began contributing code while simultaneously building commercial products on top of the kernel. This symbiotic relationship bolstered the developer community, providing much-needed resources for infrastructure and support. The legitimacy garnered by corporate sponsorship empowered the kernel to expand its reach into commercial spheres, which further energized the community.

Despite these promising developments, the journey was not without its controversies. The Linux community found itself divided occasionally over foundational principles—particularly the definitions of 'free software' and 'open source.' Disputes often arose around the direction the kernel should take in response to emerging technologies. Issues centered on the inclusion of proprietary drivers or encroachments by corporate interests highlighted the delicate nature of balancing community values with commercial viability.

Even amidst these disagreements, the kernel's growth continued unabated. Each new release not only introduced increased stability and performance but also reflected communal resilience. Version milestones became more than mere updates; they symbolized the collaborative spirit and the convergence of varied talents focusing on a common goal.

The early days of the Linux kernel laid a remarkable foundation for what would turn into an expansive journey across the tech landscape. The challenges of coding quality and community consensus, technical compatibility issues, and resource limitations transformed into victories signaled through enhanced collaboration, structured contribution models, and corporate partnerships. This transformative journey forged a vibrant ecosystem around the Linux kernel that became emblematic of what open-source software could achieve.

Today, as we look back at the trials and triumphs of the early days, it becomes evident that the very struggles shaped not only the Linux kernel but also the open-source movement at large. The kernel's ascent was a testament to the power of community, a successful example of how collective efforts can lead to revolutionary technological advances while advocating for principles of freedom and collaboration that underpin the ethos of open-source development. The lessons learned during these formative years continue to resonate today, reminding us of the extraordinary potential of communal innovation in driving technological evolution.

3. Architectural Anatomy: Understanding the Linux Kernel Structure

3.1. The Core Components

The Linux kernel, at its core, is composed of various integral components that work cohesively to provide a robust and flexible operating environment. Understanding these core components is essential for anyone aiming to negotiate the intricacies of the kernel. The architecture of the Linux kernel is designed to optimize performance, enhance security, and seamlessly manage hardware resources while supporting a wide array of applications.

One of the primary elements of the Linux kernel is the process scheduler, responsible for managing the execution of processes throughout the system. The scheduler's role is pivotal as it determines the order and duration each process runs on CPU cores, which directly affects system performance and responsiveness. Using complex algorithms like Completely Fair Scheduler (CFS), the kernel aims to distribute CPU time among all running processes fairly, thus preventing any single process from monopolizing resources. The scheduler's design also accommodates real-time prioritization, allowing time-sensitive processes to be executed without delay, which is crucial for applications such as video rendering and industrial automation.

Memory management is another critical component of the kernel that allows efficient utilization of the system's RAM. The Linux kernel employs a virtual memory architecture that allows processes to operate in their own address space, providing isolation and security between different applications. The kernel utilizes paging, where memory is divided into equal-sized blocks or pages, facilitating efficient swapping of data between RAM and storage devices. This process not only ensures optimal memory allocation but also mitigates the impact of memory fragmentation, allowing dynamically-loaded applications to run more smoothly.

Additionally, the Linux kernel features a sophisticated mechanism for managing device drivers, which are essential for facilitating communication between the kernel and hardware devices. Each driver serves as a translator, enabling the kernel to interact with different types of hardware, be it a hard drive, network interface card, or graphical processing unit. The modularity of device drivers allows them to be loaded and unloaded dynamically, thereby promoting flexibility. This design empowers developers to add new device functionality without needing to restart the entire kernel, significantly enhancing system uptime and reliability.

Moreover, the Linux kernel supports a variety of filesystems that serve as the file storage and retrieval methodology. The filesystem layer provides a uniform interface for the kernel to read and write data, regardless of its source or type. Popular filesystems supported by the kernel include ext4, Btrfs, and XFS. Each filesystem encompasses its methodologies for managing data structures, journaling, and recovery, which are crucial for ensuring data integrity and performance. A well-designed filesystem can dramatically affect the speed and efficiency at which data can be accessed, contributing to overall system performance.

Inter-process communication (IPC) is an essential component of the Linux kernel that facilitates the exchange of data between processes. Various IPC mechanisms exist, including message queues, pipes, semaphores, and shared memory. These tools allow processes to communicate and synchronize effectively, which is particularly vital for multithreaded applications or programs requiring coordination. By implementing robust IPC mechanisms, the kernel enables efficient collaboration between processes, promoting harmony in multitasking environments.

Another core aspect of the Linux kernel is its networking components, which manage communication over networks. The kernel utilizes protocols such as TCP/IP to ensure reliable transmission of data across interconnected devices. The networking stack is engineered to efficiently handle packet routing, error detection, and congestion control, adapting dynamically to network conditions. This adaptability is crucial, especially given the increasing complexity of modern networks incorporating mobile devices, IoT, and cloud services.

In terms of security, the Linux kernel has integrated features designed to protect against unauthorized access and vulnerabilities. Access Control Lists (ACLs), Mandatory Access Control (MAC) systems such as SELinux, and user namespace isolation are implementations that enhance security. By managing permissions at various levels, the kernel can safeguard sensitive data and reduce the attack surface for potential threats. Additionally, the kernel continuously evolves to integrate new security frameworks and mitigations as threats become more sophisticated, ensuring a secure execution environment for applications.

Lastly, an integral aspect of the Linux kernel's architecture is its extensibility through modules. Kernel modules are pieces of code that can be dynamically loaded into the kernel at runtime, allowing the kernel to extend its capabilities without requiring a complete recompilation. This modularity supports an agile development process, enabling developers to create custom features or drivers tailored specifically to their hardware or application needs. The kernel's support for modules continues to be a significant contributor to its success, fostering a culture of innovation and adaptation within the Linux ecosystem.

In summary, the core components of the Linux kernel—process management, memory allocation, device drivers, filesystems, IPC, networking, security features, and modular capabilities—work synergistically to create a powerful operating environment capable of meeting the diverse demands of modern computing. Recognizing how these components interact provides a foundational understanding necessary for navigating and contributing effectively to the Linux kernel ecosystem. As we continue to explore the intricacies of the kernel, we move forward with an enriched comprehension of its structural anatomy and the profound implications it has on contemporary technology.

3.2. Processes and Threads

A solid understanding of processes and threads is central to grasping the operational dynamics of the Linux kernel. In essence, processes are the units of execution in an operating system, embodying a running instance of a program, while threads represent the smaller units of execution within those processes. This distinction is critical because it influences how efficiently the system allocates resources, handles multitasking, and manages concurrency.

When an application is executed, the kernel allocates a dedicated process for it. This process is accompanied by a unique identifier known as the Process ID (PID), which the kernel uses to manage execution. Each process is given a virtual memory space, which is isolated from others, ensuring that processes do not interfere with each other's memory, thus enhancing security and stability. The kernel employs a data structure called the task_struct to maintain important information about every process, such as its state (running, waiting, or stopped), priority, and resource usage.

Creating a new process in Linux is accomplished through a system call known as fork(). When a process invokes fork(), it creates a duplicate of its own process, identical in every way except for the PID. The original process is referred to as the parent process, while the new one is the child process. This model of forking allows for easy creation of new processes, but it can introduce overhead, especially in systems with a large number of processes, due to the significant memory and CPU resources consumed.

Threads, on the other hand, are a lightweight alternative to processes. They share the same memory space of their parent process but can execute independently. This sharing of resources allows for more efficient communication between threads since they can easily share data without requiring inter-process communication (IPC) mechanisms. In Linux, threads are treated as separate processes by the kernel; they each receive their own unique thread ID but share the same process ID of their parent. This allows threads to benefit from the parent process's resource allocations while being able to execute tasks in parallel. The threading model can significantly enhance application performance, notably in multithreaded applications like web servers or databases that can benefit from concurrent operations.

The kernel's management of scheduling plays a vital role in the efficient operation of processes and threads. The scheduler is responsible for determining which process or thread should run at any given time based on various factors, such as priority and fairness. The Completely Fair Scheduler (CFS) is the default scheduling algorithm in modern Linux kernels; it allocates CPU time to processes and threads in a way that aims to give each one a fair share. By tracking the amount of execution time each process has received, CFS dynamically adjusts its scheduling decisions to balance system responsiveness with overall throughput.

When managing multiple processes or threads, the Linux kernel must address issues like synchronization and communication. Various synchronization mechanisms exist to prevent race conditions—situations where two or more processes or threads attempt to change shared data at the same time, leading to unpredictable behavior. Common synchronization primitives in Linux include mutexes, semaphores, and spinlocks.

Mutexes (mutual exclusions) are used to ensure that only one thread can access a resource at a time, while semaphores can manage access to a resource pool, allowing a specified number of threads to access it simultaneously. Spinlocks are a type of busy-wait lock; a thread will continuously check the lock until it becomes available, suitable in contexts where threads are expected to wait only briefly.

Inter-process communication (IPC) is another vital aspect of managing processes and threads. Linux provides several IPC mechanisms, such as pipes, message queues, and shared memory, which enable processes to share data and coordinate execution effectively. For example, pipes offer a straightforward means for one process to send data to another, while shared memory allows multiple processes to access the same physical memory space directly, enabling fast data exchange.

Additionally, the kernel is equipped to manage the life cycle of processes and threads. When a process terminates, the kernel must clean up resources allocated to it, a process known as "reaping." Orphaned processes, those that outlive their parent processes, are adopted by the init system, ensuring they are properly managed and do not lead to resource leaks.

The management of processes and threads impacts not only performance but also system stability and security. The kernel's ability to isolate processes enhances the protection of application data and prevents unauthorized interference. In a multithreaded application, the kernel can further enforce permissions, ensuring that threads adhere to the constraints established for the processes within which they operate.

In contemporary computing environments, where applications increasingly rely on parallelism to enhance throughput, the distinctions between processes and threads become increasingly important. Understanding how the Linux kernel organizes, schedules, and manages these entities is crucial for developers seeking to optimize application performance, manage system resources effectively, and ensure application robustness.

As the landscape of technology continues to evolve, the Linux kernel's approach to processes and threads remains a foundational aspect of its architecture. By continually optimizing scheduling algorithms, enhancing synchronization primitives, and refining IPC mechanisms, the kernel fosters an ecosystem capable of meeting the demanding performance requirements of modern applications, thus solidifying Linux's position as a critical foundation upon which countless systems are built. Moving forward, understanding the ever-shifting dynamics of processes and threads will be essential for developers and system administrators aiming to harness the full power of this versatile operating system.

3.3. Handling Memory Management

In the realm of operating systems, memory management stands as a fundamental component that determines resource allocation, efficiency, and overall system stability. Within the Linux kernel, memory management encompasses a wide range of strategies and mechanisms to handle various types of memory effectively. Understanding these aspects is critical for developers and system architects alike, as it allows for the design of applications that can make the most efficient use of the underlying hardware resources.

At the heart of Linux memory management is the concept of virtual memory, a paradigm that allows the kernel to provide the illusion of an expansive memory space for applications, even if physical RAM is limited. Each process operates within its own virtual address space, which is mapped to physical memory by the kernel. This not only isolates the memory of different processes, enhancing security and stability, but also facilitates the management of memory allocation and deallocation.

One of the primary mechanisms for managing virtual memory is paging. The Linux kernel divides memory into fixed-size blocks called pages, usually 4KB in size. This approach enables the system to load only the necessary pages into physical memory, allowing it to efficiently utilize RAM and reduce the overhead associated with managing larger memory chunks. When a process requests memory, the kernel allocates it in pages, which can be scattered throughout the physical memory, avoiding fragmentation and simplifying the swapping of pages in and out of memory.

Page swapping is an essential part of memory management, particularly in cases where the physical memory is full. When a process requires more memory than is available, the kernel employs a strategy known as paging out, where inactive pages are written to a designated area on the disk called swap space. This operation frees up physical memory for active processes. The kernel is responsible for determining which pages to swap out, typically prioritizing those that have not been accessed recently, thereby maintaining responsiveness for active applications.

The kernel implements different algorithms to determine how and when to swap pages. The Least Recently Used (LRU) algorithm is one of the most commonly employed strategies, which prioritizes keeping frequently accessed pages in physical memory. However, Linux also supports additional algorithms like the Clock algorithm, which provides a more efficient way to manage page replacement by organizing pages in a circular queue.

Another crucial aspect of memory management involves optimizing RAM usage. Linux employs techniques such as memory overcommitment, which allows applications to allocate more memory than is physically available. The kernel does this based on heuristics that predict memory usage patterns. If a process exceeds its allocated memory, the kernel may intervene by terminating the process or swapping pages to ensure system stability.

In addition to managing physical memory, the kernel uses caching as a significant optimization strategy to enhance performance. The Linux kernel maintains various types of caches, including the page cache, which stores recently accessed file data to reduce disk I/O operations. By keeping frequently accessed data in memory, the kernel can speed up file operations and improve system responsiveness. Additionally, the kernel utilizes disk caches, which manage the buffering of disk reads and writes, optimizing communication between the CPU and storage devices.

Memory leaks and overflow are significant challenges in memory management that can lead to severe performance degradation or system crashes. In Linux, the kernel has built-in mechanisms to monitor memory usage and enforce limits. Tools like the Out-Of-Memory killer are employed to identify processes that are consuming excessive resources, allowing the kernel to reclaim memory effectively by terminating those processes. Additionally, developers are encouraged to adopt best practices regarding memory allocation and deallocation when designing applications. Utilizing functions such as `malloc()` and `free()` correctly, and leveraging tools like Valgrind for memory analysis, can help identify potential leaks and optimize memory usage.

Security also plays a vital part in memory management within the kernel. The Linux kernel implements a feature called Address Space Layout Randomization (ASLR), which randomly arranges the memory address space of a process. This increases security by making it more difficult for attackers to predict the location of executed code, thereby mitigating the effectiveness of certain exploits. Furthermore, the kernel employs protections against buffer overflows, ensuring that allocated memory regions are properly defined and preventing unauthorized access to adjacent memory areas.

Numerous advanced techniques have evolved in memory management that optimize resource use further. For example, kernel developers continuously improve memory compaction—a process that reduces fragmentation by relocating allocated memory to create larger contiguous blocks. This is especially relevant in long-running applications where memory can become fragmented over time, leading to inefficient use of memory resources.

To put memory management effectively into practice, developers can utilize several tools and utilities provided by the Linux ecosystem. The `/proc/meminfo` file gives insights into a system's current memory usage, while commands like `free` and `top` can display real-time memory statistics. For debugging and profiling, the kernel provides utilities like `vmstat` and `htop`, which help visualize memory consumption and identify potential issues.

In conclusion, handling memory management in the Linux kernel is an intricate and multi-faceted task that aims to maximize performance, enhance security, and ensure system stability. From virtual memory and paging mechanisms to advanced caching strategies and strict security protocols, the kernel employs a rich set of tools and philosophies that allow it to manage the complexities of modern computing environments. As applications demand more resources and the landscape of hardware evolves, understanding these memory management principles becomes increasingly crucial for developers looking to build efficient, resilient software on the Linux platform.

3.4. Device Drivers Customization

The Linux kernel stands as a pivotal element in computing, providing the essential interface between hardware and software. At its core, it is responsible for managing system resources and ensuring that hardware devices operate smoothly and efficiently. Within this intricate system lies the essential concept of device drivers, which are critical for facilitating communication between the kernel and hardware components. Device drivers serve as the translators that enable the kernel to understand how to interact with the various pieces of hardware, from storage devices to network adapters, making them a cornerstone of kernel functionality.

Customizing device drivers can significantly enhance system performance, compatibility, and functionality. Understanding this customization begins with recognizing the foundational architecture of device drivers within the Linux kernel. Each driver is typically organized into modules, which are pieces of code that can be loaded and unloaded dynamically at runtime. This modularity allows developers to create drivers suited specifically to their hardware requirements without necessitating a complete recompilation of the kernel.

When embarking on the journey of device driver customization, the first step is acquiring a solid understanding of the kernel's driver framework. This framework categorizes drivers into several types. Character drivers, for instance, manage devices that operate with streams of data—such as keyboards and mice—while block drivers interface with devices that store data in blocks, like hard drives. Network drivers, on the other hand, are focused on facilitating communication over network devices. Familiarity with these categories is crucial for determining how best to create or modify a driver to meet specific needs.

Developers customizing device drivers will often choose to work within the Linux kernel source code to adapt existing drivers or create new ones. This process begins by locating the relevant driver code, typically housed within the /drivers directory of the kernel source tree. Here, developers have access to a plethora of existing drivers that can serve as templates or inspiration for customization. By understanding the structure of these drivers, developers can tailor functionalities such as initialization sequences, I/O controls, and interrupt handling mechanisms to align with their hardware specifications.

Once the initial driver framework is established, developers can move onto tuning and performance optimization aspects of the driver. This may involve refining how the driver handles data transfers, optimizing interrupt handling, and implementing advanced features like Direct Memory Access (DMA) for efficient data transfer. By minimizing CPU involvement in data movement processes, DMA allows for improved performance, reducing latency and maximizing throughput. Coupled with techniques such as buffering and queuing, developers can enhance overall performance and responsiveness.

Another key consideration in device driver customization is ensuring robust error handling and recovery mechanisms. The underlying hardware can sometimes present challenges such as communication errors, device failures, or timeouts. Implementing proper mechanisms can prevent a cascading failure that might affect overall system stability. There are several strategies that developers may use, such as implementing retries for failed operations or graceful degradation techniques when a device is unresponsive. This level of rigor not only contributes to system reliability but also improves the user experience.

Testing and validation are crucial stages in the custom device driver lifecycle. Developers must create comprehensive test cases to ensure that the driver functions correctly across various scenarios. These tests should encompass not only functional validation but also stress and performance testing to identify potential bottlenecks or failures under load. Tools like Kernel Self-Testing (Kselftest) enable developers to execute tests within the kernel to verify that drivers operate as intended.

In addition to functional testing, understanding the kernel's debugging features can greatly assist in diagnosing issues within custom drivers. The Linux kernel provides several debugging options, including dynamic debug and Kprobes, which allow developers to insert breakpoints and inspect the behavior of drivers at runtime. Utilizing these tools enables developers to pinpoint and resolve issues more effectively while the driver is in operation.

Cross-compiling is another essential aspect if developers intend to customize drivers for specific embedded systems or non-x86 architectures. This involves building the driver for a different architecture than that on which development is taking place, ensuring compatibility with a range of platforms. The process requires a good grasp of the kernel's build system and may necessitate the installation of cross-compilation tools to seamlessly create driver modules for different hardware architectures.

One significant benefit of device driver customization is the ability to extend support to new or proprietary hardware that may lack official driver support. Organizations often find themselves dependent on particular hardware configurations that necessitate custom solutions. By customizing device drivers, developers can bridge compatibility gaps, ensuring that even niche or specialized hardware operates seamlessly within the Linux ecosystem.

Furthermore, developers should be aware of the importance of maintaining compliance with the Linux kernel coding style and guidelines when customizing drivers. This adherence to established conventions not only ensures consistency across drivers but also facilitates community contributions and easier integration of the customized drivers into mainline kernels. Numerous resources, such as the Linux Kernel Documentation and Coding Style guidelines, serve as valuable references for developers during this process.

Engaging with the community is paramount during the process of device driver customization. The open-source nature of the Linux kernel has fostered a vibrant development community, where collaboration and knowledge-sharing are encouraged. Participating in mailing lists, attending kernel development conferences, or contributing to forums can grant developers access to a wealth of expertise and potentially important feedback on their work. Such community engagement can expedite the customization process and help identify best practices and common pitfalls.

In conclusion, device driver customization serves as a powerful avenue for enhancing the interaction between the Linux kernel and hardware devices. By understanding the architecture of the kernel, leveraging its modular framework, and applying rigorous testing and debugging practices, developers can tailor drivers to suit individual needs and drive performance improvements. This process not only bolsters system efficiency and stability but also exemplifies the collaborative spirit of the open-source community, as developers contribute to a shared goal of advancing the Linux ecosystem. As technology continues to evolve, so too will the role of device drivers, necessitating continuous customization efforts to keep pace with emerging hardware innovations.

3.5. Kernel Modules and Extensions

Kernel modules are an integral part of the Linux kernel's architecture, allowing for dynamic extension and modification of the kernel's functionality without necessitating a complete reboot. This capability provides flexibility and responsiveness, enabling developers and users to enhance system performance based on their specific needs. Over the years, kernel modules have evolved from a groundbreaking concept to a critical component of the Linux ecosystem, making understanding their function and best practices essential for anyone navigating this complex landscape.

At the core of kernel modules lies the idea of modularity. The Linux kernel can be seen as a collection of components that control hardware and manage system resources. Some of these components are required for a minimal environment to function, while others may only be needed for specific hardware or functionalities. By implementing these components as loadable modules, the kernel allows for a lean setup where only necessary drivers and features are loaded at runtime. This means that resources can be conserved, as unused modules do not occupy memory space, and system performance can be optimized based on current operational needs.

Dynamic module loading and unloading form the backbone of kernel extensibility. The primary interface for managing kernel modules is provided through the `modprobe`, `insmod`, and `rmmod` commands. The `insmod` command is used to insert a module into the kernel, while `rmmod` removes a module. `modprobe` acts as a more sophisticated interface, automatically resolving dependencies between modules. For example, if a specific module depends on another, `modprobe` will load both in the correct order without the user needing to manually manage this aspect.

Nonetheless, managing kernel modules requires an understanding of safety measures and error handling. Kernel modules operate in kernel space, which means any bugs or errors can potentially crash the entire system, leading to loss of data and stability. Robust error checking mechanisms must be implemented within modules to handle various operational scenarios and ensure graceful degradation in the face of failure. Kernel developers often make use of logging features—such as `printk()` for kernel messages—that help diagnose issues by providing insights into the module's behavior during runtime.

Creating kernel modules also involves dealing with feature dependencies. As the kernel grows and evolves, modules may become reliant on other modules and kernel features. This interdependence necessitates robust management practices to ensure that modules can be loaded in a manner where all dependencies are resolved, thus avoiding conflicts. Moreover, with the launch of new kernel versions, modules may require adjustments or recompilation to ensure compatibility. The `modinfo` command is particularly useful in retrieving metadata about a module, including its dependencies and version.

Kernel extensibility extends beyond simple device drivers. It encompasses enhanced functionalities such as network performance tuning, additional filesystems, or even implementing custom security protocols. For example, as containers have become prevalent in modern computing environments, there has been a surge in modules that facilitate container orchestration and management. This adaptability not only demonstrates a forward-thinking approach to kernel design but also underlines the principle that the Linux kernel must evolve in response to emerging technological demands.

The future of kernel modules is particularly exciting as new technologies continue to reshape the computing landscape. One promising avenue is the integration of machine learning and artificial intelligence functionalities directly into the kernel. This would allow for optimizations that adapt to workload patterns on-the-fly, potentially improving efficiency and resource management. Moreover, as cloud computing continues to dominate, kernel extensions that enhance cloud integration features or facilitate hybrid infrastructures will become increasingly important.

Another dimension to explore is the role of community and collaboration in kernel module development. The Linux kernel has always thrived on contributions from a diverse set of developers, working towards common goals. Engaging with the broader community through mailing lists, open-source projects, and conferences allows developers to share knowledge, seek assistance with complex problems, and maintain a culture of continuous improvement and mentorship. As kernel modules evolve, collective input from the community will remain paramount in ensuring the ongoing robustness and adaptability of the kernel infrastructure.

In summary, kernel modules and extensions are vital to the extensibility and dynamism of the Linux kernel. By allowing for the selective loading of features and device drivers, the kernel optimizes resource utilization and enhances performance, promoting a focus on efficiency. However, this extensibility comes with responsibilities —developers must prioritize safety, dependency management, and adaptability to create stable, powerful modules that meet the needs of users in an ever-changing technological ecosystem. As the kernel community continues to innovate and respond to emerging demands, the landscape of kernel modules will undoubtedly evolve alongside the challenges and opportunities that lie ahead.

4. Interfacing and Interaction: System Calls and APIs

4.1. Navigating System Calls

Navigating system calls is an essential part of understanding how user space interacts with the Linux kernel. System calls serve as the fundamental interface through which user applications request services from the kernel, granting them access to low-level operations such as file management, process control, and network communication. This subchapter delves into the mechanics of system calls, their significance, and the processes involved in handling requests from user applications.

At its core, a system call acts as a bridge between user space, where applications operate, and kernel space, where the kernel possesses full control over hardware and system resources. The usage of system calls is prevalent across all operating systems, but the Linux kernel offers a wealth of predefined functions that streamline interaction with the underlying system.

The mechanics of system calls begin when a user application calls a library function, often part of the C Standard Library, which serves as a user-friendly interface for invoking system calls. For example, when an application wants to read data from a file, it might call a function like read(). This process involves several layers. When the application executes the read() function, control transfers from user space to kernel space. Here, several transformations take place. The kernel must first suspend the running user application and save its state, preserve context in case of interruptions, and then switch to the appropriate execution mode.

On a low level, invoking a system call often involves using processor instructions specific to the architecture, such as the syscall instruction on x86_64 architectures. This instruction triggers a context switch to the kernel, effectively changing the processor mode from user mode to kernel mode. Within the kernel, the system call number, which identifies the desired service request, is passed through specific registers. The kernel utilizes this number to divert execution to the appropriate handler function that processes the request.

Once the kernel handler for a system call is entered, it performs the required operations, interfacing with hardware or other kernel components as necessary. This may include accessing files using the Virtual File System (VFS) interface, allocating memory, scheduling processes, or managing network connections. It's important to note that system calls typically invoke multiple kernel functions, performing various tasks to fulfill the request.

After the necessary operations are completed, the kernel prepares to return control back to the user space. This involves restoring the state of the user application and returning results, typically through registers as well. The value returned often indicates the success or failure of the operation, along with data retrieved, if applicable. For instance, a successful file read will return the number of bytes read, while an error will yield a negative value, with specific error codes populating an underlying errno variable.

In the context of performance and efficiency, system calls can be expensive due to the overhead of context switching, including the time taken to switch between user mode and kernel mode. To mitigate performance costs, applications often try to minimize the frequency of system calls. Techniques such as batching multiple calls or using buffering can help reduce the impact of context switching.

Moreover, system call interfaces can evolve over time as the Linux kernel develops and adapts. New system calls may be introduced to provide additional functionality, and existing calls may be enhanced to improve performance or security. Consequently, developers must stay abreast of changes to the system call interface, particularly when working with modules or developing applications intended for diverse kernel versions.

System call handling is not just limited to the mechanics of triggers and responses; it also encapsulates layered abstractions allowing for the easier implementation of complex tasks. For instance, abstracting file I/O operations through higher-level libraries simplifies interaction with device drivers and the kernel, making it easier for developers to build applications without needing extensive knowledge of kernel internals.

It's worth noting that system calls come with security implications. The kernel must validate every system call to prevent unauthorized access to critical system resources or data. This validation is generally achieved through permission checks, verifying whether a user has the necessary rights to execute a requested action. As the Linux ecosystem evolves, securing system calls remains a pivotal area, particularly with the rising threats in cybersecurity.

Additionally, as containerization and cloud technologies gain traction, they impose unique considerations on system calls. Managing system calls in environments with multiple isolated instances, like Docker or Kubernetes, has implications for both performance and security. Mechanisms like seccomp (secure computing mode), which allow one to limit the set of system calls a process can use, help create a more secure multi-tenant environment.

The future of system calls in the Linux kernel will likely be shaped by emerging technologies, evolving user requirements, and ongoing trends in software design. The kernel's ability to adapt and incorporate new features, such as better performance mechanisms, richer abstractions, or enhanced security measures, will ensure that the system call interface remains effective in meeting the demands of the developer community.

In conclusion, navigating system calls requires an understanding of the intricate dance between user applications and the Linux kernel. From the initial invocation to the handling of requests and returning results, system calls provide a critical pathway through which applications can leverage the core functions of the operating system. By grasping the mechanics of system calls, developers can better design applications that efficiently interact with the kernel while staying informed about performance considerations, security protocols, and the potential for future enhancements.

4.2. APIs and their Functionality

APIs, or Application Programming Interfaces, serve as an essential mechanism that facilitates communication between different software components, allowing developers to leverage the existing functionalities of the Linux kernel and build complex applications that operate atop it. Within the context of the Linux kernel, APIs offer a standardized means to access operating system services, enabling applications to request services without needing to know the intricate details of kernel operations.

The primary role of APIs within the Linux ecosystem is to simplify interactions with the kernel while abstracting away the complexities involved in system calls and other lower-level operations, making it easier for developers to create robust and efficient applications. This abstraction is crucial because it aids in promoting portability and efficiency—applications built against specific APIs can operate on any system running the same version of the kernel, independent of hardware specifics.

The behavior of the Linux kernel is largely guided by its well-defined set of APIs, which can be subdivided into several categories:

1. System Call APIs: These APIs allow user-space applications to interact directly with the kernel through system calls. Commonly used services include file manipulation (open, read, write, close), process control (fork, exec, exit), and network operations (socket creation, binding, listening). These functions encapsulate the complex low-level operations of the kernel and present them in a more manageable form. For example, instead of dealing directly with process and memory management intricacies, applications can utilize the `fork()` system call to create a new process, leaving the details of resource allocation and scheduling to the kernel.

2. Library APIs: Beyond direct system calls, many applications utilize higher-level programming libraries that wrap these system

calls into user-friendly interfaces. Libraries such as the GNU C Library (glibc) provide additional functionalities, including multi-threading, network programming, and more advanced file system operations. These libraries utilize the kernel's system call APIs but blend them with additional features, making them easier to use in higher-level programming languages.

3. Device Interfaces: Specific APIs exist for interacting with peripheral devices through device drivers. These may include direct calls to driver functions or through standardized interfaces such as the Virtual File System (VFS), which provides a uniform interface to access different filesystem types. This abstraction allows applications to operate with various storage devices, without being tied to specific device attributes.

4. Kernel Module APIs: For developers focusing on extending the kernel's functionalities, the Linux kernel provides a set of APIs designed for creating and interfacing with kernel modules. This includes functions for loading and unloading modules, as well as interfaces for interacting with various kernel subsystems (like device management and memory management). Writing kernel modules requires a deep understanding of these APIs to maintain system stability and performance, as errors at this level can lead to system crashes.

5. Networking APIs: Networking is a core component of modern operating systems, and the Linux kernel offers a comprehensive suite of network APIs. These APIs enable applications to utilize socket programming for communication over networks, offering functionalities for TCP/IP connections, UDP communication, and more. The kernel abstracts the complexities of network stack management, enabling developers to easily set up client-server architectures.

The functionality and utility of APIs within the Linux kernel can be observed not only in the ease of use they provide for developers but also in how they enhance performance and security. Performance is improved because APIs allow applications to make bulk requests or operate in asynchronous modes, reducing the overhead of frequent system calls. Security is enhanced through controlled exposure of kernel functionalities—by limiting the services available through APIs, the kernel can offer a more secure environment where unauthorized actions are minimized.

Moreover, the evolution of APIs in the Linux kernel reflects the ongoing trends in computing and the need for agility in the development process. With the rising prominence of containerization and microservices architectures, APIs are becoming more critical as components that facilitate communication in distributed systems. Kubernetes and Docker, for instance, leverage these APIs to manage workloads efficiently, extending the kernel's capabilities in cloud and containerized environments.

The future of APIs and their functionality within the Linux kernel is likely to align closely with developing technologies. As artificial intelligence (AI) and machine learning continue to permeate software development, APIs may evolve to support data processing and inference operations more seamlessly. Furthermore, with advancements in security technologies, we can expect enhanced APIs for monitoring and managing security policies within applications, further reinforcing the protective measures initiated at the kernel level.

In conclusion, APIs are indispensable within the Linux kernel ecosystem, offering a pathway for applications to harness the power of the kernel while shielding developers from its intricacies. They encapsulate core functionalities, promote interoperability, and pave the way for innovation in software development. As the kernel evolves, maintaining the relevance and robustness of these APIs will be key to the sustained growth of the Linux ecosystem, enabling developers to create sophisticated applications while optimizing performance and security.

4.3. Designing with Kernel and User Space

Designing with kernel and user space encompasses a critical understanding of how the Linux kernel interacts with user-level applications, a relationship that greatly influences system behavior, performance, and security. The Linux architecture features two distinct execution environments: user space, where applications run with limited privileges, and kernel space, where the Linux kernel operates with full access to system resources. This design choice not only ensures stability and security but also provides a robust framework for efficient resource management.

The demarcation between kernel space and user space serves multiple purposes. Primarily, by restricting user applications to user space, the kernel can enforce a layer of protection that prevents errant or malicious operations from affecting core system stability. Failures in user-level applications typically do not compromise the entire system, as they are isolated in their execution contexts. This architecture is especially crucial for enterprise systems, where reliability and availability are paramount.

Interfacing between user space and kernel space primarily occurs through system calls. When a user application requires services like file operations, networking, or process control, it invokes a specific system call, transitioning the execution context from the user space to the kernel space. This switch involves a context switch, which can incur performance overhead. Effective design practices aim to minimize these context switches, as they can be costly in terms of system resources.

Kernel developers constantly consider how to optimize the interface between user space and kernel space in terms of both performance and security. For instance, designs often focus on reducing the frequency of system calls by batching them together whenever possible. Doing so can lower the overhead associated with context switching, leading to improved application performance. Additionally, many high-performance applications leverage shared memory segments for IPC (Interprocess Communication) to bypass the overhead that comes with traditional system calls and instead allow direct access to memory regions that multiple processes can manipulate.

A major aspect of efficient design within this architecture is the consideration of user and kernel interaction through APIs (Application Programming Interfaces). APIs provide a higher-level abstraction for user space applications by encapsulating complex operations into simpler functions or methods that are easier to use. By providing libraries that wrap system calls, kernel developers can abstract away implementation details, making it easier for application developers to leverage the kernel's capabilities while adhering to best practices for performance and security. For instance, functions in the GNU C Library (glibc) provide wrappers that handle many common system calls, allowing developers to focus on building applications without delving deeply into the operational intricacies of the kernel.

Security mechanisms are crucial when designing systems that interact between user and kernel space. Security threats can stem from both poorly written applications and malicious attacks seeking to exploit vulnerabilities. Implementing strict validation on all system calls ensures only authorized and legitimate operations occur. Mechanisms such as SELinux (Security-Enhanced Linux) extend these principles by enforcing mandatory access control policies that further restrict user-space applications from performing unauthorized actions.

Moreover, protection against common vulnerabilities, such as buffer overflows and access violations, remains a focal point during the design phase. The kernel often employs techniques such as stack canaries, ASLR (Address Space Layout Randomization), and DEP (Data Execution Prevention) to protect against exploitation, enhancing the integrity of the entire operating system.

The interaction design between user space and kernel space also considers how multimedia applications and interactive processes are managed. For example, designing real-time processing capabilities through system calls and kernel modules can pave the way for high-performance applications, such as video games or industrial automation systems. Employing priority scheduling and low-latency techniques in the kernel ensures responsive execution that is crucial in real-time contexts, allowing applications to meet demanding operational requirements.

Designing with kernel and user space also requires developers to be cognizant of debugging tools and techniques. Thorough logging within both contexts ensures that interactions can be monitored and analyzed for performance bottlenecks or security vulnerabilities. Tools like strace allow developers to trace system calls made by applications, offering insights into application performance and the nature of kernel interactions. Incorporating profiling into the development cycle helps identify areas where performance can be improved by optimizing function calls or evaluating the impact of system call overhead.

In summary, designing with kernel and user space is a multifaceted endeavor that requires an understanding of how to balance performance, security, and usability. Architecting interfaces that promote efficient communication through system calls, along with leveraging APIs to simplify development, allows for the creation of robust applications that can fully utilize the capabilities of the Linux kernel. As both hardware and software landscapes continue evolving, this fundamental relationship between kernel and user space will remain critical to the advancement of innovative, reliable, and secure computing systems. Embracing best practices in this domain will be essential for developers seeking to thrive in the dynamic ecosystem surrounding the Linux kernel.

4.4. Security Mechanisms and Protocols

In the realm of software applications and systemic integrity, the significance of robust security mechanisms and protocols cannot be overstated. In the context of the Linux kernel, these layers of security are vital for protecting the kernel itself and the systems built on top of it from vulnerabilities, unauthorized access, and malicious attacks. This subchapter explores the plethora of security mechanisms, protocols, and practices intrinsic to the Linux kernel, emphasizing their role in fostering a secure computing environment.

At the kernel level, security is architected through several mechanisms designed to enforce access controls, isolate processes, and protect sensitive data. One of the fundamental principles is the principle of least privilege, which mandates that processes operate with only the permissions necessary to perform their dedicated tasks. This is achieved through a combination of user roles, permissions, and security models embedded within the kernel. The implementation of user IDs (UIDs) and group IDs (GIDs) plays a critical role in this context, allowing the kernel to differentiate between users and configure file permissions accordingly. The default permission scheme utilized by Linux is based on Unix-like permissions, applying read, write, and execute rights, thus maintaining a baseline of security against unauthorized access.

In addition to user and group permissions, the Linux kernel incorporates enhanced security modules, the most notable of which is the Security-Enhanced Linux (SELinux). Developed in collaboration with the National Security Agency (NSA), SELinux extends standard discretionary access control mechanisms by implementing mandatory access controls (MAC). This ensures that even if a malicious user gains access to a process, SELinux can restrict what that process can do, significantly limiting the potential damage and exposure of sensitive data. SELinux operates based on policies that define the access rules for resources, processes, users, and the interactions between them. Through this robust policy framework, SELinux effectively mitigates the risk of exploits, particularly in high-risk environments such as servers handling sensitive data or communications.

Another layer integral to security in the Linux kernel is the use of namespaces and cgroups (control groups). Namespaces allow for the isolation of resources among processes, making it possible to create secure environments—especially vital in containerized setups such as Docker and Kubernetes. This isolation offers a layer of defense by restricting the visibility and accessibility of system resources to different processes. Coupled with cgroups, which manage resource allocation and limits for processes, Linux can prevent runaway resource consumption, ensuring that a compromised process cannot monopolize system resources, thereby maintaining overall system stability.

The kernel employs several other security mechanisms, such as Address Space Layout Randomization (ASLR) and Data Execution Prevention (DEP). ASLR enhances memory security by randomizing the memory address space layout of processes, making it more difficult for attackers to predict where to inject code. This means that each time a process is launched, key memory addresses are randomized, preventing attackers from executing shellcode in predictable locations. DEP complements this by marking certain areas of memory as non-executable, thereby thwarting attempts to execute malicious code in those areas.

Security protocols at the communications layer are also critical components of the kernel's security framework. The Linux kernel integrates support for various encryption protocols, including Transport Layer Security (TLS) and Internet Protocol Security (IPsec). These protocols enable secure communication between networked devices, thus safeguarding data in transit from eavesdropping or tampering. By building robust networking security protocols directly into the kernel, Linux ensures that security measures are administered uniformly across applications, shielding them from vulnerabilities in lower-layer implementations.

With the growing importance of securing kernel integrity itself, technologies like kernel integrity checking and verification techniques are being integrated as well. Tools like IMA (Integrity Measurement Architecture) and EVM (Extended Verification Module) bolster kernel security through cryptographic signatures and measurements of kernel objects, including executable files and loaded modules. This ensures that only verified and trusted components can be executed, providing a mechanism to detect alterations or malicious modifications to the kernel and its modules.

As software vulnerabilities evolve, so too must the security mechanisms within the Linux kernel. The kernel's development community remains proactive in responding to threats through coordinated efforts in vulnerability management, which includes timely patching of critical security flaws. Kernel developers and maintainers conduct rigorous security reviews, focusing on existing code and new developments, to preemptively address potential vulnerabilities that could serve as attack vectors.

Furthermore, security best practices in the kernel extend to the development process itself. Secure coding practices, thorough testing, and reviewing mechanisms such as static analysis help prevent vulnerabilities from being introduced during the development phase. The open-source nature of the Linux kernel enables a broad community to contribute to this rigor, ensuring that many eyes scrutinize the code, which adds an extra layer of review and accountability.

In conclusion, the security mechanisms and protocols embedded within the Linux kernel form a multifaceted shield against a variety of vulnerabilities and attacks. From access controls, security enhancements, and isolation techniques to secure communication protocols, the kernel's design philosophy upholds principles of integrity, confidentiality, and system stability. As technology advances and the cyber threat landscape evolves, the Linux kernel's commitment to continuous improvement in security practices and methodologies will remain a paramount concern, ensuring its resilience against sophisticated threats while maintaining its reputation as a trusted foundation for countless applications and systems worldwide.

4.5. Optimizing Performance at the Interface Level

Optimizing performance at the interface level in the Linux kernel involves a meticulous examination of how the kernel interacts with user space applications, particularly through system calls, APIs, and user-level libraries. Given the critical role that these interactions play in overall system efficiency, understanding the underlying mechanics and adopting best practices can empower developers to harness the full potential of Linux while minimizing performance bottlenecks.

The interface between user space and kernel space is predominantly facilitated through system calls—requests made by applications to the kernel for various services ranging from file operations to process management. While system calls are essential for enabling this interaction, they inherently introduce overhead due to the transition from user mode to kernel mode. Each context switch involves saving the execution state of the user process and loading the state of the kernel, which consumes valuable CPU cycles. Consequently, optimizing the frequency and nature of system calls is paramount for enhancing performance at the interface level.

One effective strategy for achieving this optimization is to minimize the number of system calls made within a given application. Developers can accomplish this by batching related operations into single system calls wherever feasible. For instance, certain file operations —such as reading and writing multiple buffers or manipulating file attributes—could be combined into a single call, reducing the number of transitions between user and kernel mode. Not only does this method cut down on overhead, but it also reduces the potential latency associated with frequent context switching. Another technique combines the use of asynchronous I/O, allowing applications to issue multiple requests without blocking the execution thread, thus improving throughput and responsiveness.

Moreover, employing memory-mapped files can significantly boost performance for applications that need to handle large datasets or numerous read/write operations. By mapping a file or a block of memory directly into the address space of the calling process, user space applications can operate on the data without invoking multiple system calls. This mapping reduces the need for copying data between user space and kernel space, streamlining data access and enhancing overall efficiency.

APIs play a crucial role in abstracting the complexities of the underlying kernel functions, offering a simplified interaction model for developers. The Linux kernel is rich with a multitude of APIs designed to facilitate various functionalities, from file I/O to network communication. To optimize performance, developers should be diligent about selecting the right APIs and utilizing them effectively. High-performance libraries enabled by the kernel can abstract system calls and offer optimized pathways for frequent operations. For instance, selecting libraries like glibc, which inherently implement numerous optimizations for common tasks, can dramatically improve application performance.

Another facet of interface-level optimization involves profiling and benchmarking the application's interaction with the kernel. Tools such as strace can provide insights into which system calls are being invoked and how often, allowing developers to identify potential bottlenecks or inefficiencies. Armed with this information, they can redesign the interface strategies for interacting with the kernel to favor more efficient patterns, thereby elevating overall application performance.

Security mechanisms also factor into performance considerations at the interface level. Features such as SELinux impose certain checks and validations during system calls, which can introduce overhead. However, implementing these security protocols correctly ensures that the performance impact remains minimal while safeguarding the system. Developers should be aware of the security implications of their design choices and work to balance security requirements with performance goals.

To future-proof the interface performance in a landscape of rapidly evolving technology, it is also essential to keep abreast of emerging trends and paradigms. As cloud technologies and containerization gain traction, the interface with the kernel may evolve, requiring new optimizations focused on lightweight interactions and ephemeral environments. For example, kernel enhancements to support container orchestration could include specialized APIs or system calls tailored to handle the unique demands of containers, thereby ensuring efficient performance while maintaining isolation and security.

Ultimately, optimizing performance at the interface level calls for a holistic approach, melding efficient coding practices with a thorough understanding of the Linux kernel's capabilities. By strategically minimizing system call overhead, leveraging powerful APIs, profiling interactions, and keeping an eye on security implications, developers can craft applications that achieve peak performance without sacrificing the indispensable robustness and reliability offered by the Linux kernel.

In conclusion, as the demand for performance-driven applications continues to grow, prioritizing optimization at the interface level becomes increasingly critical. By embracing best practices and keenly understanding the Linux kernel ecosystem, developers can ensure their applications not only meet user expectations but also thrive in the competitive landscape of modern computing.

5. Concurrency and Synchronization: Ensuring Efficient Operation

5.1. Mechanisms of Concurrency Control

In the landscape of concurrent programming within the Linux kernel, concurrency control mechanisms play an essential role in ensuring that multiple processes and threads can operate simultaneously while avoiding conflicts that could lead to inconsistent data or system instability. As systems become more multifaceted, with multi-core processors and concurrent applications dominating the computing landscape, the importance of robust concurrency control mechanisms has never been clearer. This section will delve into the various methods employed within the Linux kernel to maintain concurrency, including locking mechanisms, atomic operations, and exceptions, while discussing their respective advantages and limitations.

To begin with, one fundamental approach to concurrency control in the Linux kernel is the implementation of locking mechanisms. Locks are used to prevent multiple processes from accessing the same resource concurrently, which can lead to race conditions. The kernel supports several types of locks, each suited to different scenarios. Mutexes (mutual exclusions) are a common means of enforcing exclusive access to a resource. When a mutex is acquired by one process, any other process attempting to acquire that same mutex will be put to sleep until the mutex is released. This straightforward approach helps ensure that critical sections of code are executed by only one thread at any given time, preventing data corruption.

However, mutexes can introduce performance overhead due to the blocking nature of their implementation. For performance-critical sections where low latencies are essential, spinlocks are employed. Unlike mutexes, spinlocks occupy the CPU while waiting for the lock to become available, continuously checking if the lock is free. This polling mechanism makes spinlocks appropriate for scenarios where locks are held for short durations or in situations where blocking is infeasible—such as within interrupt contexts. Spinlocks can lead to increased CPU utilization, especially if the lock is not released promptly, leading to potential performance degradation if not used judiciously.

Reader-writer locks offer a more sophisticated alternative to mutexes and spinlocks by distinguishing between reading and writing operations. These locks allow multiple threads to concurrently read shared data, significantly enhancing throughput when reads are far more frequent than writes. A writer must obtain exclusive access, blocking all other operations until the write completes. This approach strikes a balance between allowing concurrent reads and preventing data inconsistencies that could arise from concurrent writes.

Another critical concurrency mechanism within the Linux kernel involves the use of atomic operations. Atomic operations are non-interruptible tasks that ensure the correctness of shared data even when accessed by multiple threads. The kernel provides a range of atomic primitives—for example, atomic add, subtract, and bitwise operations—that maintain atomicity without requiring the overhead of acquiring locks. This feature is particularly useful for performance-sensitive code segments, where minimizing context switches and lock acquisitions can lead to notable efficiency gains.

However, while atomic operations provide a lightweight means of ensuring data consistency, their effectiveness is limited to certain scenarios. They are suitable for simple operations on simple data types but can become unwieldy when managing complex data structures or when multiple operations need to occur in a single logical transaction. As a result, developers must thoughtfully balance the use of atomic operations and locks, abiding by the principles of avoiding lock contention while minimizing overhead.

In addition to these traditional mechanisms, the Linux kernel employs techniques such as Read-Copy-Update (RCU) to facilitate safe concurrent access to shared data. RCU is a sophisticated synchronization mechanism that allows readers to access data without acquiring locks while writers create new versions of data and defer updates until all readers finish with the previous version. This non-blocking approach is particularly beneficial for read-heavy workloads and has been embraced in various subsystems to improve scalability and performance.

In navigating concurrency control, deadlocks pose one of the most significant challenges that developers must reconcile. A deadlock occurs when two or more processes are each waiting on the other to release resources, leading to a standstill. To mitigate deadlocks, kernel developers often implement strategies such as resource ordering—where locks are acquired in a consistent order across code paths—to minimize circular wait situations. Additionally, developers utilize timeouts and watchdog mechanisms to prevent processes from waiting indefinitely on a lock, thereby allowing for recovery from deadlock conditions.

As we look to the future, the demand for efficient concurrency mechanisms will only increase, driven by the ongoing shifts toward multi-threaded programming paradigms and parallel processing architectures. Emerging technologies such as hardware transactional memory (HTM) present exciting opportunities to enhance concurrency controls, allowing processes to commit or roll back changes based on conflict detection without relying on traditional locking mechanisms. This innovation could dramatically improve performance in multi-core environments, constituting a significant shift in how concurrency is approached within operating systems.

In summary, the Linux kernel employs diverse concurrency control mechanisms to ensure efficient operations in a dynamic computing environment. By leveraging locks, atomic operations, and advanced techniques like RCU, the kernel provides the foundational support required for safe concurrent execution. However, as the landscape of computing continues to evolve, the kernel's concurrency control mechanisms must adapt to meet the demands and challenges posed by increasingly complex multi-core system architectures. Continued research, development, and engagement with the developer community will be crucial for refining these mechanisms and driving future innovations in concurrency solutions.

5.2. Maintaining Synchronization Across Processes

In the Linux kernel ecosystem, maintaining synchronization across processes is paramount for ensuring data integrity and system stability during concurrent execution. The kernel's design must effectively manage multiple processes and threads to guarantee that shared resources are accessed in a controlled manner, avoiding race conditions and inconsistencies. This subchapter delves into the intricacies involved in maintaining synchronization, exploring the various mechanisms and approaches employed to achieve this critical objective.

Concurrency arises when multiple processes or threads attempt to work simultaneously, often sharing access to resources like memory, files, or devices. Without proper synchronization, concurrent access can lead to chaotic scenarios where processes overwrite each other's data or produce unpredictable outputs, severely undermining system reliability and correctness. Therefore, robust synchronization techniques are essential in the design of the Linux kernel, especially as processors become more capable of executing multiple threads in parallel.

To address synchronization needs, the Linux kernel incorporates several fundamental mechanisms, including semaphores, mutexes, and spinlocks. Each of these plays a distinct role in managing concurrent access, catering to different use cases and performance requirements. Understanding these mechanisms is vital for kernel developers aiming to write efficient, reliable code.

Semaphores are one of the simplest yet powerful synchronization primitives used in the Linux kernel. A semaphore maintains a count that indicates the number of available resources or permits. When a process attempts to access a shared resource, it must decrement the semaphore count. If the count is greater than zero, access is granted, and the process can proceed. Conversely, if the count has reached zero, the process will be blocked until another process releases the semaphore, thus signaling the availability of the resource. Semaphores facilitate synchronization across multiple processes and can be used to manage shared access to more complex data structures or resource pools.

Mutexes, or mutual exclusions, are another critical synchronization mechanism. A mutex allows only one thread to access a shared resource at any given time, providing strong protection against concurrent writes and read-modify-write operations. When a process locks a mutex, all other processes attempting to acquire the same mutex are put to sleep until it is unlocked. This blocking behavior is advantageous in scenarios with less contention on the mutex, ensuring orderly access to shared resources. The downside of mutexes is their potential to induce latency during high contention when multiple processes are competing for the same lock, necessitating careful consideration of their usage.

Spinlocks offer a lightweight alternative to mutexes and are particularly valuable in situations where threads are expected to hold locks for very short durations. Unlike mutexes, which block a waiting process, spinlocks require the waiting thread to actively poll the lock's status in a busy-wait loop. This approach eliminates the overhead of context switching associated with putting a thread to sleep but consumes CPU cycles while waiting. Spinlocks are most effective in low-latency contexts where the expected duration of the lock hold is very brief, making them well-suited for interrupt service routines or critical paths in the kernel where the overhead of sleeping would be detrimental.

While these synchronization mechanisms provide powerful tools for managing concurrency, they each have inherent limitations and trade-offs. For instance, improper usage of mutexes can lead to performance bottlenecks or even deadlocks—a situation where two or more processes are indefinitely waiting for each other to release resources. To mitigate these risks, developers must adopt best practices, such as careful ordering of lock acquisitions and implementing timeout mechanisms during locking attempts.

Another essential technique for maintaining synchronization across processes is the use of condition variables alongside mutexes. Condition variables allow threads to wait for certain conditions to be true before proceeding with their execution. A typical pattern involves a mutex being used to protect access to a shared resource and a condition variable that threads can wait on until an external event signifies that they can continue. This combination effectively enables threads to yield processor time when they cannot make progress, thus promoting efficient processor utilization.

Beyond these traditional synchronization mechanisms, the Linux kernel has introduced mechanisms like Read-Copy-Update (RCU) to enhance synchronization in scenarios characterized by high read-to-write ratios. RCU allows readers to access resources without locking, resulting in minimal latency under read-heavy workloads. Writers, instead of blocking readers, can store updates in new versions of data structures and defer the actual updates until it is safe for readers to release their references. This approach simultaneously ensures data correctness while optimizing read performance, which is particularly beneficial in systems where reads are frequent and writes are infrequent.

The advent of multi-core processors necessitates ongoing advancements in synchronization techniques as the concurrency landscape grows increasingly complex. The Linux kernel community actively explores new concepts and strategies for enhancing synchronization, translating to performance improvements across various workloads.

In summary, maintaining synchronization across processes is a multifaceted challenge that the Linux kernel addresses through a variety of mechanisms, including semaphores, mutexes, spinlocks, and condition variables. Each mechanism has its unique characteristics, tradeoffs, and appropriate use cases. By mastering these synchronization tools and adhering to best practices, kernel developers can build robust, efficient applications that effectively manage concurrent access, ensuring system stability and data integrity in a highly concurrent environment. The continual evolution of synchronization techniques

and the community's dedication to optimizing these approaches ensure that the Linux kernel remains a powerful foundation for modern
computing.

5.3. Utilizing Semaphores, Mutexes, and Spinlocks

In the realm of concurrent programming and resource management,
semaphores, mutexes, and spinlocks serve as foundational tools
within the Linux kernel, ensuring efficient operation while guarding
against data inconsistencies and race conditions. These synchronization primitives play a crucial role in determining how processes and
threads interact with one another, and mastering their utilization is
essential for any developer looking to contribute effectively to kernel
development or build high-performance applications atop the Linux
ecosystem.

At their core, semaphores are signaling mechanisms that allow
processes to communicate about the availability of resources. They
operate using a simple integer counter that represents the number
of available resources or permits. When a process wants to access a
resource protected by a semaphore, it performs a "wait" or "P" operation that decrements the counter. If the counter is greater than zero,
access is granted; the process can proceed, and the counter is reduced.
If the counter has reached zero, the process is blocked until another
process increments the counter, effectively signaling that a resource
has become available. This approach enables both mutual exclusion
and synchronization across multiple processes, making semaphores
highly versatile for managing shared resources and coordinating
activities.

Mutexes, short for mutual exclusions, are another critical synchronization primitive in the Linux kernel. They are used to protect critical
sections of code, ensuring that only one thread or process can access
a shared resource at a time. When a mutex is locked by a process, any
other process attempting to lock the same mutex is put to sleep until it
is unlocked. This blocking mechanism is crucial for maintaining data
integrity, preventing scenarios where multiple processes may modify
shared data concurrently. However, it is important to note that while

mutexes are powerful, they can introduce performance overhead due to potential blocking, especially in high contention situations.

Spinlocks serve as a complementary synchronization mechanism, particularly suited for scenarios with low latency demands. Unlike mutexes, spinlocks do not put a process to sleep while waiting for a lock; instead, they engage the CPU in a busy-waiting loop, repeatedly checking the lock until it becomes available. Spinlocks are optimal in contexts where the expected wait time is brief, as the overhead incurred from context switching is avoided. However, excessive use of spinlocks can lead to wasted CPU cycles if locks are held for extended periods, so careful consideration is needed regarding their application.

To effectively utilize these synchronization mechanisms, kernel developers must pay close attention to their specific use cases and potential pitfalls. Properly conducting race condition analyses during the design phase of code can help developers understand where shared resources may be accessed concurrently and enable them to choose the most suitable synchronization primitive. Additionally, they must be mindful of the potential for deadlocks—situations where two or more processes are indefinitely waiting for each other to release locks, which can result in system hang-ups. Implementing deadlock avoidance strategies, such as lock ordering and timeout mechanisms, can mitigate these risks.

Concurrency within the Linux kernel also extends to more advanced techniques such as Read-Copy-Update (RCU). RCU allows for highly efficient read operations without requiring locks, as readers proceed without waiting for writers to release their locks. Under this model, when a writer needs to make updates, it creates a new version of the data while preserving the current version until all readers have completed. This approach provides significant performance benefits, particularly in scenarios marked by a high frequency of read operations.

Furthermore, Linux kernel developers continually innovate and refine synchronization techniques to meet the demands of new hardware capabilities and evolving application requirements. The domain of concurrency management remains a vibrant area of research and development, as evidenced by ongoing efforts to implement more sophisticated synchronization mechanisms and manage increasingly complex workloads within the kernel.

In summary, the effective utilization of semaphores, mutexes, and spinlocks is indispensable for ensuring efficient operation within the Linux kernel. These synchronization primitives provide the necessary tools for managing concurrent access to shared resources while safeguarding data integrity and promoting system stability. By honing their understanding of these mechanisms and applying best practices in concurrency control, developers can enhance the performance and reliability of both the kernel itself and the applications built upon it. As the landscape of technology continues to evolve, these tools will remain vital in navigating the intricate dance of concurrency within the Linux ecosystem.

5.4. Debugging and Handling Deadlocks

In the complex landscape of computer systems, debugging and handling deadlocks stand out as critical areas for maintaining performance, reliability, and usability within the Linux kernel. Both debugging practices and deadlock resolution are essential for ensuring that the kernel operates seamlessly, especially given the concurrent nature of modern computing environments. This content aims to provide an in-depth overview of techniques for debugging the kernel, strategies for handling deadlocks effectively, and insights into best practices that developers should adopt while working within this intricate ecosystem.

Debugging in the Linux kernel presents unique challenges due to its complexity and the potential consequences of errors. Kernel code operates with elevated privileges, meaning that mistakes can lead to system crashes, data corruption, or security vulnerabilities. As such, debugging requires a methodical approach that balances thoroughness and caution.

One of the key tools for debugging in the kernel is the Kernel Debugger (KGDB), which allows developers to attach a debugger to a running kernel. This enables real-time inspection of kernel code, facilitating step-through debugging, breakpoints, and variable inspection. KGDB is exceptionally useful for diagnosing issues that occur in production systems, as developers can analyze kernel state without requiring a system reboot. By setting breakpoints in specific functions or paths within the kernel, developers can identify the source of bugs and analyze the stack traces to ascertain the state leading to the problem.

Another effective debugging tool is the use of print debugging via the `printk()` function. This function allows developers to log messages at various severity levels (emergency, alert, critical, etc.) and is invaluable for tracing execution flow, monitoring variable states, and gathering insights when issues arise. However, care should be taken to use `printk()` judiciously, as excessive logging can lead to performance degradation and overwhelming output, obscuring critical information amidst the noise.

Memory-related bugs, such as buffer overflows and memory leaks, are particularly common in kernel development. Tools available within the Linux ecosystem can assist in detecting these issues. For instance, `kmemleak` is a memory leak detector that operates in the kernel, identifying memory that has been allocated but not freed properly, thus allowing developers to investigate memory usage.

Additionally, the `ftrace` framework provides developers with dynamic tracing capabilities, allowing for instrumenting various parts of the kernel to gather data about function calls, execution time, and performance bottlenecks. This can be especially helpful in identifying deadlocks or performance issues arising from resource contention.

While debugging is crucial for identifying and resolving issues, handling deadlocks requires a proactive approach as well. A deadlock occurs when two or more processes are mutually waiting for one another to release resources, leaving all involved processes in a state of paralysis. In the Linux kernel, deadlocks can severely impact system performance and stability; thus, preventing and handling deadlocks is paramount.

To avoid deadlocks from occurring, developers can follow several principles. One effective strategy is to impose a strict order on resource allocation. By ensuring that all threads follow the same sequence when acquiring locks, developers can prevent circular waiting, a common cause of deadlocks. This formulaic approach requires thorough analysis of resource dependencies at design time to enforce a global order.

Additionally, implementing timeouts when attempting to acquire locks can create a safety net against deadlocks. By using timeout parameters with mutexes, developers can define a maximum waiting time for acquiring a resource. If that time is exceeded, the process can abort the attempt, avoiding indefinitely waiting states. Implementing a back-off strategy in combination with timeouts can further enhance the mechanism by allowing processes to retry obtaining the lock after a delay, reducing contention.

If a deadlock does occur, identifying the deadlock situation is essential. The Linux kernel provides several diagnostic tools and methods for uncovering deadlocks, such as the "smash" mechanism, which detects deadlocks by examining the state of all kernel threads and locks. By analyzing the thread states and resource holding patterns, developers can identify which threads are involved in the deadlock and take steps to remedy the situation.

Manual debugging of deadlocks may also involve examining core dumps or utilizing tools like SysRq commands to display the current locking state of the kernel, giving developers insights into which locks are held and which threads are waiting for them. This information can be useful for pinpointing the conditions that led to the deadlock and developing a solution.

Incorporating thorough testing methodologies into the development process can also be ineffective in catching both bugs and deadlocks early. Utilizing stress tests, concurrency tests, and scenarios designed to simulate high contention environments can uncover potential deadlocks preemptively. By running these tests in a controlled environment, developers can observe system behavior and validate the robustness of their locking strategies, locking orders, and timeout mechanisms.

Collaboration within the developer community provides additional resources for addressing common debugging and deadlock issues. Engaging in discussions on relevant mailing lists, contributing to forums, and participating in open-source communities are invaluable activities that enhance knowledge-sharing, promote best practices, and can lead to discovering existing solutions to problems faced by others.

In conclusion, effective debugging and the handling of deadlocks are critical components of maintaining the stability and performance of the Linux kernel. By utilizing appropriate debugging tools, following best practices for resource management, and implementing preventative measures and strategies, developers can navigate the complexities associated with concurrency in the kernel. These efforts contribute to building a more resilient kernel, ensuring that it performs efficiently even as it adapts to the demands of modern computing. Emphasizing continuous learning and collaboration will allow kernel developers to stay ahead of challenges, fostering an ecosystem that thrives on robustness, flexibility, and innovation.

5.5. Future Trends in Concurrency Solutions

As we look toward the future of concurrency solutions within the Linux kernel ecosystem, several trends and innovations stand poised to redefine how concurrency is managed and executed in this robust system. The evolution of hardware, advancements in software design, and increasing demands for higher performance and efficiency are driving the exploration of new concurrency strategies. This section examines the anticipated trends that will influence the design and implementation of concurrency solutions in the Linux environment.

One of the foremost trends in concurrency solutions is the shift toward greater hardware parallelism. With modern CPUs incorporating multiple cores, the Linux kernel must continue to evolve its concurrency models for optimal resource utilization. Algorithms and design patterns that facilitate fine-grained locking and concurrent data structures are gaining traction. Techniques such as lock-free programming, which allow multiple threads to operate on shared data without the need for traditional locking mechanisms, are becoming increasingly relevant. The development and adoption of lock-free data structures can significantly reduce contention and improve scalability in multi-threaded applications.

Another trend that is emerging is the closer integration of hardware transactional memory (HTM) into the Linux kernel. HTM can allow concurrent transactions among threads to be executed in a way that avoids traditional locking mechanisms. This technology provides a means for ensuring data consistency without the performance overhead typically associated with locks. As HTM becomes more commonplace in processors, the Linux kernel will need to adapt by incorporating this capability into its concurrency solutions. The potential for heightened performance, particularly in high-concurrency scenarios, makes HTM a promising area for future research and development.

In parallel computing environments, where workloads are distributed across clusters or cloud-based infrastructures, addressing concurrency through distributed computing models is also becoming essential. Innovations in frameworks that facilitate parallel programming are being integrated into the Linux kernel ecosystem. These frameworks, like OpenMP and MPI (Message Passing Interface), are paving the way for better support for large-scale, multi-core processing jobs. The kernel's ability to handle distributed tasks efficiently can optimize the utilization of resources in cloud environments, enhancing performance while managing high levels of concurrency.

Furthermore, as machine learning and artificial intelligence applications become more prevalent, there is an emerging need for concurrent execution models tailored to the unique requirements of these processing paradigms. The Linux kernel is poised to incorporate artificial intelligence-driven capabilities to dynamically manage concurrency based on workload characteristics. For example, advanced schedulers that adapt to workload patterns—prioritizing tasks based on their computational demands—could greatly improve responsiveness and resource allocation.

Moreover, the synchronization mechanisms utilized within the Linux kernel are expected to evolve significantly. As systems grow ever more complex, the need for more sophisticated synchronization primitives has never been higher. Research is ongoing into alternatives to traditional locks, such as Read-Copy-Update (RCU) and other innovative methods that minimize contention while ensuring data consistency. These advancements are vital for high-transaction environments and are likely to lead to performance enhancements that accommodate the growing parallelism of modern systems.

The role of runtime libraries will also expand in tandem with these developments. As libraries that facilitate concurrent programming enhance their capabilities, they will provide tools for developers to more efficiently manage concurrency within user-space applications. The continued improvement of libraries that abstract away the intricacies of thread management and synchronization will empower developers, allowing them to focus on creating performant applications without getting bogged down by concurrency complexities.

Lastly, community and collaboration will remain critical to the evolution of concurrency solutions in the Linux kernel. The kernel community has a tradition of fostering discussion and sharing best practices, which is essential in identifying challenges and collaboratively finding solutions to concurrency-related issues. Contributions from diverse groups—including academia, industry, and individual developers—will shape the future of concurrency in the kernel, as collective knowledge and experience drive innovative solutions.

In conclusion, the landscape of concurrency solutions in the Linux kernel is on the cusp of transformation, influenced by advancements in hardware, the rise of distributed computing, and the increasing complexity of applications that leverage multi-threading. Embracing new synchronization mechanisms, incorporating hardware-based solutions, and fostering a collaborative community will be pivotal in defining how effectively Linux manages concurrency in future computing environments. The continued focus on performance and efficiency will undoubtedly propel the Linux kernel further into the realms of scalability and innovation, ensuring its relevance in an increasingly complex technological landscape.

6. Memory Management: Allocating and Optimizing Resources

6.1. Virtual Memory Architecture

Virtual memory architecture represents a cornerstone of modern operating systems, including the Linux kernel, providing an elegant solution for managing memory resources efficiently while ensuring optimal performance and system stability. The virtual memory system gives applications the perception of a large contiguous memory space, decoupled from the actual physical memory limitations of the hardware. This sophisticated architecture underpins how memory is allocated, utilized, and reclaimed within the Linux ecosystem, enabling the robust multitasking capabilities that modern computing demands.

At its most fundamental level, virtual memory architecture allows the Linux kernel to create an abstract view of memory for each process. Every process operates in its own virtual address space, providing a layer of isolation that enhances security and stability. The separation of memory spaces ensures that one process cannot inadvertently interfere with the memory allocations of another, a significant advantage in preventing data corruption and maintaining system integrity.

The kernel employs a mechanism known as paging to implement this virtual memory architecture. Memory is divided into fixed-size units called pages, typically 4KB in size. Each process's virtual address space is mapped to these physical pages, creating a flexible structure that can grow and adapt to the processes' needs dynamically. This means that as a process requests memory, the kernel can allocate pages from different areas of physical memory, optimizing resource allocation and managing fragmentation.

Page tables serve as the backbone of this architecture, acting as a bridge between virtual addresses and the corresponding physical locations in memory. Each process has its page table, which the kernel maintains and updates as the process executes. When a virtual address is requested, the kernel consults its page table to determine the corresponding physical frame. If the mapping exists, the kernel quickly accesses the data; if not, a page fault occurs—a signal that the required page is not currently in physical memory and must be fetched from secondary storage.

One compelling aspect of this virtual memory system is its ability to facilitate demand paging. This technique allows the kernel to load only the necessary pages into physical memory when they are referenced, freezing unnecessary memory usages. This approach not only conserves resources but also speeds up process initiation, allowing application responsiveness to improve. Demand paging is particularly effective in controlling memory usage in environments where multiple applications run concurrently, a common scenario in modern multitasking operating systems.

A dual mechanism for managing memory is also embedded in the Linux kernel: paging in/out. When the physical memory becomes saturated, the kernel employs page swapping, which involves moving inactive pages to a designated area on the disk, known as swap space. The introduction of this mechanism allows physical memory to be freed for active processes, significantly expanding the perceived memory available to applications. However, it's essential to recognize that excessive paging can hamper performance, leading to increased latency due to the slower speed of disk accesses compared to RAM. Therefore, efficient management of when and which pages are swapped in and out is a critical aspect of the kernel's memory management strategy.

Optimizing RAM usage is another crucial consideration within the realm of virtual memory architecture. The Linux kernel incorporates sophisticated algorithms to track memory usage effectively. Techniques such as memory overcommitment allow the kernel to allocate more memory than available, based on heuristics that predict application behavior and memory usage patterns. This flexibility can be advantageous in high-availability environments, where applications often do not use the full memory they request.

Cache mechanisms reinforce memory utilization, enhancing performance across varied workloads. The kernel utilizes the page cache —a designated area of RAM to hold copies of frequently accessed disk data. Caching significantly reduces the time taken to read from or write to storage devices, as accessing data from RAM is orders of magnitude faster than from disk. By intelligently managing the cache, the kernel can strike a balance between performance and memory utilization, ensuring that the most pertinent data is readily accessible while still maximizing the effective use of RAM.

Moreover, addressing memory leaks and overflows is vital within the virtual memory architecture to maintain system integrity and performance. The kernel employs monitoring tools to track memory allocations and deallocations systematically, implementing best practices to prevent leaks. Techniques such as reference counting and region-based memory management help mitigate both memory overflows and leaks, allowing developers to manage memory allocation efficiently.

In addition to addressing potential pitfalls, the architecture evolves to embrace emerging technologies. As computing power continues to expand, the virtual memory system may adapt to accommodate advanced requirements, such as heterogeneous memory systems that combine different memory types (e.g., DRAM, NAND) for optimal resource allocation.

In summary, the virtual memory architecture encapsulated within the Linux kernel serves as a robust foundation for managing memory resources, facilitating optimal application performance while safeguarding system stability. Through paging, isolation, efficient resource allocation, and intelligent use of caching, the kernel ensures that memory management operates in a manner that balances both user needs and underlying hardware limitations. As technology advances, the ongoing refinement of virtual memory architecture will play an essential role in ensuring that the Linux kernel remains adept at meeting the challenges posed by evolving workloads and applications, reinforcing its position as a cornerstone of the open-source computing landscape.

6.2. Page Swapping Techniques

Page swapping techniques are a critical component of memory management in the Linux kernel, focused on optimizing how system resources are utilized and ensuring smooth performance under varying workloads. As systems run multiple processes that require more memory than may be physically available, efficient page replacement strategies become essential. The Linux kernel implements several algorithms and mechanisms to manage this dynamically, balancing resource allocation with application responsiveness. This section explores the various page swapping techniques, their mechanisms, and their significance in optimizing performance and resource utilization.

At its core, page swapping involves moving pages of memory between physical RAM and secondary storage (often referred to as swap space). The need for swapping arises primarily when the system's physical memory becomes exhausted, forcing the kernel to free memory for active processes. Thus, understanding how the Linux kernel approaches the management of pages provides insight into overall system performance and responsiveness.

One of the foundational mechanisms employed by the kernel for page swapping is the page replacement algorithm. Various algorithms have been developed, each with different strategies for deciding which pages to evict from memory. The goal is to minimize the performance impact incurred from page faults, which occur when a process requests a page that is not currently loaded into RAM. Key algorithms used in the Linux kernel include:

1. Least Recently Used (LRU): This algorithm prioritizes keeping pages in memory that have been referenced recently. It operates under the principle that pages accessed recently are likely to be accessed again soon. When a page needs to be replaced, the kernel will evict the least recently used page, freeing up space for the new

page. LRU provides a good balance between performance and efficiency, although tracking access patterns can introduce overhead.

2. Clock Replacement Algorithm: A variation of LRU, the clock algorithm uses a circular queue to maintain pages in memory. Each page is associated with a reference bit, indicating whether it has been accessed recently. When the system needs to evict a page, it scans the circular list, skipping over pages with a reference bit set to 1 while resetting the bit to 0. When it finds a page with the reference bit set to 0, it evicts that page. This method offers a more efficient way to approximate LRU without the overhead of maintaining a complete access history.

3. First-In, First-Out (FIFO): This algorithm is straightforward—pages are replaced in the order they were brought into memory. While its simplicity is appealing, FIFO often performs poorly in comparison to LRU and clock algorithms due to the risk of evicting pages that may still be in demand.

The Linux kernel's approach to swapping is further enhanced by its use of a process known as "swapping out." When a page must be swapped out, the kernel evaluates its notable criteria, including the page's activity level and its dirtiness (whether the page has been modified). Inactive pages, especially those that have not been recently accessed or have clean copies stored back on disk, are generally prime candidates for swapping. This decision-making process aims to minimize the latency introduced by page faults by ensuring that the most frequently accessed data remains in physical memory.

Developers can also leverage the swappiness parameter, an adjustable kernel setting that influences the aggressiveness of the swapping mechanism. Higher swappiness values instruct the kernel to prefer swapping out pages rather than dropping cache data, while lower values prompt the kernel to minimize swapping, retaining as much information in memory as possible. This flexibility allows system administrators to tailor memory management to the specific workload and operational patterns of their applications.

In addition to selecting pages for replacement, the Linux kernel employs various caching techniques to enhance performance. The page cache retains copies of file data in memory, allowing for rapid access and improved read times. The cache system reduces the frequency of disk I/O operations, significantly boosting the efficiency of applications that rely on file access. When the system runs low on physical memory, the kernel will reclaim cache memory, striking a balance between caching frequently accessed data and allowing room for active applications.

Another sophisticated technique employed by the Linux kernel is the use of transparent huge pages (THP). THP allows the kernel to manage memory in larger chunks, reducing page table overhead and improving overall memory access speeds. This is particularly advantageous in workloads that handle large data sets or utilize big data processing, as it minimizes the complexity induced by frequent page management and swapping operations.

Furthermore, the kernel also implements mechanisms to handle dirty pages—pages that have been modified but not yet written back to their underlying storage. The kernel will periodically flush these dirty pages to disk to ensure data integrity and consistency. Writers can be managed effectively by tracking the rate at which dirty pages accumulate, thus controlling the pressure on physical memory and reducing the likelihood of performance degradation during high writing activity.

In summary, page swapping techniques within the Linux kernel are fundamental to managing memory efficiently and optimizing the overall system performance. By leveraging various algorithms such as LRU, clock replacement, and FIFO, alongside configurable parameters like swappiness, the kernel dynamically adjusts memory usage in response to workload changes. Ultimately, page swapping serves as a crucial framework that enables Linux to run robustly, accommodating diverse applications while maintaining responsiveness and minimizing latency. As future workloads continue to evolve, ongoing advancements in page management strategies will continue to shape the memory landscape in the Linux ecosystem, ensuring its role as a pillar of modern computing remains intact.

6.3. Optimizing RAM Usage

Optimizing RAM usage in the Linux kernel is a critical concern, particularly as systems handle increasingly complex workloads and operate with limited physical memory. The Linux kernel employs a multifaceted approach to manage memory effectively, ensuring that applications run smoothly while maximizing resource allocation. This section will delve into the various strategies and techniques used to optimize RAM usage, exploring concepts from memory management architectures to caching mechanisms, and discussing their significance in maintaining system performance and responsiveness.

At the core of memory optimization is the Linux kernel's virtual memory architecture, which provides each process with the illusion of a large, uninterrupted block of memory. This abstraction is essential for memory management, allowing multiple applications to run simultaneously without interfering with each other's operations. Virtual memory is accomplished through a combination of paging and segmentation, where memory is divided into pages that can be loaded and swapped as needed. Each page can be mapped to physical memory or stored in secondary storage, allowing for a flexible allocation that adapts to the system's memory demands.

One of the critical principles underlying RAM optimization is the efficient management of physical memory through dynamic allocation and deallocation. When a process requires memory, the kernel's memory manager allocates the appropriate number of pages based on the application's needs. When pages are no longer in use, the kernel can reclaim that memory, making it available for other processes. This dynamic management ensures that physical RAM is utilized optimally, avoiding wastage and maintaining performance, particularly in multitasking scenarios.

The Linux kernel also employs various algorithms to determine how memory pages should be allocated and freed. Demand paging, for example, allows the kernel to load only the pages that a process actively uses, minimizing memory footprint. This is complemented by page replacement algorithms, such as Least Recently Used (LRU) and the Clock algorithm, which help the kernel decide which pages to evict when RAM becomes scarce. Choosing the right pages to swap out is crucial for maximizing available memory while maintaining application responsiveness.

A significant aspect of memory optimization is managing the balance between active and inactive memory. The kernel regularly monitors the usage patterns of memory pages, transitioning them between states based on their activity. Recently accessed pages are kept in physical memory, while less-used pages can be moved to swap space, freeing up RAM for active processes. This transition is vital in ensuring that high-demand applications have quick access to the resources they require without unnecessary delays caused by paging.

Caching mechanisms further enhance RAM optimization by storing copies of frequently accessed data in memory. The Linux kernel implements several types of caches, most notably the page cache, which retains copies of data from disk operations. When an application requests data, the kernel first checks the cache before accessing the slower disk. By leveraging caching, the kernel can significantly reduce the number of disk reads and writes, improving overall system performance and minimizing wear on storage devices.

In addition to traditional caching strategies, the kernel can adopt write-back caching techniques. In write-back caching, changes made to data are initially written to the cache before being asynchronously written back to the disk. This method allows the system to continue processing without waiting for disk operations to complete, effectively improving throughput and responsiveness during read and write operations.

Addressing memory leaks and overflows is also crucial for efficient RAM usage. Memory leaks occur when memory that is no longer needed is not released, leading to gradual resource depletion. The kernel implements mechanisms to detect and mitigate memory leaks, such as reference counting and slab allocation. Developers are encouraged to adopt best practices in coding to ensure proper memory management, which can include utilizing tools such as Valgrind and AddressSanitizer to analyze memory usage and identify potential leaks.

In terms of configuration, the Linux kernel offers tunable parameters that allow system administrators to adjust RAM usage strategies based on workload requirements. From modifying the swappiness value to controlling how aggressively the kernel swaps memory pages, these parameters provide a level of granularity that can optimize performance for specific applications or hardware configurations.

As applications and workloads evolve, so too will the strategies for optimizing RAM usage within the Linux kernel. Advances in hardware, such as the introduction of non-volatile memory technologies and larger memory capacities, will inform new approaches in memory management. Emerging paradigms will likely include more sophisticated memory allocation strategies, intelligent caching algorithms, and machine learning techniques to predict memory usage patterns and adapt dynamically.

In conclusion, optimizing RAM usage in the Linux kernel involves a comprehensive interplay of dynamic memory allocation, efficient caching, and proactive management of memory resources. By utilizing demand paging, employing effective page replacement algorithms, implementing robust caching strategies, and addressing potential memory leaks, the kernel ensures that available resources are maximized for performance and responsiveness. As technology advances and applications become more resource-intensive, the Linux kernel's strategies for optimizing RAM will continue to evolve, reinforcing its capability to support a diverse range of workloads and maintain its position as a leading choice in operating systems.

6.4. Caching Mechanisms Used by Kernel

Caching mechanisms in the Linux kernel play a vital role in enhancing system performance by reducing latency and increasing efficiency when accessing frequently used data. Caching optimizes the flow of data between the CPU, memory, and storage devices, ensuring that applications can operate at peak effectiveness. Understanding the intricacies of caching enables developers and system administrators to maximize the potential of their Linux-based systems. This section delves into the various caching strategies utilized in the kernel, how they operate, and their significance in the broader context of operating system performance.

At the fundamental level, caching works on the principle of storing copies of data that are frequently accessed, thereby minimizing the need to repeatedly fetch the data from slower persistent storage such as disk drives. In the Linux kernel, caching is primarily implemented through the page cache, which temporarily holds copies of file data in memory. When a process accesses a file, the kernel checks the page cache before initiating a more time-consuming disk read operation. If the requested data is present in the cache (a "cache hit"), it can be retrieved almost instantaneously, contributing to faster overall performance. Conversely, if the data is not in the cache (a "cache miss"), the kernel must read from the disk, leading to increased latency.

The page cache operates in conjunction with the buffer cache, which holds metadata and structural information about files, such as directory contents and file attributes. While the page cache focuses on actual data blocks, the buffer cache optimizes access to the file system's organizational structure. Both caches work in tandem to accelerate file system operations, ensuring that both data and metadata are readily available when accessed by applications.

To further optimize caching efficiency, the Linux kernel employs various caching strategies. One well-known approach is the use of the Least Recently Used (LRU) algorithm, which helps the kernel manage which pages to keep in the cache and which to evict when memory resources become constrained. The LRU algorithm tracks the usage of cached pages, maintaining the most recently accessed or "hot" pages in memory while periodically dismissing less frequently accessed or "cold" pages. By intelligently prioritizing which pages to retain, LRU helps to ensure that the cache remains filled with the data that applications are most likely to request, striking a balance between memory usage and performance.

Additionally, Linux uses demand-paging mechanisms to manage cache entries dynamically. This means that the kernel will only load pages into the cache when they are needed, minimizing memory overhead and ensuring that the cache remains as efficient as possible. As applications read from or write to files, the kernel automatically updates the contents of the cache, ensuring that the most current data is fast and accessible. This adaptive caching strategy helps reduce unnecessary memory consumption, which can lead to system performance degradation.

The effectiveness of caching within the Linux kernel transcends mere data retrieval. It also plays a significant role in write operations. The kernel utilizes a technique known as write-back caching, wherein write operations are initially performed on the cache rather than being immediately written to disk. This allows applications to continue executing without being delayed by slow disk write times. The kernel periodically flushes the modified data from the cache back to the underlying storage, ensuring data integrity while maintaining high performance for write-heavy workloads.

However, the presence of cached data poses challenges in terms of data consistency. To prevent issues arising from outdated information being presented to applications, the kernel implements mechanisms to synchronize the cache with the underlying storage. This includes techniques like write-through caching, where writes to the cache trigger immediate writes to the disk, ensuring that no data is lost. The kernel also provides a way to flush caches manually through system calls or commands, allowing system administrators to maintain control over cache behavior when needed.

The impact of caching extends beyond file systems; it also pertains to memory management and the efficient handling of application data. The kernel utilizes caching strategies for page tables, which map virtual memory addresses to physical addresses. By caching page table entries, the kernel reduces the overhead associated with accessing memory, enabling quicker context switches as processes interact with shared data.

As systems evolve and the demand for performance continues to escalate, caching mechanisms in the Linux kernel are also adapting. Emerging technologies such as non-volatile memory (NVM) and persistent memory present new opportunities for caching strategies, fundamentally altering how data storage and retrieval are approached. The kernel is undergoing refinements to accommodate these technologies, ensuring that caching remains relevant and efficient within modern architectures.

In addition to traditional file and memory caching, kernel developers and system architects are exploring techniques like content-aware caching, where caching decisions are made based on the nature of the data being accessed. By making intelligent caching decisions informed by application behavior and workload characteristics, it is possible to further enhance performance and resource utilization.

In summary, caching mechanisms in the Linux kernel are integral to optimizing system performance and ensuring the efficient handling of data. Through implementations like the page cache and buffer cache, along with sophisticated algorithms for managing cached data, the kernel can improve the speed of data retrieval, enhance writing efficiency, and minimize resource consumption. As caching strategies continue to evolve alongside emerging technologies and workloads, they will remain a critical component of the Linux kernel's architecture, enabling it to meet the performance demands of modern computing environments.

6.5. Addressing Memory Leaks and Overflows

In the intricate landscape of software development, particularly within the Linux kernel, memory management, encompassing the careful handling of memory allocation, optimization, and recovery, is a crucial domain of focus. Memory leaks and overflows are two pervasive issues often encountered in the development process, requiring significant attention from developers to maintain system performance and reliability.

Memory leaks occur when a program allocates memory but fails to release it back to the system after usage, leading to a gradual increase in memory consumption. This issue can culminate in performance degradation, as the available memory dwindles, causing applications to slow down, freeze, or even crash due to insufficient memory. The Linux kernel, with its vast ecosystem and multitude of running processes, is prone to the ramifications of memory leaks, which can affect overall system stability. Hence, addressing memory leaks is paramount.

Efficient strategies to prevent memory leaks begin with robust coding practices. Developers must ensure that every allocation made by the kernel, typically through functions like `kmalloc()` for dynamic memory allocation, is paired with a corresponding deallocation through `kfree()` when the memory is no longer needed. Adopting a vigilant approach to memory management involves thorough reviews and analyses, where developers must examine the code for potential paths where memory allocated may remain unreturned to the system, particularly in error handling routines where the likelihood of resource leaks can increase.

To actively monitor memory usage and identify leaks, developers can leverage various tools available within the Linux ecosystem. One popular tool is `kmemleak`, which functions similar to garbage collection mechanisms but specifically targets kernel memory. This tool scans for allocated memory regions and cross-references them against the addresses that have been freed, effectively identifying memory that has been allocated but not released properly. When employed during testing and debugging phases, kmemleak can provide critical insights into memory handling, ultimately reducing the instances of leaks in the production environment.

Furthermore, rigorous testing methodologies play a pivotal role in addressing memory leaks. Developers can integrate unit tests that specifically evaluate memory usage in their kernel modules, ensuring that every allocation is validated and properly managed. This approach not only helps detect leaks early in the development cycle but fosters a culture of accountability around resource management amongst developers. Additionally, employing tools like Valgrind in user space can assist in spotting memory errors and leaks during kernel module development, providing developers with clear reports on misuse and helping them track down potential leaks effectively.

Memory overflows, on the other hand, present a significant security risk whereby a process writes more data to a memory buffer than it can accommodate. This action can lead to corruption of adjacent memory, resulting in undefined behavior or exposing the system to attacks like buffer overflows, which can be exploited by malicious actors to gain unauthorized access or escalate privileges. The Linux kernel must maintain stringent protocols for handling memory boundaries to mitigate overflow risks.

To safeguard against memory overflows, the kernel utilizes robust memory management practices, including data structure size checks and bounds checking on buffers during allocation. Developers can make use of functions that limit data copies to a specified length, ensuring that the memory allocated can accommodate the required data size without running the risk of overflow. In addition, the implementation of safe string manipulation functions like strncpy() and snprintf() that include size parameters reduces the likelihood of buffer overruns by enforcing boundaries on input sizes.

In parallel, employing compiler features such as stack canaries and Address Space Layout Randomization (ASLR) can further fortify protective barriers against memory overflows. Stack canaries, which are special values placed on the stack, can help detect unexpected modifications during program execution, signaling an overflow attempt. Similarly, ASLR makes it more difficult for attackers to predict the memory addresses where processes or data are loaded, thereby hindering their exploitation tactics.

The kernel's continuous monitoring and application of techniques such as kernel address sanitizers and memory bounds checking reinforce the importance of memory integrity. These layers of strategies collectively form a resilient framework against both memory leaks and overflows, where proactive safeguards are put in place to prevent resource mismanagement and secure kernels against potential threats.

As technology continues to advance, addressing memory leaks and overflows within the Linux kernel remains an ongoing effort intensified by the growing complexity of systems and applications it supports. Developers and maintainers must remain alert to emerging trends, adopting new practices and technologies that promote effective memory management and ensure that the Linux kernel remains not only robust and high-performing but secure against the vulnerabilities that memory mismanagement can introduce.

In conclusion, the management of memory leaks and overflows within the Linux kernel is an area marked by vigilance, proactive coding practices, and the integration of robust monitoring tools. Through a combination of thorough code reviews, adherence to memory allocation protocols, and the implementation of protective features, developers can ensure that the kernel operates efficiently and securely, sustaining the foundation of modern computing environments and safeguarding against the risks posed by memory mismanagement.

7. Device Drivers Demystified: Bridging Hardware with Software

7.1. Role and Importance of Device Drivers

The role of device drivers within the Linux kernel ecosystem is pivotal, serving as the crucial link between the operating system and hardware peripherals. As fundamental components of the kernel's architecture, device drivers are responsible for managing the interactions between the software—and by extension the Linux kernel—and the hardware devices installed on a system. This section delves into the integral importance of device drivers, illuminating their functions and highlighting why they are necessary for the seamless operation of hardware within the Linux environment.

In essence, device drivers function as translators that bridge the architecture of the operating system with the idiosyncratic nature of hardware devices. Each device, whether it be a hard drive, network card, or graphics processor, has its own set of features and requirements to operate effectively. Device drivers encapsulate these hardware complexities, presenting a consistent interface to the kernel that abstracts away the intricacies of the underlying hardware. This abstraction allows the kernel to provide a uniform API for applications, regardless of the specific hardware in use.

The importance of device drivers expands significantly when considering the diversity of hardware available in today's computing landscape. From standard components like keyboards and mice to specialized devices such as embedded sensors and high-performance computing cards, the Linux kernel must accommodate a vast array of device types. Each of these devices comes with its own command set, initialization processes, and operational quirks that must be encapsulated within a driver. This variety illustrates the necessity of a well-designed driver architecture to ensure that the kernel can interact with all relevant hardware seamlessly.

Device drivers not only translate commands and manage data flow between the operating system and devices; they also play a critical role in resource management. By controlling access to hardware resources, drivers can ensure that multiple applications can operate efficiently without conflicts. For instance, in a multi-threaded environment, a network driver can manage incoming and outgoing packet streams, allocating bandwidth effectively and ensuring that the transmission of data is prioritized according to current system demands. This resource management capability is essential for maintaining system stability, particularly in environments where hardware is shared amongst various processes and applications.

Furthermore, device drivers are instrumental in maintaining system performance. High-quality drivers can optimize hardware capabilities, enable advanced features, and minimize latency in communications between the kernel and the hardware. For example, modern network drivers can optimize data transmission using techniques such as offloading processing tasks to the hardware, improving overall throughput and latency. Such optimizations result in a more efficient use of CPU resources, allowing the kernel to focus on managing processes rather than continuously servicing hardware operations.

The development and maintenance of device drivers play a pivotal role in the growth of the Linux kernel's capabilities. The open-source model encourages collaboration among developers and hardware manufacturers to create and improve drivers over time. This collaborative environment ensures that newly released hardware can quickly be supported, broadening the range of devices that can effectively operate under Linux. Moreover, community contributions help address bugs and vulnerabilities in drivers, promoting overall system reliability and security.

The flexibility and modularity of the Linux kernel allow for the dynamic loading and unloading of device drivers. This modular approach means users can install, manage, or update drivers without the need for a complete system reboot. Such capabilities enhance system uptime and user experience, particularly on servers or systems requiring high availability. Additionally, this adaptability accommodates hardware upgrades, as users can load the appropriate drivers for newly added devices, streamlining the integration process.

Device drivers also facilitate crucial error handling and recovery mechanisms. They monitor the status of the hardware and report failure conditions or resource conflicts back to the kernel. Through the use of error codes and logging mechanisms, drivers help maintain overall system health by allowing the kernel to react appropriately to hardware errors, such as failing disks or unresponsive devices. Effective error handling within drivers minimizes the impact of hardware failures on the overall system, improving resilience and reliability.

Moreover, as technology advances and hardware evolves, the scope of device drivers is continually expanding. With the increase in the Internet of Things (IoT) devices, for instance, the Linux kernel must adapt to interact with a multitude of new sensors and devices with varied communication protocols. Developments in virtual reality, blockchains, and artificial intelligence also prompt further diversification in device driver development, demonstrating their evolving role in modern computing.

In summary, the role and importance of device drivers within the Linux kernel ecosystem cannot be overstated. Functioning as crucial intermediaries that facilitate communication between the hardware and the operating system, device drivers enable a wide range of applications to operate effectively and enhance overall system performance. As the landscape of hardware continues to change and expand, the adaptability and innovation in device driver development will remain central to the ongoing evolution of the Linux kernel and its capabilities.

7.2. Developing Custom Drivers

Developing custom drivers for the Linux kernel is a pursuit that blends creativity with technical acumen, enabling developers to tailor the kernel's functionality to meet specific hardware requirements and operational needs. This process involves several detailed steps, from understanding the foundational concepts of driver architecture to mastering the intricacies of kernel development. By achieving proficiency in custom driver development, practitioners can not only enhance the Linux kernel's capabilities but also contribute to its vibrant ecosystem.

The initial phase in developing custom drivers begins with a firm understanding of the different types of drivers within the Linux ecosystem. Primarily, device drivers fall into three main categories: block drivers, character drivers, and network drivers. Block drivers manage devices that store data in blocks, such as hard drives or USB drives, while character drivers interface with devices that process streams of data, such as keyboards or mice. Network drivers, on the other hand, handle the transmission and reception of data packets over network interfaces. Familiarity with these categories helps developers identify the appropriate architectural framework for their custom driver.

Once the type of driver is established, developers must then engage with the Linux kernel's infrastructure. The kernel is modular by design, allowing developers to load and unload drivers dynamically without the need for system reboots. This modular approach paves the way for iterative development and testing, enabling developers to refine their drivers through immediate feedback. The primary tools for driver development include the Linux kernel source code, documentation available in the kernel (often found in /Documentation), and the kernel header files that define interfaces, functions, and commands available for driver function.

During the actual coding phase, developers typically utilize the C programming language, as it is the language in which the Linux kernel is written. The first task involves creating a basic driver skeleton that incorporates essential functions. A typical driver includes initialization and cleanup functions, allowing the kernel to manage the driver's lifecycle. The initialization function is invoked when the driver is loaded, populating vital structures and registering the driver with the kernel. Conversely, the cleanup function is executed when the driver is unloaded, ensuring that resources are released appropriately.

Key structures for drivers include `file_operations`, a fundamental structure that defines the operations that the kernel allows on a file accessed through the driver. By populating this structure with function pointers, developers inform the kernel how to handle read, write, open, and close operations for the device managed by the driver. This approach encapsulates the functionality that the driver exposes, creating cohesive interaction between the device and the user space applications.

After establishing the core functionality, developers need to address the interaction between the driver and the underlying hardware. Establishing communication with the hardware may involve dealing with registers, interrupts, and mode settings specific to the device. Accessing device registers typically requires knowledge of the hardware specifications and potentially the use of functions like `ioremap()` for mapping memory allocated for device registers. Moreover, setting up interrupts through the Linux kernel's interrupt handling APIs ensures that the driver can appropriately respond to events from the hardware, enabling timely communication within the system.

Debugging and testing are critical components of the driver development process. The Linux kernel provides a rich set of debugging tools, including kernel log messages that can be output using `printk()`. By employing careful logging practices, developers can diagnose issues arising from incorrect hardware communication or logical errors in the driver code. Using the Kernel Debugger (KGDB) is another useful tactic, enabling developers to attach a debugger for real-time code inspection and stepping through their code.

The final stages of custom driver development involve rigorous testing. Developers should create comprehensive test cases that validate driver behavior under various conditions to ensure robustness and reliability. Additionally, collaborating with end-users to gather feedback during the testing phase is critical, as it provides insights into practical use cases and unforeseen issues that may arise during real-world operation.

In addition to technical skills, becoming an effective contributor to the Linux community revolves around building collaborative relationships. Engaging with existing kernel developers through mailing lists, attending conferences, and partaking in open-source events fosters a culture of shared knowledge. By drawing from the experience of others and contributing back to the community, developers can ensure their custom drivers remain aligned with the kernel's developing standards.

In conclusion, the process of developing custom drivers for the Linux kernel is inherently complex and multifaceted. It involves understanding driver architecture, leveraging appropriate coding practices, engaging in thorough testing, and building collaborative relationships within the ecosystem. By diligently following best practices and remaining receptive to feedback, developers can create effective, efficient custom drivers that extend the functionality of the Linux kernel and contribute positively to its evolving landscape.

7.3. Techniques for Troubleshooting

In the world of software development, particularly concerning complex systems like the Linux kernel, troubleshooting is an essential skill that every developer must acquire. The ability to diagnose, isolate, and resolve issues not only enhances personal proficiency but also contributes to the overall health of the kernel and the ecosystem surrounding it. This chapter focuses on techniques for troubleshooting within the Linux kernel, providing a comprehensive framework that integrates cause identification, testing methodologies, and practical remediation strategies.

Troubleshooting within the Linux kernel environment begins with a fundamental understanding of the architecture and components of the system. Familiarity with the kernel's structure helps developers pinpoint where an anomaly is likely to have occurred, whether it be within device drivers, memory management, process scheduling, or networking. Acquiring a holistic view of how different components interact will significantly reduce the diagnostic overhead, as it allows developers to form educated hypotheses about the cause of an issue.

One of the cornerstones of effective troubleshooting is the ability to reproduce issues consistently. Establishing a controlled environment where specific conditions lead to the observable problem can provide invaluable insights into the underlying cause. Utilizing containerization or virtual machines to replicate the production environment allows developers to manipulate variables and observe outcomes without jeopardizing live systems. This practice not only assists in isolating the problem but also enhances the understanding of how the kernel interacts with specific hardware or software configurations.

Once a problem has been identified, logging emerges as an indispensable tool. The Linux kernel is equipped with robust logging mechanisms that can capture diagnostics at various levels of the system. Developers can utilize `printk()` to generate log messages, which—when strategically placed within critical sections of code— can provide a trail of execution paths leading to the point of failure. Setting appropriate logging levels (emergency, alert, critical, etc.) allows developers to filter the noise and focus on messages pertinent to their current investigation.

Moreover, analyzing logs generated by the kernel can provide a retrospective view of operational anomalies. Tools such as `dmesg` can be utilized to display kernel ring buffer messages, revealing critical notifications, warnings, and error states that have occurred during runtime. Understanding patterns in log messages helps developers recognize recurrent issues and facilitates informed decisions about which areas of the kernel require attention.

Within the context of kernel development, various debugging tools can be employed to gain deeper insights into system behavior. The Kernel Debugger (KGDB) allows developers to attach a debugging interface to the kernel, stepping through code execution, examining memory states, and inspecting variable values. This real-time access to kernel internals effectively eliminates guesswork, allowing developers to pinpoint the exact point of failure in the code.

Another advanced diagnostic tool is ftrace, which provides dynamic function tracing capabilities within the kernel. By instrumenting functions to log their entry and exit, ftrace enables developers to track execution flow and identify potential performance bottlenecks, potentially revealing sections of code that exhibit erratic behavior under specific conditions. Coupling ftrace with performance analysis can also help identify correlations between high system load and specific routines or areas in the kernel, facilitating targeted optimizations.

When it comes to memory management, tools like kmemleak and valgrind can be employed to identify memory-related issues. Memory leaks—where allocated memory is never freed—can escalate over time, leading to resource exhaustion. kmemleak systematically monitors kernel memory allocations, alerting developers to memory that remains allocated without a corresponding deallocation. In userspace applications, valgrind serves a similar purpose, detecting memory errors and providing comprehensive reports of memory management violations, thus acting as an essential aid during the development and tightening of the kernel's memory handling capabilities.

Networking issues also merit specific troubleshooting techniques given their complexity and the critical role they play in kernel functionality. Tools such as tcpdump and wireshark can facilitate packet capturing and analysis, enabling network flow debugging in real-time. Examining packets at various layers assists in diagnosing communication pitfalls between the kernel and network devices, facilitating quick resolutions to connectivity issues.

As issues are diagnosed, developers must rigorously test proposed solutions. Implementing a systematic testing approach, ideally using unit tests, can help validate changes before they are integrated into the main kernel or sent to production environments. Continuous integration systems that automate testing for every kernel build facilitate regression testing, ensuring that new changes don't introduce failures tied to previously resolved issues.

Furthermore, community engagement is a critical aspect of troubleshooting within the Linux ecosystem. Kernel developers often share knowledge and tips through mailing lists and forums, allowing collective experiences with similar issues to become invaluable resources. Collaboration not only accelerates issue resolution but also fosters a sense of community responsibility, as developers contribute to shared documentation and troubleshooting guidelines, creating a legacy of learning.

Lastly, thorough documentation is an essential facet of effective troubleshooting. Recording findings, solutions, and implemented fixes contributes to an evolving knowledge base that can guide future development and troubleshooting efforts. Clear documentation serves as both a reference for the original developer and a resource for others who may encounter similar challenges.

In conclusion, troubleshooting within the Linux kernel is a multifaceted practice that integrates technical expertise, systematic methodologies, and community engagement. Employing thorough logging, utilizing diagnostic tools, engaging in effective memory management practices, and maintaining an open dialogue with the kernel development community empowers developers to resolve issues efficiently and effectively. As technology continues to evolve, these troubleshooting techniques will remain paramount in ensuring the ongoing robustness and reliability of the Linux kernel ecosystem.

7.4. Driver Compatibility Layers

Driver compatibility layers are an essential aspect of the Linux kernel's architecture that enable the seamless interaction and integration of various hardware devices with the operating system. This subchapter will explore the intricate workings of driver compatibility layers, their architecture, and their significance in maintaining system stability and performance while supporting a wide variety of hardware. By bridging the gap between the kernel and diverse hardware, driver compatibility layers play a pivotal role in the overall flexibility and adaptability of the Linux ecosystem.

At the core of driver compatibility layers lies the concept of abstracting device-specific functionalities from the core kernel code. This approach allows developers to create drivers that seamlessly interact with diverse hardware, independent of the specific implementations for each device. It enables the Linux kernel to remain hardware-agnostic, meaning that the same kernel can manage a wide variety of devices without needing extensive modifications to core components. Instead, kernel developers can focus on core functionalities while hardware manufacturers can create drivers tailored to their products.

One prominent example of a compatibility layer is the use of the Generic Device Interface (GDI). The GDI provides a standardized abstraction that enables device drivers to interact with specific hardware features while adhering to the kernel's interface. This standardization can greatly streamline the driver development process, allowing device manufacturers to leverage existing kernel frameworks instead of developing complex interfaces from scratch.

The Linux kernel also employs the concept of modules, which can be dynamically loaded or unloaded based on the devices present in the system. This modular approach allows for easy updates and enhancements to drivers without requiring a complete kernel recompilation or reboot, leading to greater system uptime and flexibility. Custom drivers can be created to fit into the modular framework, allowing seamless integration of new devices, existing devices, or peripheral functionalities as technology evolves.

In addition to traditional drivers, compatibility layers support virtualization and containerization technologies. For example, Virtual Function I/O (VFIO) allows guest virtual machines to access devices directly, enabling performance close to bare-metal conditions. This is particularly important in cloud computing, where resource optimization and rapid provisioning of services are paramount. The kernel provides compatibility layers to manage these interactions efficiently, facilitating the integration of guest operating systems with host hardware.

While the benefits of driver compatibility layers are widely recognized, their implementation is not without challenges. One significant concern is the maintenance of the compatibility layer as hardware evolves. The kernel's driver compatibility layers must continuously adapt to accommodate new protocols and features introduced in the latest hardware revisions. This requires an active community of developers to remain engaged in maintaining compatibility while ensuring no loss of performance or functionality.

Furthermore, the potential for performance degradation can arise when using compatibility layers due to the additional abstraction layers introduced. Driver compatibility layers must be carefully designed to minimize overhead and ensure that hardware-specific optimizations are not lost during interactions. Performance monitoring and optimization practices must be implemented to ensure that the system functions smoothly, particularly in high-demand environments such as enterprise servers or data centers.

Security considerations also play a crucial role in the management of driver compatibility layers. As with any abstraction, vulnerabilities can be introduced at the compatibility layer level, potentially exposing the kernel to malicious exploits. The kernel community prioritizes security, continuously testing and auditing driver compatibility layers to identify and rectify vulnerabilities before they can be leveraged by attackers.

Ultimately, the successful implementation of driver compatibility layers not only enhances the interoperability of the Linux kernel but also fosters a collaborative environment for developers to share knowledge and best practices. Open-source development empowers contributions from a diverse array of developers, generating valuable insights into the complexities of hardware interactions and enriching the kernel's capabilities.

In conclusion, driver compatibility layers represent a vital component of the Linux kernel architecture that enables seamless hardware integration, promotes modularity, and enhances overall system performance. By providing standardized interfaces and supporting numerous devices, the kernel can maintain its flexibility and adaptability amidst the rapid pace of technological innovation. The ongoing engagement of the developer community in maintaining and evolving these compatibility layers ensures that the Linux kernel remains a premier choice for a wide range of applications, from personal computing to enterprise-level solutions.

7.5. Collaborating with the Linux Community

Collaborating with the Linux community is a central tenet of the ecosystem surrounding the Linux kernel, reflecting the principles of transparency, inclusivity, and shared responsibility that have defined its evolution since its inception. This collaborative spirit is not limited to the submission of patches or contributions of code; it encompasses a wide array of social interactions that foster innovation, learning, and problem-solving among developers, users, and stakeholders alike.

At the heart of collaboration within the Linux community lies the kernel mailing list. This list serves as the primary communication channel and feedback loop for developers, maintainers, and users, distributing patches, discussing kernel features, and solving issues. The kernel mailing list is renowned for its high standards, where technical discussions are met with critical reviews and constructive criticism. Engaging with this community requires an understanding of netiquette and respect for the technical expertise of others. It is essential for contributors to present their ideas clearly, provide justifications for their patches, and invite feedback in a way that encourages dialogue.

Participating in this collaborative environment offers tremendous benefits. Developers can tap into a rich reservoir of collective knowledge, drawing upon the expertise of established contributors who possess a deep understanding of various kernel subsystems. This engagement can lead to mentorship opportunities and enhanced technical acumen, further elevating the quality of contributions made. By asking questions, sharing experiences, and openly collaborating on solutions, developers can foster meaningful relationships that strengthen the fabric of the Linux community.

Open-source conferences and events play a considerable role in nurturing collaboration within the Linux ecosystem. These gatherings, such as LinuxCon, the Embedded Linux Conference, and various local meetups, provide platforms for developers to share their work, discuss emerging trends, and forge connections with fellow kernel developers. Attending talks, workshops, and panel discussions enables participants to expand their horizons, learn about cutting-edge developments, and engage in hands-on coding sessions.

Furthermore, many conferences offer opportunities for contributors to present their patches, gather real-time feedback, and discuss their ideas with the kernel maintainers. Such interactions can significantly influence the direction of their work, ensure alignment with community values, and enhance the chances of their contributions being accepted into the mainline kernel.

The collaborative culture of the Linux community strongly emphasizes diversity and inclusion, acknowledging that varied perspectives contribute to more robust solutions and innovations. Initiatives aimed at promoting underrepresented groups within the tech sphere help to cultivate a more equitable environment by supporting newcomers as they navigate the complexities of kernel development. Programs such as outreach efforts, mentoring programs, and coding sprints often aim to provide resources, education, and opportunities for individuals who may lack access to the kernel development community.

Moreover, embracing collaborative practices extends to code contributions. The process of submitting patches to the Linux kernel is formal yet inclusive, allowing developers to sequentially present their work for review. Developers are encouraged to document their patches clearly, explaining the purpose of changes, the benefits they bring, and any potential impact on existing code. The process of engaging with maintainers and responding to feedback is iterative, creating a dynamic environment where contributors can learn from their experiences and refine their skills.

When collaborating with the Linux community, understanding the role of maintainers becomes vital. Each subsystem within the kernel typically has one or more maintainers responsible for guiding its development, reviewing patches, and preserving the integrity of the codebase. Whether through personal conversations or formal patch requests, establishing and nurturing relationships with maintainers can be instrumental in ensuring that contributions resonate with project goals and standards.

As collaboration becomes integral to the journey in the Linux community, contributing to documentation also plays a significant role in fostering growth. Comprehensive and clear documentation empowers existing members and newcomers alike, simplifying learning curves and facilitating contributions. Developers who take the initiative to improve and clarify kernel documentation are enhancing the community's knowledge base and promoting collaboration among users and developers.

The landscape of community collaboration continues to evolve alongside technological advancements. New platforms for sharing knowledge, such as online forums, Git repositories, and documentation wikis, provide relevant spaces for collaboration and communication. The transition to a more virtual environment, particularly in light of recent global events, has demonstrated the resilience of the Linux community as members find innovative ways to interact, contribute, and foster connections in a digital context.

In conclusion, collaborating with the Linux community is a multifaceted endeavor that encompasses a wealth of interactions, opportunities, and resources. By participating meaningfully in mailing lists, engaging with peers at conferences, embracing diversity and inclusion, maintaining strong relationships with maintainers, and actively contributing to documentation, developers can nurture the spirit of collaboration that lies at the heart of the Linux kernel. The strength of this collaborative ethos not only empowers individual growth but also reinforces the vitality of the Linux ecosystem as a whole, ensuring its continued relevance and advancement in the face of evolving technological challenges.

8. Networking and Communication: The Lifeline of the Kernel

8.1. Networking Basics and Concepts

In navigating the vast landscape of the Linux kernel, networking basics and concepts form a fundamental cornerstone in understanding how systems communicate and share resources. The Linux kernel's networking subsystem is extensive and sophisticated, providing support for a myriad of protocols and enabling seamless communication between devices, whether on the same network or across the globe. This chapter aims to introduce the foundational aspects of networking as it pertains to the kernel, emphasizing key concepts, protocols, and structures that underpin effective network communications.

At its essence, networking refers to the practice of connecting computers and other devices in order to share resources, data, and services. This connectivity can take various forms, including local area networks (LANs), wide area networks (WANs), and the ever-expanding internet. Each connection facilitates data transmission, opening the door to a wide array of applications—from web browsing and file sharing to multimedia streaming and cloud services. For the Linux kernel, networking provides a critical channel through which applications can conduct real-time operations, necessitating a deep understanding of the underlying protocols and infrastructure.

The building blocks of networking in the Linux kernel rely on the Internet Protocol Suite, often abbreviated as TCP/IP. This suite defines how data packets are formatted, addressed, transmitted, routed, and received across networks, ensuring seamless communication between disparate devices. The prominence of the TCP/IP model stems from its versatility and robustness, making it the de facto standard for internet communications. Within this model, two key protocols stand out: Transmission Control Protocol (TCP) and User Datagram Protocol (UDP).

TCP is a connection-oriented protocol that establishes a reliable communication channel between two endpoints. It ensures the orderly transmission of data through features such as error detection, message acknowledgment, and retransmission of lost packets. This reliability makes TCP ideal for applications requiring accuracy and completeness, such as web browsing and email. By contrast, UDP is a connectionless protocol, providing faster data transmission with minimal overhead. UDP does not guarantee delivery or order, making it suitable for applications where speed is crucial and some data loss is acceptable, such as video streaming or online gaming.

When a user application intends to send or receive data, it interacts with the networking subsystem exposed by the Linux kernel through APIs. These APIs hide the complexities of the underlying protocol stack, allowing developers to focus on application logic rather than low-level networking intricacies. The socket API is particularly noteworthy, as it provides a powerful interface for creating endpoints for communication, listening for incoming connections, and sending or receiving data. This abstraction significantly simplifies the developer experience and encourages the implementation of diverse networking functionalities.

To facilitate networking, the Linux kernel employs various data structures and protocols that organize and route packets effectively. Networking layers within the kernel are derived from the 7-layer OSI model, but condensed into a simpler structure in the TCP/IP model. These layers include the Link Layer, Internet Layer, Transport Layer, and Application Layer. The Link Layer encompasses protocols managing the physical connection to the network, such as Ethernet, while the Internet Layer is responsible for the logical addressing and routing of packets, utilizing protocols like IP (Internet Protocol) to deliver data across networks. The Transport Layer employs TCP or UDP to ensure data is sent reliably or efficiently, depending on the requirements.

Routing, another vital concept in networking, involves sending packets to their destination through intermediary devices known as routers. Routers maintain routing tables that facilitate the decision-making process regarding the optimal path for packet delivery.

The Linux kernel provides robust routing capabilities, allowing for dynamic management and configuration of routing tables, which can be influenced by routing protocols such as RIP, OSPF, or BGP. Understanding how routing works within the kernel helps developers ensure that their applications can communicate effectively across various network topologies.

As security remains a paramount concern in networking, the Linux kernel implements several mechanisms to safeguard data transmitted across networks. Technologies such as the IPsec suite provide encryption and authentication at the IP layer, ensuring that sensitive information can traverse potentially insecure networks securely. Additionally, the kernel's support for firewalls and other security tools further enhances protection against unauthorized access and malicious attacks.

In recent years, emerging trends in networking have outlined the direction for the future of kernel integration. With the rise of cloud computing and virtualization, container technologies like Docker and Kubernetes necessitate efficient networking solutions that can seamlessly connect isolated applications. The Linux kernel's advancing capabilities in networking must adapt to meet these demands, providing features for service discovery, load balancing, and scalability across distributed systems.

In conclusion, networking basics and concepts within the Linux kernel encompass a rich tapestry of protocols, tools, and technologies designed to facilitate communication and resource sharing in modern computing environments. A firm grasp of these foundational elements equips developers and system administrators to build applications capable of thriving in interconnected landscapes, ensuring efficiency, reliability, and security. As network technology continues to evolve, mastering these fundamental concepts will remain instrumental in leveraging the full capabilities of the Linux kernel and fostering a thriving, interconnected digital ecosystem.

8.2. Understanding Protocols and Interfaces

Understanding protocols and interfaces in the context of the Linux kernel is vital for developing effective networking solutions and creating systems that can communicate seamlessly. Protocols serve as the rules and conventions governing the exchange of data between devices, while interfaces act as the mediums through which these protocols are implemented and managed within the kernel. By dissecting both protocols and interfaces, developers can gain insights into creating more responsive, efficient, and secure network communications within the kernel ecosystem.

The networking stack in the Linux kernel is fundamentally built on established protocols dictated by the TCP/IP model, which segments networking activities into a series of manageable layers, commonly referred to as layers of abstraction. At the core of this design lies the Internet Protocol (IP), a critical component that standardizes how data packets are delivered between devices across various networks. Understanding IP involves both version 4 (IPv4) and version 6 (IPv6), each with its own specifications, addressing schemes, and capabilities.

Protocols define behaviors for data transmission and reception; they incorporate rules for how data packets are structured, addressed, and processed. Building on IP are higher-level protocols like Transmission Control Protocol (TCP) and User Datagram Protocol (UDP). TCP, a connection-oriented protocol, ensures reliable data transfer by implementing error-checking mechanisms, data segmentation, and reordering, making it suitable for applications such as file transfer and web browsing. UDP, by contrast, is lightweight and connectionless, favoring speed over reliability—ideal for streaming applications where timeliness is paramount, and losing some data is acceptable.

As developers work with these protocols, they must navigate interfaces that facilitate communication between the kernel and user space applications. A key interface utilized in Linux networking is the socket API, which abstracts the complexities of protocol interactions. Sockets allow applications to create endpoints through which they can send and receive data, effectively managing communication with the underlying networking stacks. This abstraction simplifies the programming model, enabling developers to focus on application logic rather than intricate protocol implementation details. By using sockets, developers can open connections, send commands, and receive data seamlessly, regardless of the underlying transportation protocol being employed (TCP/UDP).

Internally, the kernel provides data structures that represent both protocols and socket state. For instance, when establishing a TCP connection, the kernel maintains control structures that track socket states, manage queueing mechanisms for sending and receiving data, and handle error recovery. These internal states reflect the operational status of each connection, allowing the kernel to optimize data flow based on current network conditions.

The Linux kernel also incorporates several additional layers of abstraction and protocols, including the Link Layer, which governs communication over physical media (e.g., Ethernet). Within this layer, drivers interact with hardware interfaces and are responsible for packet transmission and reception, ensuring packets are delivered to the correct network interface. Protocol subsystems within the kernel, such as the Netfilter framework, can extend this further, enabling packet filtering, network address translation (NAT), and various security measures.

An important consideration while implementing protocols and interfaces is ensuring proper security measures are in place. Security protocols like IPsec provide layers of encryption and authentication, securing data transmissions over potentially insecure networks. Understanding how to leverage these security protocols is vital for maintaining data integrity and confidentiality, especially for sensitive applications within enterprise environments.

The rapid advancement of networking technologies necessitates continuous evaluation of existing protocols and interfaces within the kernel. As trends such as cloud computing, Internet of Things (IoT), and edge computing emerge, the Linux kernel must adapt to evolving networking paradigms. This requires not only enhancements to existing protocols but also the potential development of new interfaces that ensure seamless operation with emerging technologies.

In summary, comprehending protocols and interfaces within the Linux kernel framework is crucial for effectively managing network communications. It equips developers with the knowledge to design robust networking applications by embracing the fundamental networking protocols, utilizing efficient socket APIs, and ensuring secure data transfer. This understanding serves as a foundation for building future-proof systems capable of navigating the dynamic landscape of networking technologies.

8.3. Routing and Switching Mechanisms

Networking is at the heart of modern computing, enabling seamless communication between devices and forming the backbone of the internet. Within the Linux kernel, networking encompasses a rich array of mechanisms, protocols, and concepts that facilitate this interaction. Understanding the underlying principles of networking in the Linux kernel, including routing and switching mechanisms, is essential for developers, system administrators, and anyone interested in the workings of this powerful operating system.

Routing and switching are fundamental processes that determine how data packets traverse networks. Routing involves the decision-making process for determining the best path for packets to reach their destination across interconnected networks. In contrast, switching refers to the movement of packets within the same network, typically functioning within a local area network (LAN). Both processes play a crucial role in network efficiency, reliability, and performance.

The networking subsystem of the Linux kernel provides a sophisticated framework for routing and switching. Among the mechanisms utilized are routing tables, which maintain information about the paths available for directing packets. Each entry in a routing table specifies destination addresses, the associated gateway, and the metrics determining the best path for routing a packet. The kernel uses these tables to make real-time decisions based on the current network topology, ensuring that data is transmitted with the most efficient routing path.

Dynamic routing protocols, such as Routing Information Protocol (RIP) and Open Shortest Path First (OSPF), complement static routes by enabling automatic updates to routing tables based on changing network conditions. These protocols allow routers to communicate with one another to share information about reachable networks, providing adaptability as network configurations shift over time. The Linux kernel integrates support for these protocols, enhancing its capability to manage diverse network environments.

In terms of switching, the Linux kernel encompasses the mechanisms to process and forward packets within local networks. The concept of bridging is crucial here, allowing the kernel to connect multiple Ethernet networks seamlessly. By creating a bridge device within the kernel, packets can be forwarded based on MAC addresses, efficiently distributing data across devices on the same network segment. This capability facilitates communication within LANs, enabling devices to interact without requiring routing through a central network device.

Furthermore, the kernel's involvement extends to Ethernet switching, where the kernel can manage the behavior of Ethernet frames, handling tasks such as packet filtering, spanning tree protocols (STP), and network address translation (NAT). These features contribute significantly to enhancing network reliability and performance. The use of VLANs (Virtual Local Area Networks) enables network segmentation, allowing logical separation of traffic for security or management purposes while leveraging the same physical infrastructure.

As networking protocols evolve, the Linux kernel must remain adaptive to incorporate new technologies. With the emergence of Software-Defined Networking (SDN) and Network Function Virtualization (NFV), the role of networking in the kernel is shifting. SDN introduces a paradigm where network control is decoupled from the physical hardware, enabling programmatic management of the network. The Linux kernel increasingly supports this shift, allowing for higher-level abstractions to manage routing and switching functions dynamically.

Security plays an equally pivotal role in networking, and the Linux kernel integrates mechanisms for ensuring secure communications. Protocols such as IPsec facilitate encryption and integrity checks for IP packets, enabling secure transmission over potentially insecure channels. Other security layers, such as TLS (Transport Layer Security), further bolster secure communications at higher layers within the protocol stack.

As we assess future trends in networking technologies, the integration of advanced concepts such as Internet of Things (IoT), edge computing, and 5G networks will require the Linux kernel to adapt and expand its networking capabilities. These technologies necessitate dynamic routing, efficient resource management, and robust security protocols to support the increasingly connected devices and services proliferating in today's digital ecosystem.

In summary, routing and switching mechanisms within the Linux kernel underpin the essential processes that facilitate data communication across networks. Through dynamic protocols, robust tables, bridging capabilities, and a keen focus on security, the kernel ensures efficient, reliable, and secure data transmission. As technology progresses and networking demands intensify, the kernel will continue to evolve, adapting to meet emerging trends and maintaining its critical role at the heart of modern networking solutions.

8.4. Security in Networking Protocols

In the vast landscape of technology, networking has become an essential pillar that underpins the seamless operation and communication of systems. Within this domain, securing networking protocols emerges as a primary objective, ensuring that data transmitted across networks remains confidential, integral, and available. The Linux kernel, as a robust and adaptable operating system, incorporates a variety of strategies to enhance security in networking protocols. This subchapter explores the significance of security in networking, the protocols involved, and how the Linux kernel addresses these challenges.

At the heart of networking security lies the understanding that various threats can jeopardize data transmission. Cyber-attacks, unauthorized access, and data interception are just a few potential vulnerabilities that can exploit inadequacies in communication protocols. As data packets traverse networks, they may pass through multiple nodes, making them susceptible to interception and manipulation. Thus, ensuring the integrity and security of these packets is of paramount importance.

The Linux kernel employs several security mechanisms to fortify networking protocols. One of the foundational elements is encryption, which encodes data in such a manner that only authorized parties can decipher it. This process employs cryptographic algorithms that transform plaintext into ciphertext, making intercepted data unreadable without the proper keys. Two widely adopted encryption protocols are Secure Sockets Layer (SSL) and its successor, Transport Layer Security (TLS). These protocols provide secure communication over the internet by establishing secure connections between clients and servers, ensuring that sensitive information, such as login credentials and financial data, remains protected.

The kernel's support for IPsec (Internet Protocol Security) further extends its capability to secure data at the network layer. By authenticating and encrypting IP packets, IPsec provides a level of security that protects data at its source and ensures secure transit. This is particularly beneficial in Virtual Private Network (VPN) implementations, where secure connections are established over potentially untrusted networks. The Linux kernel's IPsec implementation supports various modes, such as transport and tunnel modes, allowing flexibility based on the specific use case and required level of security.

Moreover, the kernel incorporates additional layers of security governed by its networking stack, such as the Netfilter framework. Netfilter is a powerful subsystem that enables packet filtering, allowing administrators to set rules governing which packets can enter or leave the system. This approach enhances security by providing a mechanism to block malicious traffic and prevent unauthorized access. Newer technology like the nftables framework builds on this foundation, simplifying and streamlining how firewall rules are defined and implemented.

Another key aspect of networking security in the Linux kernel is the use of access control lists (ACLs). ACLs allow for more granular control over who can access network resources. By defining rules specifying the permissions granted to users or groups, the kernel can enforce strict access policies. For instance, sensitive network interfaces can be configured to accept packets only from trusted sources, mitigating the risk of unauthorized access.

Security in networking protocols also hinges on authentication mechanisms, which ensure that only legitimate users can access resources or data. The kernel supports various authentication methods, including password-based authentication, Public Key Infrastructure (PKI), and certificate-based authentication. By establishing robust authentication protocols, the Linux kernel ensures that data can only be accessed or modified by authorized users.

Intrusion detection and prevention systems (IDPS) complement the security mechanisms embedded within the Linux kernel's networking protocols. These systems monitor network activities for malicious behavior, providing real-time alerts to potential threats. The integration of tools such as Snort and Suricata into the kernel infrastructure helps bolster overall security by enabling detection and response capabilities to emerging vulnerabilities and exploitation attempts.

As technology evolves, the Linux kernel's approach to securing networking protocols must adapt accordingly. Emerging trends such as software-defined networking (SDN) and the proliferation of Internet of Things (IoT) devices present unique challenges that necessitate innovative security strategies. The kernel community must remain proactive in refining security protocols to address evolving threats, leveraging community contributions to stay ahead of risks associated with increasingly decentralized and interconnected systems.

In conclusion, security in networking protocols is a multifaceted challenge that the Linux kernel continuously addresses through a variety of mechanisms and protocols. From encryption and authentication to access controls and intrusion detection systems, the Linux kernel implements a comprehensive approach to safeguarding data transmissions. As networking technologies evolve and new security threats emerge, the kernel's commitment to adapting and enhancing its networking security measures will ensure that it remains a reliable foundation for secure communications in an interconnected digital world.

8.5. Future Networking Trends and Kernel Integration

Future Networking Trends and Kernel Integration

As technology continues to evolve, the landscape of networking is witnessing transformative changes that demand robust adaptation from the Linux kernel. These shifts are not merely trends but rather paradigms that redefine how data communications occur, enabling new applications and enhancing existing frameworks. Understanding these future networking trends is integral for developers, administrators, and enthusiasts who aim to leverage the capabilities of the Linux kernel in a rapidly changing environment. In this context, we will explore several key trends and discuss how these developments necessitate advanced kernel integration to ensure optimal performance, security, and scalability.

One of the most prominent trends shaping the future of networking is the growing ubiquity of Internet of Things (IoT) devices. The proliferation of connected devices—from smart home appliances to industrial sensors—has resulted in an exponential increase in network traffic and a significant need for a more efficient handling of data. As IoT devices continue to multiply, the Linux kernel must adapt its networking stack to accommodate the unique requirements of these devices, often characterized by low power consumption, minimal bandwidth, and the need for real-time data processing. Kernel integration will be crucial in ensuring that networking protocols can efficiently manage the vast array of IoT devices while maintaining responsiveness and reliability.

Relatedly, the rise of 5G networks promises a paradigm shift in networking capabilities, providing significantly increased bandwidth, reduced latency, and improved connectivity. The potential of 5G not only enhances mobile data services but also lays the groundwork for innovations like smart cities and advanced telemedicine applications. The Linux kernel must continue to evolve its networking infrastructure to fully harness the capabilities offered by 5G. This includes improving protocols that capitalize on low latency and high throughput while ensuring that security is maintained in high-speed data communications.

Another trend is the embrace of software-defined networking (SDN) and network function virtualization (NFV). SDN decouples the control plane from the data plane in networking devices, enabling a centralized view of the network that can be easily programmed and managed. In tandem, NFV allows network functions to be virtualized and hosted on standard servers rather than proprietary hardware, providing greater flexibility and efficiency. The Linux kernel's architecture must effectively support these technologies, facilitating the integration of dynamic configuration and management tools that allow for real-time updates and optimizations of network functions. This evolving framework will enable administrators to tailor networking capabilities to the specific requirements of their environments while reducing costs and enhancing scalability.

Likewise, the momentum of cloud computing continues to exert significant influence on networking trends. As more applications move to cloud-based services, the need for efficient, reliable networking solutions becomes critical. The Linux kernel is poised to play a significant role in this shift, optimizing how it handles traffic between cloud services and on-premises systems. Enhancements in cloud-native technologies and container orchestration, exemplified by Kubernetes, necessitate seamless kernel-level support for managing network resources effectively. This includes implementing network policies, load balancing, and service discovery mechanisms to ensure that containerized applications can communicate efficiently and securely across distributed environments.

In parallel, the increasing emphasis on security in networking frameworks cannot be overlooked. With the rise in cyber threats, there is a pressing need for robust security measures to protect data transmitted over networks. The Linux kernel must integrate advanced security protocols and practices that safeguard against potential vulnerabilities in the networking stack. Techniques like end-to-end encryption, intrusion detection systems (IDS), and secure access controls will be essential in addressing these challenges. The kernel's continuous evolution will integrate these security measures, ensuring that they are intrinsic to networking solutions rather than being an afterthought.

Machine learning and artificial intelligence (AI) are also making their mark on networking, enabling smarter decision-making and automated optimization of resources. As algorithms evolve, the Linux kernel will need to incorporate capabilities for processing large volumes of data and making real-time adjustments in network configurations based on predictive analysis. This integration could extend to automating network management tasks, enhancing performance, and identifying potential issues before they impact operations.

Finally, as trends converge toward more collaborative and interconnected systems, the need for open communication channels and standardization becomes increasingly relevant. The Linux kernel, being the pillar of open-source collaboration, must continue fostering environments where developers can contribute, innovate, and share knowledge effectively. As new networking technologies emerge, combined efforts among the community will be crucial to developing standards that ensure interoperability and security across diverse systems and platforms.

In conclusion, the future of networking trends and their integration with the Linux kernel presents a landscape rich with opportunities and challenges. As we move further into an era marked by IoT, 5G, SDN, cloud computing, enhanced security, and the utilization of AI, the kernel must adapt robustly to these developments. Continuous innovations in networking will not only enhance the performance and capabilities of the Linux kernel but also ensure that it remains at the forefront of modern computing, providing the groundwork for applications that redefine how we interact, communicate, and innovate in an increasingly connected world.

9. Kernel Development: Tools and Techniques

9.1. Comprehensive Suite of Development Tools

The Linux kernel development ecosystem is rich with tools and techniques designed to empower developers, streamline workflows, and enhance collaborative efforts. This subchapter delves into the comprehensive suite of development tools available, reflecting the importance of an effective toolkit when navigating the complexities of kernel development.

A foundational element in the development toolkit is the integrated development environment (IDE). While kernel development is typically carried out in text editors or command-line tools, there are specialized IDEs that offer features such as code navigation, syntax highlighting, and integrated debugging tools. Editors like Visual Studio Code, Eclipse, and JetBrains CLion can significantly enhance productivity by providing intelligent code completions, error highlighting, and version control integration that simplifies management of code changes.

Version control systems (VCS) are equally crucial for any kernel developer. Git, the predominant version control system used in kernel development, allows developers to manage code changes, track contributions, and collaborate efficiently with others. Learning Git commands for branching, merging, rebasing, and pull requests is essential to navigate the patch submission process and handle potential conflicts arising from multiple developers working on the same codebase. The community's strong adherence to Git best practices ensures that contributions maintain the integrity and quality of the kernel.

Makefiles play a critical role in organizing the build processes for the kernel and its modules. Using Makefiles, developers can define dependencies and build instructions systematically, enabling the compilation of the kernel or specific modules with simple commands. Understanding how to write and modify Makefiles is essential for ensuring that the kernel code compiles correctly, linking to the necessary resources efficiently while preventing build-time issues.

Automated testing tools are an integral part of ensuring code reliability and quality. The kernel community employs various testing frameworks, such as Kernel CI (Continuous Integration) and kselftest, to assess changes consistently and quickly. These frameworks enable automated testing of kernel functionality, ensuring that newly submitted patches do not introduce regressions or break existing features. Developers benefit from integrating these testing routines into their workflow, as they provide immediate feedback on code quality.

Debugging tools are indispensable for plumbing the depths of kernel interactions. Strace and Ltrace are user-space tools that can trace system calls made by applications, enabling developers to monitor and analyze interactions with the kernel. For kernel-space debugging, tools such as KGDB and ftrace facilitate real-time examination and analysis of kernel code execution. These debugging capabilities are instrumental in diagnosing complex issues, optimizing performance, and enhancing the kernel's behavior reliability.

Documentation is an often underrated yet critical tool within the development workflow. Engaging with the kernel's extensive documentation, found within the source tree and in the kernel's code comments, is fundamental for developers seeking to understand subsystems, APIs, and the expected behavior of code components. Tools like Doxygen can generate documentation from source code comments, aiding in keeping information current and accessible.

Parenting the kernel also involves managing various configuration files that guide its building and operational parameters. The kernel's configuration system, relying on .config files generated through tools like make menuconfig, make xconfig, or make gconfig, allows developers to easily select features and modules to include in their build. Mastering this configuration process enhances a developer's ability to tailor the kernel to specific hardware, feature sets, and performance needs.

Monitoring tools provide insights into how the kernel performs in real time. Utilities such as `top`, `iotop`, and `vmstat` offer developers a window into kernel resource usage, allowing them to identify bottlenecks or inefficiencies. These tools empower developers to make informed decisions when optimizing code, resulting in improvements in performance, responsiveness, and stability.

As kernel development evolves, staying current with the tools is paramount. With emerging technologies, such as containers and cloud-native infrastructures, new development tools tailored to interact with these innovations are continually being introduced. The rise of DevOps practices, where development and operations functions are integrated, emphasizes collaboration with operational tools that span the kernel, application code, and cloud environments.

In summary, the comprehensive suite of development tools available to Linux kernel developers encompasses a broad range of utilities designed to enhance productivity, collaboration, and code quality. Familiarity with IDEs, version control systems, automated testing, debugging tools, documentation practices, configuration systems, and monitoring utilities is paramount for mastering kernel development. As technology advances, embracing emerging tools and practices ensures that developers can not only contribute to the growth of the kernel but also adapt successfully to future networking and computing challenges.

9.2. Version Control Systems and their Importance

In the intricate world of software development, particularly within the realm of operating systems, version control systems (VCS) serve as critical tools for managing code changes, facilitating collaboration among developers, and preserving the integrity of projects. This subchapter delves into the significance of version control systems in the context of Linux kernel development, highlighting their vital role in maintaining a cohesive and dynamic development environment.

The landscape of software development, particularly in large-scale projects like the Linux kernel, involves contributions from numerous developers across diverse locations. Given this collaborative essence, ensuring that changes made by one developer do not adversely affect the work of others is paramount. Version control systems facilitate this by allowing developers to track code modifications, collaborate seamlessly, and revert to previous versions if necessary.

At the core of any version control system lies the concept of repositories—structured collections of files that are tracked over time as developers make modifications. The Linux kernel primarily utilizes Git, a distributed version control system that has become synonymous with open-source collaboration. Git empowers developers to clone repositories, create branches for experimenting with new features, and submit patches for review. Its ability to handle large repositories, manage branching effectively, and maintain a clear history of changes makes it an ideal choice for the intricate and ever-expanding Linux kernel.

One of the standout features of Git is its ability to manage branches effectively. Branches allow developers to isolate their work, creating an environment where they can experiment with new ideas without affecting the main codebase. This isolation helps minimize disrupted workflows and encourages creativity, as developers feel free to prototype without the fear of breaking existing functionality. When a feature is stable, changes can be merged back into the main branch, ensuring the integrity of the shared codebase while allowing multiple lines of development to coexist.

Collaboration within the Linux kernel community hinges on the ability to share contributions effectively. Developers can submit patches —small modifications to the codebase—through the kernel mailing list or via pull requests in Git. This process encourages peer review, where fellow developers scrutinize proposed changes for quality and adherence to coding standards. This peer review mechanism ensures that only high-quality contributions make it into the mainline kernel, thus upholding its overall integrity.

The significance of version control systems extends beyond mere code management; they also enhance accountability within the development community. By maintaining a detailed history of changes, Git enables developers to identify who made modifications, when, and the reasons behind those changes. This auditability is vital for understanding the evolution of the kernel and identifying when a particular bug was introduced—an invaluable resource when addressing issues and debugging the code.

In addition to accountability, version control systems also promote transparency. The open-source philosophy championed by the Linux kernel encourages developers to share their contributions openly, allowing for broader community engagement and fostering a culture of collaboration. Anyone can contribute to the kernel, suggest improvements, or report bugs—all supported and facilitated by the documentation and audit trails maintained by the version control system.

Regarding troubleshooting, version control systems can play a pivotal role in resolving issues that arise from code changes. When encountering bugs introduced by recent modifications, developers can quickly revert back to a stable version of the codebase, allowing them to isolate problems and minimize downtime. This capability is crucial for maintaining system stability, especially in a project as large and complex as the Linux kernel, where unintended interactions can lead to significant complications.

With the fast-paced nature of technology and the increasing complexity of modern systems, version control systems will continue to evolve alongside development practices. Emerging trends such as continuous integration (CI) and continuous delivery (CD) leverage version control to automate testing and deployment processes, ultimately leading to faster releases and more reliable software. Teams working on the Linux kernel must stay attuned to these advancements, adapting their workflows to enhance efficiency and responsiveness to community needs.

In conclusion, version control systems play an invaluable role in the development of the Linux kernel, serving as the backbone for collaboration, accountability, and transparency within the community. Tools like Git enable developers to manage code effectively, engage with one another constructively, and maintain the integrity of the kernel as it evolves. As technology advances and the importance of open-source contributions continues to grow, the integration and optimization of version control practices will remain a cornerstone of successful Linux kernel development.

9.3. Refactoring and Code Quality Measures

Refactoring and Code Quality Measures in the Linux kernel development context emerge as essential practices aimed at enhancing code maintainability, readability, and performance. Within the collaborative ecosystem of the Linux community, the implications of code quality stretch beyond individual contributions, influencing overall productivity, collaboration, and the kernel's evolution over time. This subchapter will explore the significance of refactoring, typical strategies employed, and ongoing measures to uphold code quality standards within the kernel.

Refactoring refers to the systematic process of restructuring existing code without altering its external behavior. The intent is to improve code organization, clarity, and efficiency, making it easier to understand, modify, and enhance in the future. As the Linux kernel continues to expand, it accumulates contributions from a myriad of developers, each bringing their own coding style and paradigms. Consequently, maintaining a cohesive codebase that adheres to accepted coding standards becomes paramount. Developers frequently engage in refactoring activities to ensure that new functionality can be integrated smoothly into existing structures.

The significance of refactoring extends to performance optimization as well. The kernel must maintain efficient use of system resources, and old code can often harbor inefficiencies that hinder performance. By analyzing algorithms and data structures used within kernel components, developers can optimize performance-critical paths, enhancing throughput and reducing latency in key operations. For instance, refactoring may involve converting nested loops into more efficient forms or replacing inefficient data structures with better-suited alternatives. Such refinements contribute to an overall enhancement of the kernel's responsiveness and resource management capabilities.

Adopting a consistent coding style is a fundamental aspect of quality measures in kernel development. The Linux kernel community adheres to coding standards detailed in the "Linux Kernel Coding Style" document. These guidelines encompass naming conventions, indentation practices, commenting protocols, and function organization, among other criteria. A uniform coding style not only improves readability but also facilitates peer reviews and collaborative efforts, as developers share a common understanding and expectation of how the code is structured.

Continuous integration (CI) practices are another critical aspect of maintaining code quality within the Linux kernel. As new patches and contributions are submitted, automated systems can evaluate their compliance with established coding standards, as well as execute testing protocols to validate their functionality. Integrating CI tools fosters an environment of rapid feedback, allowing developers to correct issues promptly and ensuring that the introduction of new code does not break existing functionality.

Code review processes form an integral component of the Linux kernel development workflow. When developers submit patches, these contributions are subjected to thorough scrutiny by peers and maintainers. This collaborative review process not only ensures adherence to coding standards but also allows for the sharing of knowledge and best practices. Engaging in code reviews empowers developers to critique each other's work constructively while fostering a sense of shared ownership within the community.

Moreover, extensive testing frameworks exist within the kernel to bolster code quality. Unit tests, integration tests, and kernel self-tests (kselftest) provide mechanisms to validate and verify the intended functionality of kernel modules and components. The systematic testing of patches before they are merged ensures that changes do not introduce regressions, enabling the kernel to maintain stability across releases and iterations.

Addressing technical debt is another crucial facet of refactoring and code quality measures in kernel development. Technical debt accumulates as quick fixes and temporary solutions pile up while transitioning towards more permanent, elegant resolutions. Developers must routinely identify and address these instances to maintain long-term health within the codebase. This proactive approach not only mitigates the complexity of existing code but also paves the way for smoother future enhancements and modifications.

Documentation is often an overlooked aspect of code quality. Well-documented code, including clear comments and design outlines, eases the onboarding process for new contributors and facilitates maintenance. Documenting the intent and functionality of complex code segments is particularly essential in the kernel, where the intricate interaction of various subsystems can be daunting for newcomers. In addition to in-code documentation, maintaining an updated user manual and development guides ensures that users and contributors have access to essential resources.

In conclusion, refactoring and code quality measures are intrinsic to maintaining the integrity, sustainability, and performance of the Linux kernel. By engaging in systematic refactoring, adhering to coding standards, implementing continuous integration practices, fostering collaborative code review processes, and emphasizing rigorous testing and documentation, the kernel community continues to uphold the robust quality of its codebase. As the kernel evolves and technology advances, these practices will remain vital in ensuring that the Linux kernel not only meets current demands but also anticipates and adapts to future challenges and innovations in the computing landscape.

9.4. Continuous Integration Practices

In the fast-paced and rapidly evolving landscape of software development, particularly in the realm of the Linux kernel, Continuous Integration (CI) practices stand as a foundational element for enhancing collaboration, accelerating development cycles, and ensuring the stability and reliability of contributions. Continuous Integration constitutes a systematic approach that allows developers to integrate code changes into a shared repository frequently, often several times a day. This collaborative practice minimizes integration problems, fosters rapid feedback, and promotes quality in the development process.

At the heart of CI practices for the Linux kernel is the use of automated testing frameworks that are integrated into the workflow of kernel development. These frameworks run predefined tests whenever there's a code change, allowing developers to catch regressions and bugs early in the development cycle. The kernel community has adopted tools such as KernelCI, which performs various tests, from booting different kernel configurations to running performance benchmarks, to ensure that the submitted patches do not introduce new issues. These automated tests provide immediate feedback, giving developers a clear understanding of how their changes impact the stability and performance of the kernel.

For contributors, understanding the CI pipeline specific to the kernel is essential. As patches are submitted to the mainline or a development branch, the CI system automatically retrieves the changes and triggers a series of tests. This process includes compiling the kernel, running static analysis tools, executing unit tests, and performing integration tests to verify that the entire system behaves as expected. Successful completion of these tests is often a prerequisite before patches are accepted, ensuring a commitment to quality and robustness throughout the development lifecycle.

Engaging with CI practices also improves collaboration within the Linux kernel community. As multiple developers contribute simultaneously, CI provides a structured environment where integration takes place in a controlled manner. The use of CI fosters a culture of shared responsibility, where contributors are held accountable for their changes, knowing that their code will undergo rigorous scrutiny before becoming part of the official kernel. This transparency encourages a more cohesive development ecosystem and enhances trust among community members.

In addition to automated testing, CI practices often involve code review processes. Developers are encouraged to submit patches to the Linux mailing list, where they are reviewed by peers and maintainers who provide feedback and suggestions. This review process is bolstered by CI as reviewers can reference the results of automated tests when evaluating a submission. By integrating testing outcomes into the review process, maintainers can make more informed decisions regarding code quality and overall contribution acceptance.

Beyond testing and review, CI practices have implications for continuous documentation and knowledge sharing within the community. As patches are developed, it is necessary to maintain clear and comprehensive documentation that accompanies changes, ensuring that the intent and functionality of code are well-understood. CI systems can automate aspects of documentation generation, ensuring that the latest modifications are reflected in the kernel's broader documentation framework, streamlining the knowledge transfer process among existing and new contributors.

Furthermore, CI practices facilitate easier adjustments and adaptations in response to new features or changing requirements in the Linux kernel. As the landscape of technology continues to shift, evolving standards and emerging capabilities necessitate that kernel developers remain agile. Adopting CI allows the community to swiftly incorporate new features while ensuring that existing functionality remains intact. This adaptability is crucial as the kernel serves not only as the foundation for operating systems but also as the backbone for a multitude of embedded systems, cloud environments, and IoT devices.

Looking into the future, the ongoing evolution of CI practices in the Linux kernel community promises further enhancements. Advancements in processing capabilities, artificial intelligence, and machine learning can be harnessed to improve automated testing and predict potential integration issues before they arise. Implementing CI/CD (Continuous Delivery) methodologies will become increasingly vital for speeding up the deployment of kernel updates and patches, reducing the time between coding and release, thus allowing for more rapid innovation cycles.

In summary, Continuous Integration practices represent an essential component of the development process within the Linux kernel community, promoting quality, collaboration, and rapid feedback among contributors. Through automated testing, structured workflows, peer reviews, and documentation processes, CI enhances the kernel's robustness against bugs and regressions, fostering a culture of transparency and support among developers. As technology continues to evolve, so too will the CI practices that drive kernel development, ensuring that the Linux kernel remains at the forefront of innovation and adaptability in an ever-changing digital landscape.

9.5. Future of Kernel Development Practices

The Linux kernel has long served as the backbone of countless operating systems, providing critical functionality foundational to modern computing. As technology evolves, the practices surrounding kernel development must also adapt to meet new challenges and opportunities. This evolution of practices will necessitate both the enhancement of existing methodologies and the adoption of new tools that foster innovation and ensure the kernel remains secure, efficient, and accessible to a broader audience.

One of the most significant trends shaping the future of kernel development practices is the increasing emphasis on automation in the development lifecycle. Continuous Integration (CI) and Continuous Deployment (CD) practices are already being employed throughout the kernel community to enhance collaboration and maintain high standards of code quality. As these practices mature, their integration will become even more robust, enabling developers to automate the testing of new patches and ensure that merges into the mainline kernel are seamless and devoid of regressions. This increased reliance on automation will not only improve the quality of the kernel but also expedite the delivery of features and patches, keeping pace with the rapid technological advancements occurring in the industry.

The need for heightened security will also drive changes in kernel development practices moving forward. As cyber threats become increasingly sophisticated, ensuring the integrity of the kernel against potential vulnerabilities will require the adoption of proactive security measures. This includes rigorous code reviews focused on security, the integration of static and dynamic analysis tools, and a broader commitment to security-focused coding practices among developers. There will likely be an increased focus on training and awareness programs within the kernel community to ensure that contributors understand the importance of writing secure code and can recognize potential vulnerabilities.

Collaboration within the kernel community will continue to be a core value that drives its success. With the rise of remote work and global collaboration exemplified during recent events, fostering inclusiveness and diversity will be an essential part of the community's evolution. Future development practices will increasingly prioritize attracting contributors from varied backgrounds, encouraging diverse perspectives on problem-solving, and establishing mentorship programs that help onboard newer developers into the community. The kernel's growth depends not only on technical skills but also on cultivating a supportive environment that promotes shared learning and collective responsibility.

Open-source principles will continue to guide kernel development practices, but they must also adapt to rapidly changing technological landscapes. As technologies like machine learning, artificial intelligence, and blockchain become more prevalent, kernel practices will increasingly need to accommodate these innovations. This may involve defining new standards for kernel interactions with these emerging technologies, creating additional protocols, or developing compatibility layers that facilitate smooth integrations.

The demand for performance optimization will also be a driving factor behind future development practices. As the variety of devices using Linux continues to expand, from embedded systems and IoT devices to cloud computing platforms, the kernel must evolve to provide robust performance across diverse use cases. This will necessitate ongoing investment in profiling, benchmarking, and performance tuning practices, as well as encouraging developers to take ownership of efficiency in their contributions. The adoption of predictive analysis tools that can anticipate performance bottlenecks and recommend optimizations before they manifest publicly will add a new layer of sophistication to performance management in kernel development.

In terms of tooling, the future of kernel development practices will see expanded use of integrated development environments (IDEs) and enhancement of debugging tools. As development environments become more sophisticated, with advanced features like intelligent code suggestions, seamless integration with version control systems, and robust debugging capabilities, they will empower developers to maintain and enhance kernel code more efficiently. Continuous advancement in tooling will provide developers with the capabilities they need to address the growing complexity of kernel components and ensure high-quality submissions.

The kernel's future is not without challenges. As the community grows, maintaining a cohesive and productive collaborative environment will require active efforts to foster communication, establish transparent governance structures, and ensure adherence to common standards. Open channels of communication through mailing lists, forums, and regular community events will strengthen relationships, helping to bridge divides across geographies and experiences while also serving as a means of sharing knowledge and addressing issues as they arise.

In summary, the future of kernel development practices will be characterized by increased automation, a heightened focus on security, greater collaboration, adaptability to emerging technologies, optimization for performance, improved tooling, and a commitment to inclusivity within the community. By embracing these changes, the Linux kernel will continue to thrive as a powerful, flexible, and essential technology, capable of supporting the demands of the modern digital world and pushing the boundaries of what is possible in computing. As we forge ahead into this dynamic future, the kernel community's commitment to innovation, governance, and collaboration will ultimately dictate its success and longevity.

10. The Patchwork Process: Contributing to Kernel Development

10.1. Understanding the Patch Workflow

Understanding the patch workflow is essential for anyone looking to contribute to the Linux kernel development process. This workflow outlines the steps involved in submitting changes, managing patches, and obtaining approval from maintainers. As a contributor, familiarizing yourself with the patch workflow will enable you to navigate the complexities of kernel development effectively and ensure your contributions align with community expectations while enhancing the overall quality of the kernel.

The patch workflow begins with the identification of a problem or feature enhancement relevant to the kernel. This could stem from an observed bug, performance issue, security vulnerability, or an improvement idea. Before proceeding with code changes, it is crucial to research the existing codebase to ensure familiarity with the relevant subsystems and to avoid duplicating efforts already addressed by previous work.

Once the initial analysis is completed, the next step is to create a patch. Patches represent the difference between the old and new versions of the code, detailing the changes made. For kernel contributions, patches must conform to specific coding and formatting guidelines outlined in the kernel documentation. Utilizing tools such as `git diff` simplifies the patch creation process by generating the necessary output based on local changes.

As part of the patch creation process, developers must adhere to the kernel's submission guidelines, including providing a clear commit message encapsulating the rationale behind the changes. A good commit message should explain the problem being addressed, detail how the changes resolve it, and visualize any consequences for existing code. The kernel community values well-defined commit messages, recognizing that they vastly improve the reviewing process and help maintainers understand the intent behind the patch.

Once the patch is prepared and the commit message is crafted, the next step is to submit the patch for review. Traditionally, the Linux kernel submission process has relied heavily on mailing lists, specifically the Linux Kernel Mailing List (LKML). When sending a patch to the mailing list, developers should ensure it is formatted correctly and is tagged appropriately to capture the attention of maintainers and reviewers. Including a "Cc:" line in the email can help notify relevant parties who might be interested in the changes.

Following patch submission, maintainers will review the patches, assessing their quality, adherence to coding standards, and overall impact on the kernel. This review process can involve back-and-forth communication, with maintainers providing feedback on the patch. Contributors should be prepared to address any comments, questions, or suggestions for improvement, further refining the patch based on community input.

If the patch meets the maintainers' criteria, it is likely to be accepted into the kernel. Upon acceptance, the patch is typically merged into the next release branch during the kernel development cycle. Depending on the urgency and significance of the change, some patches may be queued for immediate integration; others may be bundled and integrated with future patch sets.

The patch workflow also features aspects of tracking and managing patches over time. Contributors should maintain a record of submitted patches to assess their current status—whether pending, accepted, or rejected. Utilizing tools like Git helps streamline the patch tracking process, providing version control features that allow contributors to observe changes, address issues in previously accepted patches, or withdraw patches if they are found to be unnecessary.

Furthermore, as patches proliferate within the kernel, maintaining a coherent and structured archive becomes increasingly important. The Linux community uses Patchwork—a web-based patch tracking system—to organize and monitor patches submitted to the kernel. This tool can provide a visual overview of submitted patches, their statuses, and the history of discussions surrounding them, serving as an invaluable resource for both contributors and maintainers.

In summation, understanding the patch workflow is foundational for effectively participating in Linux kernel development. The workflow encompasses identifying a problem, creating a well-defined patch, submitting it for review, and engaging with maintainers throughout the process. Establishing a successful patch submission involves adhering to community guidelines, crafting articulate commit messages, and actively participating in discussions. By navigating this workflow proficiently, developers can make meaningful contributions that enhance the quality and performance of the Linux kernel while becoming integral members of the collaborative community that drives its success.

10.2. Engaging with the Kernel Mailing List

Engaging with the Kernel Mailing List is crucial for anyone looking to contribute to the Linux kernel development process. This vibrant communication channel serves as the primary platform for developers to discuss patches, propose changes, and collaborate on issues related to kernel development. Understanding the practices, etiquette, and expected behaviors associated with the mailing list is key to effectively participating in this collaborative ecosystem.

The kernel mailing list is not just a forum for submitting patches; it is a dynamic community where developers engage in technical discussions, share insights, and solicit feedback on their work. To make the most of this platform, potential contributors should start by familiarizing themselves with the mailing list's archives, which contain a wealth of discussions covering a multitude of topics—from technical problems and solutions to community governance and development processes.

When a developer is ready to submit a patch, the process should begin with a thorough review of the existing coding standards and submission guidelines. The Linux kernel community has established specific conventions to ensure consistency and clarity across contributions.

By adhering to these guidelines, developers can help maintain the high standards expected of kernel contributions, which will enhance the likelihood of their patches being favorably received.

Crafting a well-structured email to the mailing list is equally important. The subject line should be concise yet descriptive, indicating which subsystem or issue the patch addresses. This clarity aids maintainers in filtering and prioritizing patches, ensuring they focus on relevant contributions. In the body of the email, developers should provide a clear explanation of the problem being solved, the rationale behind their proposed changes, and any potential implications that could affect the kernel's functionality. Including references to any relevant discussions or issue trackers can also strengthen the submission.

As patches are submitted and reviewed, it's vital to engage with feedback constructively. The mailing list is a space for collaborative critique, and developers should be open to suggestions and revisions from peers and maintainers. This process may involve additional discussions to clarify points, explain decisions, or further enhance the code based on community feedback. By maintaining a receptive attitude and fostering productive dialogue, developers contribute positively to the collaborative spirit embodied by the kernel community.

Maintainers play a crucial role in the kernel mailing list, acting as gatekeepers who assess and approve patches. They are responsible for ensuring the quality and stability of the kernel, which can involve asking for additional information, seeking clarifications, or requesting further testing before merging changes. Being responsive to their requests is essential for developers, as it reflects professionalism and respect for the development process.

In addition to technical content, engaging in discussions about broader issues is an important aspect of participation on the mailing list. Topics such as community inclusivity, governance changes, and long-term strategies can greatly influence the direction of the kernel. Contributing to discussions on these matters is encouraged, as developers can share their perspectives and contribute to the collective decision-making process.

Another valuable practice when engaging with the kernel mailing list is to welcome newcomers and assist them in navigating their first contributions. Mentorship plays a vital role in fostering a thriving community. By supporting newer developers, experienced contributors can help cultivate a culture of inclusivity and collaboration, ensuring that knowledge and best practices are continually shared.

Finally, successful engagement with the kernel mailing list goes beyond just one-off interactions. Building relationships within the community, participating in kernel-related events or conferences, and following discussions over time allows contributors to understand the nuances of the community better. This sustained engagement can lead to recognition within the community, opening doors for collaboration on future projects and enhancing overall personal growth as a kernel developer.

In conclusion, engaging with the kernel mailing list is essential for aspiring contributors looking to make meaningful contributions to the Linux kernel development process. By following established guidelines, effectively communicating submissions, engaging constructively with feedback, and fostering community relationships, developers can navigate the complexities of the kernel mailing list and become valuable members of the kernel community. This proactive approach not only solidifies their contributions but also enriches the collaborative culture that defines the Linux kernel ecosystem.

10.3. Best Practices for Patch Submissions

In the expansive realm of Linux kernel development, contributing new code or features often involves navigating a well-defined patch submission workflow. This workflow is crucial for ensuring that contributions meet the community's standards for quality, stability, and maintainability, as the Linux kernel is a collaborative effort involving thousands of developers across the globe. Understanding the patch workflow not only empowers developers to effectively submit their changes but also fosters a culture of respect and professionalism within the community.

The journey to contributing a patch begins with identifying an area in the kernel codebase that could benefit from improvement. This could be a bug fix, a performance enhancement, a new feature, or a security vulnerability that requires addressing. Before diving into coding, it's important for developers to familiarize themselves with the code related to the issue they intend to tackle. This exploration might involve reading source code, referencing documentation, or consulting community resources to ensure a comprehensive understanding of the kernel's architecture and goals.

Once a developer has pinpointed the problem and thoroughly examined the relevant code, they can proceed to create a patch. This involves making code changes in a local development environment, followed by compiling the kernel to ensure that the modifications do not introduce any errors. Developers often use version control systems like Git to manage their code changes efficiently. When creating a patch using Git, it's best practice to ensure that the commit is atomic —meaning it addresses a single issue or makes a single enhancement to maintain clarity when reviewing.

The creation of a clear and descriptive commit message is integral to this process. A well-crafted commit message captures the essence of the changes made, explaining the problem, how the patch resolves it, and any implications that the change may have on the existing codebase. This clarity not only helps maintainers understand the context of the patch during reviews but also serves as documentation for future developers who engage with the code.

Once the patch is prepared and the commit message is finalized, the next step in the workflow is to submit the patch for review. Traditionally, patches are sent via email to the Linux Kernel Mailing List (LKML) or relevant subsystem-specific lists. The email should include the patch as an attachment or as a properly formatted inline message. It is important to follow the community's conventions for mailing list submissions, including adding appropriate tags to the subject line, such as the subsystem being modified (e.g., "net: fix issue with packet routing"), to facilitate prioritization and categorization by the maintainers.

Following submission, the patch enters a review phase where maintainers and fellow developers evaluate the contributions. This stage is characterized by constructive feedback and discussion, wherein maintainers may request modifications, seek clarifications, or highlight potential concerns regarding the submission. Engaging respectfully with the feedback is vital; developers should be open to incorporating suggestions and making adjustments to improve their patches, as this iterative process is essential for maintaining the quality and integrity of the kernel.

If a patch is accepted, it will eventually be merged into the mainline kernel during the integration period. Kernel maintainers manage this merging process, usually aligned with the planned release schedules of new kernel versions. At this point, developers may also want to engage with the community to address any issues or additional discussions that arise, especially if their patch influences broader system functionality.

As patches continue to accumulate within the community, effective tracking of submissions and their statuses is paramount. Developers often utilize tools like Patchwork, a web-based patch tracking system, to monitor the state of their patches, manage resubmissions, and maintain an overview of ongoing discussions. Having a clear view of the status of contributions aids developers in planning and prioritizing their work efficiently.

As collaborative contributions mature, the Linux community emphasizes the importance of sustaining a culture of inclusivity and respect. This means that while the patch workflow serves as a formalized process for submissions, there exists a broader ethos around kindness and patience in collaboration. Engaging with less experienced contributors, sharing knowledge, and providing mentorship are essential practices that form the backbone of the kernel development community.

In conclusion, understanding the patch workflow is crucial for anyone looking to contribute to the Linux kernel. By identifying issues, crafting well-defined patches with descriptive commit messages, submitting to the appropriate mailing lists, responding to feedback, and actively participating in the community's culture, developers can effectively navigate the complexities of kernel development. The patch workflow not only enhances individual contributions but also reinforces the collaborative spirit that defines the Linux kernel, ensuring its continued evolution as a premier open-source project.

10.4. Maintainers and their Role

In the Linux ecosystem, maintainers occupy a critical role that is foundational to the collaborative development process, ensuring the integrity, quality, and evolution of the kernel. As the project has grown and matured, the structure of maintainers has adapted to accommodate the increasing complexity of contributions from a diverse community of developers and organizations. Understanding the role of maintainers within this collaborative framework underscores their impact on the Linux kernel project and the broader open-source movement.

Maintainers are responsible for overseeing specific subsystems of the kernel. Each subsystem can encompass a variety of components, including file systems, networking protocols, device drivers, and more. The designation of these roles allows maintainers to cultivate expertise within their particular areas, ensuring that contributions align with the technical requirements and strategic vision of their assigned subsystems. This specialization is crucial, given the breadth and depth of the Linux kernel codebase.

The primary responsibilities of maintainers include reviewing submitted patches, providing feedback to contributors, and ultimately deciding whether to accept or reject changes. This process is vital in ensuring that patches meet certain criteria, such as adherence to coding standards, compatibility with existing features, and an understanding of performance implications. Reviewers often engage in discussions with contributors, encouraging dialogue that may lead to refinements before a patch is merged into the mainline kernel. This collaborative interaction helps ensure high-quality contributions while also fostering a sense of community around the project.

Maintainers also act as a bridge between the kernel development community and users. By monitoring issues raised by users in forums, mailing lists, or bug reports, maintainers can identify potential problems or areas of improvement in their subsystems. This feedback loop enables the kernel to evolve according to the needs of its user base, illustrating a responsive approach to community engagement. Furthermore, maintainers can facilitate the communication of changes in functionality or updates to features through effective documentation, ensuring that users remain informed and can adapt to any modifications effectively.

However, maintainers face challenges as they juggle numerous responsibilities in an environment characterized by rapid change and high expectations. With the pace of contributions increasing, maintaining a careful balance between accepting new patches and ensuring that the code quality remains consistent can be daunting. This demands a level of organization, time management, and communicative engagement that can be intense, as the number of submissions can fluctuate greatly depending on the release cycle and the introduction of new features.

To support this work, maintainers utilize various tools and methodologies. Systems like Patchwork, which tracks submitted patches, allow maintainers to manage the review process efficiently. This organizational capability enables maintainers to prioritize patches based on importance, necessity, and readiness for integration. Moreover, automated testing frameworks such as KernelCI are employed as part of the review process to validate patches automatically before integration, further ensuring that the quality is maintained.

As the kernel faces new challenges driven by developments in technology—such as the emergence of cloud computing, Internet of Things (IoT), and artificial intelligence—maintainers also play a role in guiding the kernel's strategic direction. They are often at the forefront of discussions regarding potential enhancements and must consider how changes might affect the overall architecture and performance of the kernel. This requires a capacity for foresight, an understanding of technological trends, and a willingness to advocate for necessary changes or resources within the community.

Maintainers also serve as mentors to new contributors entering the kernel development space. By engaging actively with newcomers, they can share insights into best practices, kernel architecture complexities, and the expectations of the community. This mentorship fosters the growth of the community, introducing diverse perspectives and talents, and ensuring that the Linux kernel remains a thriving open-source project.

As we reflect on the essentiality of maintainers within the Linux kernel ecosystem, it becomes clear that they are not merely gatekeepers but rather pivotal figures who ensure that the project progresses while retaining an inclusive, collaborative culture. Their expertise, dedication, and leadership drive the continuous evolution of the Linux kernel, solidifying its place as a cornerstone of modern computing. In the face of ongoing challenges and opportunities, maintainers will remain vital to navigating the future trajectory of the Linux kernel, balancing innovation with the enduring commitment to quality and community values.

10.5. Emerging Patterns in Collaborative Development

In the evolving landscape of collaborative development, particularly within the Linux kernel community, emerging patterns reflect the convergence of technical innovation, community dynamics, and the increasing complexity of modern computing environments. These patterns not only shape how contributions are made but also influence the collaborations that form the backbone of this globally distributed open-source project. This subchapter aims to illuminate these emerging patterns, exploring key themes that are redefining the collaborative development process in the Linux kernel ecosystem.

One prominent pattern in collaborative development is the shift towards more structured and transparent contribution processes. The Linux kernel has long been characterized by its meritocratic approach, where contributions are evaluated based on their technical quality and relevance rather than the contributor's status. However, as the community has expanded, the introduction of platforms such as Git and mailing lists has formalized how contributions are tracked and assessed. Developers now adhere to specific coding standards and documentation practices that enhance clarity and facilitate smoother peer reviews.

The use of automated testing and Continuous Integration (CI) tools has also emerged as a significant trend. The integration of automated testing into the submission process allows for timely feedback regarding the functionality and stability of patches before they are accepted. By identifying issues early in the development cycle, the Linux kernel community enhances the overall quality of contributions, fosters accountability, and accelerates the integration of new features. This shift towards automation reflects a broader industry-wide trend of adopting CI practices to boost efficiency and streamline workflows.

A shift towards improving security practices in collaborative development is another pattern taking hold. With cybersecurity threats on the rise, the need for secure coding practices has become increasingly paramount. Developers are now more conscious of potential vulnerabilities in their contributions, leading to heightened emphasis on code reviews that prioritize security assessments. Additionally, security-focused tools are being integrated into the development pipeline to automatically analyze patches for vulnerabilities, reinforcing the community's commitment to building a secure and resilient kernel.

The kernel community has also recognized the importance of diversity and inclusion in fostering a thriving ecosystem. Efforts to cultivate a more diverse pool of contributors by encouraging participation from underrepresented groups are reshaping the collaborative landscape. Initiatives like mentorship programs, outreach efforts, and diversity-focused events are becoming more commonplace, allowing more collaborators to engage in kernel development from various backgrounds. This inclusivity not only enriches the community but also leads to improved problem-solving and innovation, as diverse perspectives contribute to a more comprehensive understanding of challenges faced in kernel development.

The trend towards cross-disciplinary skills development is an emerging pattern that is gaining traction among contributors. As the Linux kernel operates at the intersection of various domains—such as networking, embedded systems, and security—developers are encouraged to broaden their expertise beyond traditional kernel development. This cross-pollination of skills allows contributors to bring fresh insights and ideas into the kernel, addressing complex challenges and leveraging advancements in related fields. Encouraging interdisciplinary learning fosters a culture of continuous improvement, where contributors support one another in mastering new technologies and paradigms.

Furthermore, the rise of cloud computing, containerization, and microservice architectures has prompted the Linux kernel community to adapt its collaborative development practices to meet the needs of modern infrastructure. The integration of virtualization technologies into the kernel has enabled developers to create solutions that cater specifically to the demands of cloud environments. By embracing these emerging trends, the community positions itself to remain relevant and innovative, continuously adapting to the changing landscape of technology.

Collaboration is increasingly transcending traditional boundaries, with the Linux community connecting with external stakeholders, industry partners, and research institutions. These partnerships facilitate knowledge exchange and resource sharing, further enhancing collaborative efforts. Engaging with external entities provides developers with insights into emerging technologies, reinforces the adaptability of the kernel, and opens new avenues for innovation.

As we look to the future, the emerging patterns in collaborative development are likely to continue shaping how the Linux kernel evolves. The synthesis of automation, inclusivity, security awareness, and cross-disciplinary skills will likely yield a more robust and cohesive community, poised to tackle tomorrow's challenges. The health of the collaborative development ecosystem hinges on the community's ability to embrace these emerging trends, ensuring that it remains at the forefront of innovation in the ever-expanding realm of open-source computing. By collectively championing collaboration, the Linux kernel community can foster continuity, resilience, and an enduring commitment to excellence that propel it into the future.

11. From Compilation to Boot: The Kernel in Action

11.1. Compiling the Kernel: Step-by-Step Guide

Compiling the Linux kernel marks the gateway to customizing your system at a fundamental level, allowing you to optimize performance, add support for new hardware, or even strip away unnecessary components to streamline operation. This step-by-step guide will walk through the process of compiling the kernel from source, illustrating the necessary steps and considerations to ensure a successful build.

Begin by preparing your environment. Ensuring that your system has the necessary packages and tools installed is crucial for a smooth compilation process. The specific packages will depend on your distribution; for example, on Debian-based systems, you might need `build-essential`, `libncurses-dev`, `bison`, and `flex`. You can install these packages with a command such as:

```
sudo apt-get install build-essential libncurses-dev bison
flex libssl-dev libelf-dev
```

Next, download the kernel source code. You can obtain the latest stable version from the official kernel release website or through your distribution's repositories. It's common to use `wget` or `curl` for this purpose:

```
wget https://cdn.kernel.org/pub/linux/kernel/v5.x/linux-5.
x.tar.xz
```

Extract the downloaded tarball:

```
tar -xf linux-5.x.tar.xz
cd linux-5.x
```

Once you've navigated to the kernel source directory, the next step involves configuring the kernel options. Linux provides various configuration menus to tailor the kernel to suit your needs. The most common configuration tool is `make menuconfig`, which opens a friendly interface in your terminal, allowing you to toggle options, enable or disable features, and select the necessary modules. You can initiate this process with:

```
make menuconfig
```

Alternatively, if you're recompiling using existing settings, you can copy the current configuration file:

```
cp /boot/config-$(uname -r) .config
```

After configuring the kernel to your specifications, you'll prepare to compile. The process often involves three primary commands: `make`, `make modules`, and `make install`.

First, run:

```
make
```

This command compiles the kernel and can take some time, depending on your hardware capabilities. Once the compilation completes, if your kernel includes modules that need to be built, you should run:

```
make modules
```

Next, you will want to install these modules into the appropriate directory. This ensures that your system recognizes them during boot:

```
sudo make modules_install
```

After successfully compiling the kernel and modules, it's time to install the newly built kernel. This can be done using:

```
sudo make install
```

This command updates the bootloader configuration for you and copies the new kernel and its associated files to `/boot`.

Next, you need to update your bootloader configuration. If you're using GRUB, you can often run:

```
sudo update-grub
```

This step ensures that the bootloader recognizes the newly compiled kernel, allowing you to select it during the boot process.

Reboot your system to boot into your newly compiled kernel:

```
sudo reboot
```

During the boot process, you should see the new kernel version in the GRUB menu if everything was configured correctly. Once the system is up, you can verify that you are running the new kernel by executing:

```
uname -r
```

If the output reflects the version you compiled, congratulations, you've successfully compiled and booted into a new kernel!

However, if you encounter boot issues, don't panic. The kernel compilation process can be intricate, and several factors could contribute to problems during boot. Utilize the boot options to troubleshoot. Adding a recovery mode or alternative kernel option in the boot menu can assist in diagnosing issues.

Moreover, common recommendations after a failed boot include reverting to the previous working kernel entry and examining boot logs, accessible through the system's journal:

```
journalctl -b -1
```

Through these logs, you can receive insights into what went wrong, allowing you to troubleshoot the issue effectively.

In summation, compiling the Linux kernel involves downloading the source, configuring it, compiling it, and then installing it alongside an considerate update of the bootloader. Engaging in this process empowers you to tailor the kernel to your specific needs while greatly enhancing the performance and functionality of your system. As with any significant changes, patience, attention to detail, and a willingness to troubleshoot will stand you in good stead as you embark on your kernel compilation journey.

11.2. The Boot Process Unveiled

The Linux kernel's boot process is a complex yet fascinating sequence, representing the seamless transition from hardware initialization to a fully operational operating system. Understanding this process provides valuable insights into the kernel's functionality and the mechanisms behind system readiness. This section will delve into the various stages involved in the boot process, starting from power-on through to the invocation of user-space processes leading to a fully functional system.

The boot process commences when a computer receives power. This triggers the hardware, initiating the power-on self-test (POST) routine, conducted by the Basic Input/Output System (BIOS) or Unified Extensible Firmware Interface (UEFI). During POST, critical hardware components, such as RAM, CPU, and peripheral devices, are tested to ensure proper functionality. If any hardware malfunctions are detected, the boot process will be halted, usually accompanied by an error message or beep codes that indicate the nature of the issue.

Once the POST completes successfully, the BIOS/UEFI locates the boot loader on a specified storage device, typically a hard disk drive or a solid-state drive. The boot loader is a small program responsible for loading the kernel into memory along with necessary initial configurations. In Linux systems, the most common boot loaders are GRUB (Grand Unified Bootloader) or LILO (Linux Loader).

When the boot loader activates, it presents users with a boot menu from which they can select their preferred kernel or boot option. Upon selection, the boot loader loads the specified kernel image into memory. This kernel image is typically compressed to reduce its size and may also be accompanied by an initial RAM disk (initrd or initramfs). The initial RAM disk provides essential drivers and device nodes necessary for the kernel to mount the root file system.

After loading the kernel and the initrd, the boot loader transfers control to the kernel by executing it. This marks the beginning of the kernel's initialization phase. Upon execution, the kernel first initializes its internal subsystems, such as memory management, process scheduling, and interrupt handling. The kernel sets up virtual memory, establishes a process table, and prepares to manage system resources.

As part of its initialization, the kernel also sets up necessary hardware drivers to effectively communicate with the various devices installed on the system. During this phase, the kernel detects hardware presence, initializes device drivers, and configures parameters critical for system operation. The kernel will read configuration details from the initial RAM disk, which often contains the necessary modules for handling particular hardware devices, especially critical in systems with variable hardware setups.

Following hardware initialization, the kernel mounts the root file system, allowing it to access critical resources needed to continue the boot process. The kernel uses the root file system to read configuration files, load additional modules, and track device status. The transition to the root file system also signifies the kernel's shift from initializing hardware to preparing user-space services.

Once the kernel has mounted the root file system, it invokes the "init" process, often located at /sbin/init. The init process functions as the first user-space program and serves as the parent for all other processes started in the system. Init reads its configuration files, commonly /etc/inittab or its replacements in modern systems, determining what services and user-space programs will be initiated. This step is where the transition to multi-user mode takes place, preparing the system for regular operations.

The init system can vary across distributions, with several popular implementations, such as Systemd, Upstart, or SysVinit. Systemd, in particular, has gained traction for its streamlined approach to service management and parallelized booting, contributing to faster boot times and more efficient resource utilization.

As the init process launches various system processes and services, it also initializes login prompts, graphical sessions, and background daemons. This represents the culmination of the boot process, with kernel operations transitioning smoothly into user-space activities, ultimately leading to a fully functional Linux operating system.

An important aspect of understanding the boot process is recognizing the efficiency of boot-time optimizations. Modern Linux distributions implement various optimizations, including parallel processing during service startups, reduced initramfs sizes, and using pre-compiled kernels to improve boot times. These measures significantly enhance the user experience by minimizing the duration from power-on to a ready-to-use system.

In summary, the boot process of the Linux kernel is a meticulously coordinated series of events that transitions from hardware initialization to a fully operational system. It encompasses stages such as POST, boot loader execution, kernel initialization, root file system mounting, and user-space service startup. Understanding this vital process offers valuable insights into the inner workings of the Linux kernel and the elegant orchestration of components that enable modern computing experiences.

11.3. Configuration Options and Customization

Configuration options and customization within the Linux kernel are paramount as they enable users to tailor the system to meet their specific requirements and optimize performance for various hardware setups and application needs. Customization can range from enabling specific features, modifying performance parameters, or entirely removing unnecessary components to streamline the kernel. This aspect allows for substantial flexibility, efficiency, and adaptability, making Linux a preferred choice for a broad range of applications—from embedded systems to enterprise servers.

The process of configuration begins with building the Linux kernel from its source code, during which users can specify the options that will be compiled into the kernel. This is conducted using a configuration tool that provides a menu-driven or command-line interface to select features and options. Commonly used tools include `make menuconfig`, `make xconfig`, and `make oldconfig`. Each tool presents a detailed hierarchical structure of available options, allowing users to navigate various submenus that correspond to kernel features, device drivers, file systems, networking options, and more.

As users progress through the configuration, they will encounter a plethora of options categorized into sections. For instance, users can enable or disable support for specific hardware drivers based on the peripherals attached to the system. This selective inclusion of modules is crucial for performance optimization, as unnecessary drivers can bloat the kernel and consume system resources. Similarly, users can adjust file system options to cater to their particular storage solutions, enhancing read and write performance or enabling specialized features like encryption or journaling.

Another significant aspect of configuration is setting kernel parameters that govern core behavior. These parameters control various system settings, such as memory management, process scheduling, and networking configurations. They can be adjusted at build time as well as at runtime through /proc or /sys interfaces, allowing administrators to fine-tune system performance without recompiling the kernel. For example, the /proc/sys directory contains files representing tunable parameters, and by modifying these files, users can influence aspects of kernel behavior, such as adjusting the swappiness value to control memory swapping behaviors.

Custom kernel configurations also empower users to experiment with different kernel features, allowing for enhanced performance or additional functionality. For example, they can enable support for preemptive multitasking for real-time applications, optimize CPU scheduling algorithms for specific workloads, or implement advanced power management features to extend battery life in portable devices. Administrators can utilize kernel boot parameters to further customize behavior during the boot process, letting them specify features such as single-user mode, debugging options, and hardware-specific configurations.

Beyond functionality, configuration options and customization foster an environment of security. By enabling or disabling specific kernel features, users can address security concerns relevant to their implementation. For example, disabling unused networking protocols can minimize attack surfaces, while certain security-focused options can enhance the resilience of the system against potential exploits or vulnerabilities.

Following kernel configuration and compilation, users must also consider the maintenance of their customized kernels. As new kernel versions are released, users might want to track upstream changes and apply relevant updates to their custom versions. Managing patches and configuration adjustments effectively enables users to harness advancements in hardware and software improvements introduced by the kernel community while retaining the benefits of their tailored setup.

Customization is not limited solely to the kernel's configuration. Users can augment kernel functionality through the development and inclusion of loadable kernel modules (LKMs). These modules enable users to extend the kernel's capabilities dynamically without recompiling it, accommodating hardware changes or enabling new features as needed. This modular approach not only improves efficiency by allowing the kernel to remain lean but also facilitates rapid adaptation to changing workloads or device requirements.

In conclusion, configuration options and customization within the Linux kernel are instrumental in optimizing system performance, enhancing security, and adapting to user needs. The ability to tailor the kernel through careful selection of features, management of kernel parameters, and the utilization of loadable kernel modules empowers users to create environments that align closely with their operational requirements. These practices serve as cornerstones for efficiency and flexibility, ensuring that Linux remains a powerful and versatile platform in the ever-evolving landscape of technology. As users engage deeply with the kernel, they establish not only a customized environment but also an ongoing relationship with the dynamic development community that continues to shape the future of Linux.

11.4. Troubleshooting Boot Issues

Troubleshooting boot issues in the Linux kernel is a crucial skill that can be indispensable for system administrators, developers, and enthusiasts alike. When a system fails to boot or encounters boot-related problems, having a structured approach to identify, diagnose, and resolve these issues can save significant time and effort. This guide provides a comprehensive overview of techniques and common problems associated with the boot process, enabling effective troubleshooting of boot issues in the Linux kernel.

The boot sequence initiates as soon as power is supplied to the machine, and the boot loader takes control after the POST (Power-On Self-Test) phase. A variety of factors can create problems at this stage, preventing the kernel from loading or functioning correctly. Troubleshooting begins by observing any error messages or unusual behavior during the boot process. Familiarity with the boot sequence can help pinpoint where issues may arise.

The first step in diagnosing boot issues often involves checking the system logs. If the kernel fails to boot successfully, error messages may still be logged during the boot process, accessible through `dmesg` or within the `journalctl` command. Accessing logs from a previous boot attempt can provide essential clues about what transpired leading up to the failure. For example, executing `journalctl -b -1` shows logs from the previous boot, which might reveal troubles with hardware detection, failed services, or configuration issues that prevented successful booting.

Another common point of failure is the boot loader configuration. If the GRUB bootloader (the most widely used bootloader for Linux systems) is misconfigured, it may prevent the kernel from loading correctly. Users can edit `/etc/default/grub` to adjust kernel parameters or ensure that the correct options are selected. After making any changes, remember to update GRUB to apply these modifications, using the command `sudo update-grub` in Debian-based systems or equivalent commands based on the distribution in use.

It is also crucial to verify the integrity of the installed kernel image and associated files. The `ls` command can show the contents of `/boot`, allowing users to ensure that the kernels listed are present and correctly configured. In the case of a custom or rebuilt kernel, ensure that the installation of the kernel was performed correctly using `make install` and that the associated files are accurately reflected in the `/boot` directory. This step is particularly important if multiple kernel versions are present in case the wrong version is attempted for boot.

Filesystem issues can also cause boot failures, particularly if the root filesystem is not mounting correctly. Booting into a recovery mode or using a live CD/USB can help troubleshoot filesystems. In this scenario, performing filesystem checks using the `fsck` (File System Check) command can identify and resolve inconsistencies that might affect the ability to mount the root filesystem.

Hardware-related problems, such as incompatible drivers or misconfigured hardware components, can hinder the boot process as well. To diagnose these issues, utilize the kernel's boot options. Another powerful tool is the `apport` system, which captures and analyzes crash reports. Booting the system with options like `nomodeset` to bypass graphical issues or `noapic` to disable APIC-related features can sometimes circumvent hardware-related issues, allowing access to logs for further diagnosis.

If the kernel is compiled from the source, it's crucial to ensure that configuration options were correctly selected. Missing support for essential filesystems—such as ext4 or XFS—can result in a failure to mount partitions necessary for booting. Review the kernel configuration using tools like `make menuconfig` to verify that all required components are indeed compiled into the kernel or as loadable modules.

During boot, the kernel requires certain init scripts and services to complete the boot process successfully. If any of these services fail, the boot process may hang. Since systemd is commonly used in modern Linux distributions, monitoring the status of units during boot can reveal which services are failing. Users can check for service status with `systemctl status <service-name>` in recovery mode.

Lastly, engaging with the broader Linux community resources—such as mailing lists, forums, or issue trackers—can provide additional support if boot issues persist. Often, others may have encountered similar experiences, leading to shared solutions or insights that accelerate troubleshooting.

In summary, troubleshooting boot issues in Linux involves a systematic approach encompassing log analysis, boot loader verification, filesystem checks, hardware diagnosis, and configuration validation. Understanding the boot process and utilizing available tools effectively allows users to identify and resolve issues quickly, leading to a functional and responsive Linux system. By sharpening these troubleshooting skills, system administrators and developers can maintain optimal system operation and enhance their expertise in the Linux ecosystem.

11.5. Kernel Parameters and Overrides

Kernel parameters and their overrides represent a crucial aspect of configuring the Linux kernel to tailor its behavior and functionality to specific use cases. By understanding and utilizing these parameters, system administrators and developers can enhance system performance, optimize resource management, and enforce security measures. This section will delve into the structure of kernel parameters, the methods for modifying them, and the implications of such adjustments on system behavior.

Kernel parameters are configuration settings that define how the kernel operates. These parameters operate at various levels, influencing everything from memory management to process scheduling and networking behavior. Each parameter can be accessed, modified, and monitored to ensure optimal system performance and responsiveness. They are typically housed within the `/proc/sys` directory, which presents an interface for real-time configuration of kernel settings, allowing users to query and adjust parameters dynamically without requiring a system reboot.

The context within which kernel parameters can be set varies. Some parameters can be altered at runtime, while others may require the kernel to be recompiled with the desired settings. Adjusting parameters that can be modified at runtime is generally facilitated through the `sysctl` command, which provides a standardized method for viewing and modifying kernel parameters. For instance, altering the `vm.swappiness` parameter, which determines the balance between swapping out runtime memory versus freeing up page cache, can be adjusted using:

```
sysctl -w vm.swappiness=10
```

This command effectively tells the kernel to be less aggressive about swapping memory, which can enhance performance for certain workloads. The change will persist only until the next reboot unless it is added to the `/etc/sysctl.conf` file, allowing for persistent settings across restarts.

The modification of kernel parameters serves several purposes, including enhancing performance, optimizing resource allocation, and enforcing security measures. For example, by tweaking the `kernel.pid_max` parameter, which determines the maximum allowable process ID, a system can accommodate a broader range of concurrent processes, thereby optimizing resource usage for multi-threaded applications. Similarly, expanding the `fs.file-max` parameter increases the maximum number of open file descriptors, allowing processes to handle more connections and files simultaneously.

Importantly, kernel parameters also have a profound impact on system security. Parameters within the `/proc/sys/kernel` directory can be adjusted to impose restrictions, such as enabling or disabling address space layout randomization (ASLR) through `kernel.randomize_va_space`. Additionally, the use of `kernel.keysroot` allows configuration of a keyring for enhanced security. By understanding these parameters, system administrators can enforce stringent security policies that control how the kernel handles inbound and outbound traffic and manages sensitive data.

Furthermore, the overriding of kernel parameters can take form through boot-time options. For instance, users can specify kernel parameters at boot by modifying the bootloader configuration—typically GRUB—to pass parameters directly to the kernel on startup. This method involves appending parameters to the `GRUB_CMDLINE_LINUX` variable in the GRUB configuration file. For example:

```
GRUB_CMDLINE_LINUX="quiet splash vm.swappiness=15"
```

After modifying this configuration, the bootloader requires updating with `update-grub`, ensuring that the specified settings take effect during the next boot sequence.

In recent kernel versions, managing kernel parameters has been further streamlined with the introduction of interfaces such as the sysfs filesystem, accessible through `/sys/`. This offers an alternative, hierarchical way to manipulate kernel parameters, providing an intuitive structure for complex configurations. Parameters in sysfs are often linked directly to kernel subsystems, allowing for smoother interactions with device management and driver settings.

When adjusting kernel parameters, caution and testing are essential components of the process. Misconfigured parameters can lead to instabilities or unwanted behaviors within the system. It is advisable to monitor the effects of any changes made to kernel parameters closely, capturing system logs and making adjustments based on observed performance and stability metrics.

In summary, kernel parameters and their overrides are integral to customizing the Linux kernel to meet specific operational and performance needs. By gaining a comprehensive understanding of available parameters, utilizing the appropriate commands for modification, and respecting best practices for testing and monitoring, users can tailor their kernel environments effectively. The ability to adjust kernel behavior enhances both performance and security, providing a dynamic response to the ever-evolving demands of technology. Embracing kernel parameters and their overrides paves the way for a finely tuned system primed for efficient operation across diverse workloads and use cases.

12. Security Safeguards: Antivirus and Malware Defense

12.1. Principles of Kernel Security

In the fast-paced and ever-evolving landscape of technology, security remains a paramount concern within the realm of kernel development. As the backbone of countless systems, the Linux kernel faces numerous threats from malicious actors and vulnerabilities that could jeopardize the integrity and performance of the systems built upon it. The principles of kernel security are fundamental to safeguarding against these threats and ensuring that the kernel operates reliably in a variety of environments.

Kernel security principles fundamentally focus on the integrity, confidentiality, and availability of system resources. The kernel's privileged position means that its security is critical; any vulnerability within the kernel can potentially lead to a complete compromise of the entire operating system. Thus, maintaining a strict separation between user space and kernel space is fundamental, as it minimizes the risk of unauthorized access and secures sensitive operations against potential exploitation by malicious software.

Access control mechanisms are central to kernel security principles. The Linux kernel employs a robust user and group ID (UID/GID) model to enforce permissions on various system resources. This mechanism ensures that only authorized users can access or modify specific files, directories, or devices. Implementing additional layers of security, such as by utilizing access control lists (ACLs), further refines the permissions model, allowing more granular control over user access rights.

Mandatory Access Control (MAC) systems, such as Security-Enhanced Linux (SELinux) or AppArmor, augment traditional discretionary access control mechanisms by enforcing strict policies governing how processes can interact with each other and with system resources. By employing a policy-based approach, these systems ensure that even if users gain unauthorized access to a process, the MAC framework will limit what that process can do, effectively containing potential damage. This approach enhances the overall resilience of the kernel against unauthorized access and exploitation.

Another pivotal principle is the concept of least privilege. The kernel should operate using the minimum privileges necessary to perform its tasks. This principle applies not only to the kernel itself but also to user-level applications and services executed by the kernel. By restricting processes and services to necessary permissions, the kernel limits the potential impact of a security breach, ensuring that any exploit does not grant an attacker undue control over system resources.

In addition to controlling access and privileges, regularly applying security patches is a critical security measure within the kernel lifecycle. Vulnerabilities are often discovered after a kernel release, necessitating timely updates to address known weaknesses. The active Linux community remains vigilant in identifying and reporting security issues, ensuring that maintainers can distribute timely patches. System administrators must stay proactive in applying these patches, optimizing their systems' security postures and mitigating risks effectively.

Continuous monitoring of kernel activities and resource usage can also bolster kernel security. Tools such as audit frameworks and intrusion detection systems enable administrators to track system changes, log access attempts, and identify potential anomalies before they escalate into significant breaches. Through runtime monitoring and auditing, threats can be detected early, allowing for rapid mitigation.

Kernel security is not a static endeavor; rather, it must evolve in response to emerging threats and technological advancements. As systems integrate with new technologies such as cloud computing, IoT, and decentralized architectures, the security mechanisms within the kernel must adapt accordingly. This includes extending security

protocols to cover new communication interfaces and devices, fortifying APIs, and implementing robust data encryption methods.

Emerging technologies also usher in the need for adaptive security
mechanisms, particularly in light of sophisticated attacks that exploit
modern system vulnerabilities. Innovations such as machine learning
can facilitate smarter security responses, enabling proactive threat
detection by analyzing patterns and behaviors within the kernel.

As we look ahead, the principles of kernel security will remain at
the forefront of development and integration efforts, ensuring that
the Linux kernel not only provides robust functionality but also
maintains a secure and reliable environment for all applications and
deployments. In summary, understanding the principles that underpin kernel security principles, implementing appropriate security
measures, and staying abreast of emerging technologies will empower developers and administrators to safeguard their systems and
minimize risks in an increasingly complex technological landscape.

12.2. Implementing Security Measures

Implementing security measures in the context of the Linux kernel
is a critical aspect of ensuring that the operating system remains
resilient against threats while providing a robust and stable computing environment. Given the kernel's position as the core component
of the OS, effective security practices must be ingrained throughout
its architecture. This discussion will outline the various security
measures that can be implemented, ranging from access controls and
memory protections to real-time monitoring, thus creating a comprehensive security posture for the Linux kernel.

As the primary interface between hardware and applications, the
kernel must govern access to system resources with stringent security
policies. One foundational measure is the implementation of Mandatory Access Control (MAC) systems, such as Security-Enhanced
Linux (SELinux) or AppArmor. These frameworks extend the traditional discretionary access control (DAC) model provided by basic
Unix file permissions by enforcing policies that restrict how processes

and users can access objects within the kernel. Through finely-tuned policies, SELinux can protect critical system components, preventing unauthorized access or modifications and reducing the likelihood of compromise.

To bolster security further, the principle of least privilege should be prioritized. This principle ensures that processes operate with the minimum permissions necessary to perform their tasks, thereby minimizing the potential impact of vulnerabilities. For example, by configuring specific daemons or services that run with lower privileges, the kernel mitigates risks associated with privilege escalation attacks. This granular control allows system administrators to enforce strict security measures within both user and kernel spaces.

In conjunction with access controls, employing memory protections is vital to kernel security. The kernel must ensure that processes executed in user space are isolated from each other, preventing them from corrupting or accessing each other's memory. The implementation of features such as Address Space Layout Randomization (ASLR) randomizes the memory address space assigned to processes, complicating the task for potential attackers seeking to exploit memory corruption vulnerabilities. Additionally, protective measures against buffer overflows—such as stack canaries and executable space protection—help to safeguard against common vulnerabilities that can be leveraged for exploitation.

Another critical area of focus involves real-time monitoring and logging of system activities. Kernel subsystems can be configured to maintain logs of security events and access attempts, providing insights into unusual activities that may indicate an attempted breach. Tools such as Auditd, which records system calls and access events, can capture critical data necessary for forensic analysis should an incident occur. Intrusion Detection Systems (IDS) can complement this monitoring by analyzing system behaviors in real time, alerting administrators to potential attacks based on predefined attack patterns or suspicious anomalies.

As the complexity of modern computing designs continues to proliferate, so do the potential attack vectors; thus, the kernel must remain adaptable. Encouraging a culture of regular security patching is vital in maintaining kernel security. Developers and maintainers must keep abreast of vulnerabilities discovered in kernel code, as timely patching directly guards against newly identified threats. This practice extends to ensuring that all third-party drivers and modules adhere to the same security protocols and are updated regularly in tandem with kernel releases.

Kernel security also emphasizes the importance of secure boot and integrity checking mechanisms. Secure Boot helps ensure that only trusted components load during the boot process, preventing the execution of unauthorized or malicious code. Similarly, tools (such as IMA/EVM—Integrity Measurement Architecture/Extended Verification Module) can provide cryptographic validation of kernel components and configurations at runtime, assuring system integrity even amid hardware or firmware alterations.

Education and training within the kernel development community play a pivotal role in cultivating security awareness. Developers must stay informed about secure coding practices, known vulnerabilities, and the latest security measures applicable to the kernel. Active participation in secure coding workshops or training programs can further enhance their understanding and establish a culture that prioritizes security at every development stage.

As we look ahead, the landscape of kernel security will continue evolving alongside emerging technologies. Integrating artificial intelligence and machine learning into security measures represents a new frontier that can provide adaptive and proactive defenses. By leveraging patterns in system behavior, these technologies can improve threat detection and response times, complementing existing security measures.

In conclusion, implementing security measures in the Linux kernel demands a multifaceted approach that emphasizes access controls, memory protections, real-time monitoring, and rigorous patching practices. Proactively establishing policies that govern user permissions, maintaining vigilance against vulnerabilities, and fostering a culture of awareness within the development community will help ensure the kernel remains stable, resilient, and secure against evolving security threats. As technology advances and new challenges arise, the kernel's adaptive security mechanisms will be crucial in safeguarding the system's integrity and protecting sensitive data. Through collaboration and ongoing education, the Linux kernel community can develop a comprehensive security posture that addresses both current and emerging threats.

12.3. Malware Defense Mechanisms

In the ever-evolving landscape of cybersecurity, malware defense mechanisms have become paramount, especially within the context of the Linux kernel, which underpins a multitude of systems worldwide. This subchapter delves into the essential strategies and techniques employed to safeguard systems against malware threats, underscoring the proactive approach taken within the kernel development community to protect the integrity, confidentiality, and availability of data.

The kernel serves as the core interface between hardware and software, making it a prime target for malicious actors seeking to exploit vulnerabilities that could lead to system compromise. Consequently, developing effective malware defense mechanisms requires a multifaceted approach encompassing prevention, detection, and response strategies.

At the foundation of these defenses is the principle of least privilege, which restricts user permissions to the minimum necessary for tasks. By limiting the access levels of processes and applications, the kernel effectively mitigates the potential for unauthorized modifications to critical system components. This principle applies universally within the kernel's architecture, reinforcing the security model that insulates low-level functions from higher privilege levels.

Moreover, mandatory access control (MAC) systems such as Security-Enhanced Linux (SELinux) and AppArmor are critical frameworks implemented within the kernel to enforce stringent security policies governing how processes interact with each other and system resources. These policies prescribe specific permissions and actions allowed for each process, significantly reducing the potential attack surface for malware. SELinux, for instance, utilizes a policy-driven mechanism to provide robust protection by confining processes to predefined roles, thus preventing unauthorized access to sensitive files or resources.

Another important aspect of malware defense within the kernel is the use of secure boot mechanisms. Secure boot ensures that the kernel and its components are authenticated before loading, thereby preventing unauthorized alterations to the boot process. This verification process guards against rootkits and bootkits that seek to compromise the system at launch time by ensuring that only trusted components are executed during boot-up.

In addition to these preventive measures, real-time monitoring systems play a vital role in detecting malware activity. Tools like `auditd` and audit frameworks integrated into the kernel facilitate the tracking of system calls and file accesses, thereby identifying anomalous behavior that may indicate a breach. Moreover, intrusion detection systems (IDS) can monitor network traffic and system activities to flag suspicious actions in real time, prompting immediate investigation and remediation.

Another layer of defense involves the promotion of secure coding practices throughout the kernel development community. Ensuring that kernel developers are aware of potential vulnerabilities and adhering to best practices can significantly reduce the risk of malware introduction through exploitable code. This can include strategies to avoid buffer overflows, null pointer dereferences, and improper input validation—common vectors that malicious code can exploit to gain elevated privileges within the kernel.

As the landscape of threats diversifies, incorporating machine learning and artificial intelligence into malware defense mechanisms represents an exciting frontier in enhancing kernel security. By leveraging these technologies, systems can analyze vast amounts of behavioral data in real time, identifying patterns typically indicative of malware activity. Automating responses based on predictive models can enhance adaptability against evolving threats, leading to more resilient defenses.

The kernel community also continually emphasizes the importance of patch management in maintaining security. Promptly addressing vulnerabilities as they are uncovered ensures that systems remain fortified against known exploits. Operating system maintainers are proactive in releasing security patches, and users are encouraged to apply these updates consistently, fortifying their systems against emerging malware.

Lastly, collaboration within the Linux community remains a pivotal aspect of malware defense. Developers and security experts routinely share their findings on vulnerabilities, exploits, and strategies for fortified defenses. This collaborative ethos fosters a proactive approach to system security, empowering organizations and individuals to stay ahead of potential threats by leveraging shared knowledge.

In summary, malware defense mechanisms within the Linux kernel focus on a proactive, multi-layered approach to safeguard systems against threats. By implementing principles of least privilege, mandatory access controls, secure boot methods, real-time monitoring, and predictive analytics, the kernel continually adapts to meet the challenges posed by malware. Coupled with an emphasis on secure coding practices, vigilant patch management, and collaboration within the community, these defenses create a resilient framework that protects the integrity of the Linux ecosystem in today's dynamic threat landscape. As technology advances, ongoing innovations in malware defense will fortify the kernel's position as a trustworthy foundation for computing systems worldwide.

12.4. Security Patch Applications

In the fast-paced and rapidly evolving landscape of technology, the implementation of security patches stands as a crucial practice to uphold the robustness and safety of the Linux kernel. The kernel operates at the core of the operating system, serving as the interface between hardware and user-level applications. Given its fundamental role, ensuring that the kernel remains fortified against vulnerabilities and exploits is paramount.

Security patches are updates to the kernel aimed at correcting flaws in the code that may be exploited by malicious actors or lead to system instability. These flaws could represent bugs, vulnerabilities, or design weaknesses that have been identified through security audits, community feedback, or by security researchers. When a vulnerability is discovered, the priority is to develop and deploy a security patch as swiftly as possible to mitigate risk and protect users from potential exploits.

The process of security patch application starts with vulnerability discovery. Tools and methodologies such as static analysis, dynamic analysis, and fuzz testing are employed to identify gaps in the kernel's defenses. Once vulnerabilities are identified, developers, typically working within a dedicated security response team or volunteer group, initiate the creation of a patch. This involves diagnosing the root cause of the vulnerability, writing code to rectify the issue, and thoroughly testing the patch to ensure it resolves the problem without introducing new issues—a step known as regression testing.

Once a patch has been prepared, it follows a set submission process that typically includes a clear and concise explanation of the vulnerability, how the patch addresses it, and any potential implications for users or system performance. Proper documentation is essential; it aids in transparency and helps maintainers and users understand the necessity of the patch they are about to apply.

The submission of security patches is often made to the kernel mailing list, where it undergoes peer review from the community.

This collaborative review process not only helps ensure the technical accuracy of the patch but can also surface additional considerations, such as performance impacts or interactions with other subsystems. The community's diverse expertise enhances the robustness of the patch, reinforcing the ethos of collaboration that defines the Linux kernel development process.

Once the patch passes review and is accepted by maintainers, it is integrated into the kernel source code and made available for end-users to apply. In many cases, distributions will prepare these patches as part of their update cycles, allowing users to benefit from enhanced security without necessitating manual interventions. Effective communication channels, including distribution-specific announcements and community forums, can inform users about the importance of applying security updates and provide guidance on the update processes.

The implementation of security patches also necessitates ongoing vigilance. After applying a security patch, it is essential for users and administrators to monitor for any adverse effects. Checking for system logs, conducting performance tests, and confirming that the kernel behaves as expected can help ascertain that the patch has been successfully deployed and does not disrupt existing functionalities.

In addition to addressing immediate vulnerabilities, the kernel security patching process integrates seamlessly into ongoing maintenance and support frameworks. Long-Term Support (LTS) versions of the kernel, which are especially relevant in enterprise environments, prioritize the timely release of security patches while ensuring that the stability and performance of the kernel are not compromised. This structured approach not only fosters user trust but also enhances system longevity, allowing administrators to confidently employ the kernel in mission-critical environments.

Furthermore, as the security landscape evolves, so too do the tools and methodologies employed for vulnerability management and patch application. Advances in artificial intelligence and machine learning can aid in automating vulnerability detection, enabling timely response organizations and developers alike. Predictive analytics can help prioritize patches based on the severity of vulnerabilities and the potential impact on affected systems.

Looking to the future, the kernel's security patch application processes are likely to continue evolving. Emerging technologies and resource constraints will necessitate agile methodologies that ensure secure systems performance without compromising user experience. The kernel community's commitment to continuous improvement, coupled with thriving collaborative engagement, will be crucial in addressing the challenges of tomorrow's security landscape.

In summary, the application of security patches within the Linux kernel ecosystem is a multifaceted process that encompasses vulnerability identification, patch development, testing, review, deployment, and ongoing user engagement. Through the diligence of the community and adherence to best practices, the kernel remains a resilient and secure foundation for countless systems worldwide, emphasizing the importance of collective responsibility in safeguarding its integrity against threats. As technology continues to advance, the ongoing evolution of patch application processes will ensure that the Linux kernel remains well-equipped to face new challenges in an increasingly complex digital framework.

12.5. Emerging Security Technologies

Emerging Security Technologies

In today's digital landscape, where cyber threats are increasingly sophisticated and pervasive, the significance of robust security technologies cannot be overstated. The Linux kernel, as a fundamental component of countless systems, must be equipped with the latest and most effective security measures to safeguard against potential vulnerabilities. This section delves into the emerging security technologies that are shaping the future of kernel security, highlighting advancements that integrate with the Linux environment to bolster security postures across a diverse array of applications.

One pivotal aspect of emerging security technologies is the integration of artificial intelligence (AI) and machine learning (ML) into security frameworks. These technologies offer the capability to analyze vast amounts of data in real time, identifying patterns indicative of potential cyber attacks or anomalies. For the Linux kernel, AI-driven security solutions can enhance threat detection systems, allowing for proactive identification of vulnerabilities or unusual behavior in system processes before they lead to exploitations. By integrating AI algorithms into kernel security measures, administrators can respond to security events with greater accuracy and speed, ultimately improving system resilience.

Another critical development in security technology is the rise of software-defined security (SDSec). SDSec abstracts security measures and allows for more Agile security configurations within virtualized environments. With the increased adoption of virtualization and containerization, the Linux kernel's ability to dynamically enforce security policies in response to evolving threats is paramount. SDSec enables administrators to deploy security measures that can adapt to changes in the network environment, ensuring that all elements— from virtual machines to the underlying hardware—maintain robust and cohesive security postures. This flexibility enhances the kernel's capability to combat a variety of strategies employed by cyber attackers.

The introduction of new cryptographic protocols also plays a vital role in emerging security technologies. The Linux kernel leverages encryption methods not only to protect data in transit but also to fortify stored data against unauthorized access. Modern cryptography standards—such as elliptic curve cryptography (ECC)—are being increasingly integrated, providing stronger security with reduced computational overhead. The ability to employ these advanced cryptographic standards within the kernel allows applications to establish secure communication channels and protect sensitive information efficiently.

With the increasing nexus of devices connected via the Internet of Things (IoT), specialized security technologies designed for IoT integration have gained prominence. These technologies ensure that the multitude of connected devices maintain security without compromising their performance or user experience. The Linux kernel must adapt to this expanding scope by incorporating lightweight security protocols that cater specifically to resource-constrained devices common in IoT applications. Solutions such as micro-segmentation can limit the attack surface for IoT devices by creating isolated environments, thus mitigating potential threats.

Moreover, the growing significance of container security has ushered in the need for sophisticated security technologies that protect containerized applications running on the Linux kernel. Tools such as container runtime security solutions are emerging, providing security mechanisms specifically tailored for the dynamic nature of container ecosystems. Such solutions implement security features such as runtime monitoring, image scanning, and vulnerability assessments to ensure that container images do not contain known vulnerabilities before deployment. Integrating these technologies within the kernel environment allows containerized applications to run securely while adhering to best practices in security management.

Another focus area in emerging security technologies is the advancement of multi-factor authentication (MFA) systems. As single-factor authentication continues to be compromised, transitioning to MFA becomes essential to safeguard access to critical systems interfacing with the Linux kernel. Implementing PAM (Pluggable Authentication Modules), the kernel can support various MFA methods—including hardware tokens, biometric scans, and one-time passwords—enforcing stricter access control across user-space applications.

Additionally, security measures must evolve to encompass emerging threats associated with cloud and virtual environments. Cloud security solutions are being designed to address the specific challenges of securing shared resources outside traditional on-premises infrastructure. These solutions involve developing frameworks that integrate seamlessly with the Linux kernel while permitting secure data inter-actions across multiple cloud instances and ensuring data integrity and confidentiality.

Lastly, enhanced incident response capabilities represent another vital area of development within emerging security technologies. The integration of centralized logging systems, such as the Linux Audit Framework, allows for the comprehensive collection of security-related events to facilitate real-time monitoring and analysis. By im-plementing structured logging practices, organizations can conduct forensic investigations following breaches, helping them understand the nature of the attack and build better defenses to prevent future incidents.

In conclusion, emerging security technologies are essential compo-nents in bolstering the Linux kernel's defenses against potential threats. By incorporating AI and ML, software-defined security, ad-vanced cryptographic protocols, IoT-specific security measures, con-tainer security solutions, multi-factor authentication, and enhanced incident response capabilities, the kernel is better equipped to endure the challenges of a rapidly evolving threat landscape. As security risks continue to grow, so too will the strategies and technologies neces-sary to ensure the ongoing integrity, confidentiality, and resilience of the Linux ecosystem. Embracing these developments will not only safeguard the kernel itself but also protect the countless systems and applications that rely on this foundational technology.

13. Virtual Machines and Containers: Extending Kernel Capabilities

13.1. The Basics of Virtualization

In the realm of technology advancements, virtualization has emerged as a powerful paradigm that enables resource optimization and efficiency in computing. Within the Linux kernel, virtualization allows multiple operating system instances to run concurrently on the same physical machine, effectively abstracting hardware resources and providing users with the flexibility to deploy applications in isolated environments. Understanding the basics of virtualization, its implementation in the kernel, and the potential of related technologies is vital for developers, system administrators, and those keen on harnessing the capabilities provided by modern computing infrastructures.

At its core, virtualization involves the creation of virtual instances that simulate physical hardware. A hypervisor—the software layer that enables this abstraction—sits between the hardware and the guest operating systems. It manages the distribution of resources such as CPU, memory, and I/O between the virtual machines (VMs) or containers, ensuring that each instance operates independently and efficiently. The two primary types of hypervisors are Type 1, or bare-metal hypervisors, which run directly on the host hardware, and Type 2, or hosted hypervisors, which run atop an existing operating system.

The Linux kernel provides robust support for virtualization, with the KVM (Kernel-based Virtual Machine) module being a prominent example. KVM allows the kernel to function as a Type 1 hypervisor, leveraging its existing scheduling and memory management capabilities. By transforming the kernel into a hypervisor, KVM enables the creation of virtual machines that can run unmodified guest operating systems, effectively turning any Linux system into a host for VMs. This integration minimizes overhead, as the kernel efficiently manages resources and mediates interactions between the VMs and the underlying hardware.

Kernel support for hypervisors extends beyond KVM, with other technologies such as Xen and VMware also playing significant roles in the Linux virtualization landscape. Xen, a hypervisor that has garnered widespread use in enterprise environments, offers high-performance virtualization through paravirtualization and hardware-assisted virtualization techniques. Meanwhile, VMware has developed its own hypervisors and virtualization tools that can run alongside Linux, allowing the kernel to act as a host for its dynamic ecosystem of products.

Containerization is another critical aspect of virtualization technologies, allowing developers to package applications along with their dependencies into lightweight, portable containers. Unlike full VMs, which virtualize entire operating systems, containers share the host operating system's kernel, significantly reducing resource overhead and improving performance. The primary containerization technology in the Linux ecosystem is Docker, which utilizes Linux kernel features such as namespaces and cgroups (control groups) to implement isolation and resource management for containers.

Optimizing performance for VMs and containers is essential for ensuring efficient resource utilization and responsiveness. Techniques such as tuning resource limits using cgroups, adjusting I/O scheduling, and leveraging caching mechanisms can significantly enhance the performance of virtualized environments. For instance, prioritizing I/O for specific VMs can minimize latency for critical applications, while utilizing efficient storage backends can improve data access speeds for containerized services.

Security considerations are paramount when working with virtualization technologies. Both VMs and containers introduce specific security challenges that need to be addressed to protect the underlying host and other instances. Secure practices include implementing strict access controls, regularly updating kernels and applications to patch vulnerabilities, and employing security hardening measures specific to virtualization technologies. For example, running VMs in isolated environments and utilizing MAC systems like SELinux can mitigate risks associated with cross-instance attacks or unauthorized access.

The future of virtualization holds exciting prospects as emerging technologies continue to influence its capabilities. With the expansion of edge computing, IoT, and serverless architectures, the demand for lightweight, efficient virtualization solutions will escalate. Innovations in the Linux kernel, such as enhanced container orchestration and dynamic resource allocation based on predictive analytics, will further drive the adoption of virtualization technologies.

In conclusion, the basics of virtualization encapsulate a powerful framework for resource management, providing developers and system administrators with the tools necessary for efficient computing practices. With robust support from the Linux kernel, virtualization technologies such as hypervisors and containerization solutions enable the deployment of isolated environments, ensuring optimal performance, reliability, and responsiveness. By mastering the principles and mechanisms of virtualization, users can unlock the full potential of the Linux kernel, navigating an increasingly complex technological landscape while meeting the demands of modern applications.

13.2. Kernel Support for Hypervisors

Kernel Support for Hypervisors

The Linux kernel stands as a robust and versatile platform for virtualization, providing essential support for hypervisors that enable the coexistence of multiple operating system instances on a single physical machine. This subchapter delves into the kernel's architecture and features that facilitate hypervisor functionality, exploring how it assists in managing virtual machines (VMs) and intersecting with container technologies.

The foundation of kernel support for hypervisors in the Linux environment is primarily represented by the Kernel-based Virtual

Machine (KVM) module. KVM transforms the Linux kernel into a Type 1 hypervisor, allowing it to run multiple VMs with each having its own private virtualized hardware resources, including CPU, memory, and storage. One of the critical advantages of KVM is its ability to leverage existing kernel components, such as scheduling and memory management, to efficiently manage virtualization. This integration means that the kernel can optimize resource distribution and enhance performance for hosted VMs with minimal overhead.

KVM operates by utilizing the hardware virtualization extensions provided by modern processors, such as Intel's VT-x and AMD's AMD-V technology. These extensions enable the kernel to execute guest operating systems directly on the host CPU, significantly reducing performance overhead compared to traditional software-based virtualization methods. The utilization of virtualization extensions not only improves execution speed but also allows for better isolation between VMs, critical for ensuring security and stability across different instances.

Kernel support goes beyond just providing a virtualization environment. It provides essential device management, enabling virtual devices that represent physical hardware. These virtual devices facilitate the interaction between guest operating systems and physical resources. For instance, various drivers within the kernel can be utilized by KVM to emulate networking interfaces, storage controllers, and graphics devices. The abstraction simplifies the deployment of diverse guest OS types, from Linux distributions and Windows to specialized operating systems, ensuring compatibility across various hardware architectures.

One of the key features of the Linux kernel that aids in hypervisor support is the implementation of virtual memory management tailored for virtual machines. Each VM maintains its own virtual address space, just like a physical machine, while the kernel manages the mapping between virtual memory pages and physical memory. This separation ensures each VM operates in isolation, providing security and preventing data leaks between virtual instances. The kernel's memory management unit (MMU) plays a crucial role here, handling the translation between virtual and physical addresses in a manner that guarantees efficient access to memory while allowing for memory overcommitment.

Another critical aspect of kernel support for virtualization involves resource allocation and management through cgroups (control groups). Cgroups allow administrators to manage and allocate resources, such as CPU bandwidth, memory limits, and I/O access, ensuring that each VM operates within predefined constraints. This capability is particularly important in multi-tenant environments, where resource contention is a concern. By utilizing cgroups, administrators can enforce quality of service (QoS) and prevent any single VM from monopolizing resources, thereby ensuring predictable performance across all virtual instances.

Security remains a fundamental priority in hypervisor support. The Linux kernel incorporates several measures to secure both host and guest systems from potential attacks. For hypervisor functionality, maintaining the integrity of the kernel is crucial, as any vulnerabilities could compromise the entire virtualization environment. Kernel features such as SELinux or AppArmor can be deployed to enforce strict access control policies that govern interactions between the kernel and running VMs, minimizing the risk of exploitation through misconfigured sections.

Moreover, the concept of paravirtualization can be leveraged alongside KVM to enhance performance further. Paravirtualized drivers allow guest operating systems to communicate directly with the kernel, bypassing the overhead associated with emulated devices. This technique improves performance by reducing latency when accessing virtualized resources, particularly in environments where I/O operations are critical.

As virtualization technologies evolve, the Linux kernel will continue to adapt, supporting the emergence of new features and refining existing capabilities. For example, the integration of container technologies, such as Docker and Kubernetes, emphasizes the relevance of lightweight virtualization solutions and necessitates robust kernel-level support. The kernel's ability to manage both VMs and containers creates a cohesive environment where both technologies can thrive, offering similar benefits while addressing different use cases.

Furthermore, as the Internet of Things (IoT) continues to expand, the kernel must adapt to manage a large number of lightweight, resource-constrained devices through virtualized solutions. The ability to run multiple guest operating systems efficiently and securely in such scenarios will prove essential as more devices seek to connect in an increasingly interconnected world.

In conclusion, kernel support for hypervisors within the Linux kernel is founded on sophisticated architecture and optimized management of virtualized resources. By integrating KVM and other virtualization technologies, the kernel provides robust support for multiple instances of operating systems, making it a preferred choice for enterprise solutions and cloud environments. The ongoing evolution of virtualization technologies, combined with the kernel's adaptability, positions the Linux kernel to remain at the forefront of virtualization solutions as the landscape continues to change. As new challenges and use cases for virtualization emerge, the Linux kernel will undoubtedly evolve to meet the demands of a diverse and interconnected world.

13.3. Containerization Technologies

Containerization technologies represent a groundbreaking advancement in the deployment and management of applications, vastly influencing the ecosystem surrounding the Linux kernel. By allowing applications to be packaged with all their dependencies into isolated units known as containers, this technology has transformed the way software is developed, deployed, and scaled. This subchapter delves into the operating principles of containerization technologies, their integration with the Linux kernel, and the operational advantages they confer in contemporary computing environments.

At the foundation of containerization lies the concept of boxes, which provide process isolation by utilizing kernel features such as namespaces and cgroups (control groups). Namespaces allow the container to have its isolated instance of an environment, including its process ID (PID) space, user IDs, network interfaces, and filesystem structure. Each container operates independently, unaware of the processes running outside of it, thus ensuring that applications function without interference.

Cgroups, on the other hand, are employed to manage and limit the resource allocation for containers, enabling the kernel to allocate CPU, memory, and I/O bandwidth efficiently. By implementing limits and quotas at the container level, cgroups ensure that no single application can monopolize the host's resources, which is critical for maintaining system stability, particularly in multi-tenant environments.

A robust and widely-adopted containerization technology is Docker. Docker leverages the capabilities of the Linux kernel, enabling developers to create, deploy, and manage containers seamlessly. Docker's architectural components include the Docker Engine, which is responsible for building and running containers, and the Docker Hub, a registry for sharing container images. The simplicity and accessibility of Docker have catalyzed its adoption, making it the gold standard for container orchestration in development operations (DevOps) environments.

The integration of containerization technologies with the Linux kernel offers numerous operational advantages. One significant benefit is resource optimization. By using containers, multiple applications can successfully run on the same host without the overhead associated with full virtual machines. While virtual machines require the emulation of an entire operating system stack, containers share the host operating system's kernel, drastically reducing resource consumption and improving application startup times.

Beyond resource efficiency, containerization technologies enhance the development and deployment workflows of applications. The encapsulation of an application and its dependencies within a container ensures a consistent environment across various stages of development, testing, and production. This "build once, run anywhere" philosophy addresses the age-old problem of "it works on my machine," where discrepancies between development and production environments can lead to significant issues. Containers eliminate these discrepancies, providing developers with confidence that their applications will behave consistently in any environment.

In modern microservices architectures, where applications are broken into smaller, independently deployable components, containers provide an ideal solution. Each microservice can run in its container and be developed, tested, and scaled independently of others. This modular approach enhances agility, allowing developers to iterate quickly and deploy changes without risking disruption to the entire application. The orchestration of these containers can be managed using platforms like Kubernetes, which automates deployment, scaling, and management of containerized applications in production environments.

However, while containerization technologies offer extensive benefits, they also introduce unique challenges that need to be addressed. One significant concern is security. As containers share the host kernel, vulnerabilities within one container could potentially impact others running on the same host. Therefore, implementing security measures is crucial. This includes leveraging MAC systems such as SELinux and AppArmor to enforce stricter access controls, ensuring that each container has limited privileges and is sandboxed from others.

Furthermore, managing secrets and sensitive information within container environments poses challenges. Incorporating secure methods for managing sensitive data—such as environment variables, external secret management tools, or encrypted storage solutions—is vital for maintaining confidentiality.

As the landscape of container technology continues to evolve, so too must its integration with the Linux kernel. Enhancements to the kernel's capabilities, such as improved resource management, enhanced security features, and expanded namespaces, will contribute to the continued growth and efficiency of containerization technologies.

In conclusion, containerization technologies leverage the capabilities of the Linux kernel to facilitate the isolation and management of applications in lightweight packages. The integration of features like namespaces and cgroups allows for efficient resource sharing, while tools such as Docker provide an accessible framework for developers to build and deploy applications consistently. As the industry embraces containerization, ongoing advancements and the creative adaptation of these technologies will shape the future of application development and deployment in the Linux ecosystem, ensuring robust performance, scalability, and security in increasingly complex computing environments.

13.4. Optimizing VM and Container Performance

In the relentless pursuit of efficiency in computing environments, the optimization of virtual machines (VMs) and containers has emerged as a critical area of focus. Both technologies harness the power of the Linux kernel to provide isolated environments for applications, yet their performance characteristics and requirements differ significantly. Achieving peak performance in both VMs and containers necessitates an understanding of kernel operations, resource management standards, and the specific optimizations that can be applied to maximize efficiency.

Virtual machines represent a complete emulation of physical hardware, running their kernels, operating systems, and applications. The performance of VMs is heavily dependent on the efficiency of the hypervisor layer managing these VMs—a layer that can introduce overhead in resource allocation, context switching, and I/O operations. This overhead can be mitigated through careful configuration and tuning of the hypervisor settings, resource limits, and memory management strategies inherent to the Linux kernel.

In contrast, containers share the underlying kernel of the host operating system, allowing for a lighter-weight implementation compared to VMs. This shared architecture augments the potential for rapid startup times, lower resource consumption, and higher density in application deployments. However, to optimize container performance effectively, developers must leverage kernel features such as control groups (cgroups) and namespaces to manage resource distribution, isolation, and security effectively.

One significant driver of performance optimization for both VMs and containers lies in resource allocation, with both solutions requiring precise limits to ensure that optimal performance is achieved without significant contention. The Linux kernel's implementation of cgroups allows administrators to set limits on CPU, memory, and I/O bandwidth, enabling tailored performance tuning for specific workloads. This is critical in scenarios where multiple VMs or containers coexist on a single host and may compete for resources.

When addressing VM performance, it is essential to consider the configuration of virtual hardware. Ensuring that virtual CPUs (vCPUs) are mapped efficiently to physical CPU cores can alleviate resource contention and reduce scheduling overhead. Techniques such as CPU pinning, where vCPUs are assigned to specific physical cores, can enhance performance by limiting context-switching penalties, particularly important in environments with real-time constraints or performance-sensitive applications.

For containers, networking optimizations become paramount to achieving streamlined communication between services. The introduction of technologies like eBPF (Extended Berkeley Packet Filter) allows for dynamic tracing and monitoring of network operations, enabling developers to optimize network paths, reduce latency, and ensure reliable throughput. Optimizing networking performance can drastically enhance the responsiveness of applications, especially in microservices architectures where inter-container communication is frequent.

Disk I/O operations also require careful consideration in both VMs and containers. Implementing storage solutions that utilize direct access methods and optimized filesystems can minimize I/O latencies and bolster performance. For containers, utilizing storage drivers that are designed for performance, such as overlayFS or flock-based systems, can enhance the overall responsiveness of applications through effective management of storage layers.

Monitoring tools play an essential role in optimizing performance, providing insights into resource usage patterns, system health, and potential bottlenecks. Tools such as `top`, `htop`, and `iotop` allow administrators to track real-time performance metrics, enabling quick identification of resource contention or over-utilization. Additionally, profiling tools, such as `perf`, provide deeper insights into where optimizations can be made by analyzing function call performance and resource allocation logs.

Furthermore, understanding the resource requirements of specific applications within VMs and containers provides a framework for optimization. Containers may utilize different resource layers depending on their operational contexts—adapting performance tuning based on anticipated workloads enables systems to allocate resources dynamically, enhancing responsiveness according to varying demands.

As technology continues to advance, keeping a keen eye on emerging trends will influence optimization techniques for VMs and containers. Innovations in hardware virtualization, such as hardware-assisted technologies (Intel VT-x and AMD-V), are expected to provide further enhancements to virtualization performance. Similarly, the adoption of edge computing requires tailored performance strategies that prioritize response times and resource management capabilities in decentralized architectures.

In summary, optimizing VM and container performance is a multifaceted endeavor that requires a comprehensive understanding of kernel operations, resource management techniques, and application-specific requirements. By effectively utilizing features within Linux, administrators can finely tune resource allocation, optimize I/O operations, and leverage monitoring tools to enhance performance. As the landscape of technology evolves, continuous refinement of these optimization strategies will ensure that both VMs and containers deliver the performance and responsiveness required to meet the demands of modern computing environments. The ongoing development of tools and techniques in this realm highlights the Linux kernel's central role in shaping the future of virtualization and containerization technologies.

13.5. Security Considerations and Challenges

In the context of the Linux kernel, security considerations and challenges are paramount as the landscape of technology evolves and the complexity of systems increases. The kernel, being the core of the operating system, interacts closely with hardware, processes user commands, and manages system resources, which makes it a significant target for security breaches. Understanding the security implications and navigating the challenges inherent in kernel development and operation is crucial for maintaining the integrity, confidentiality, and availability of systems built on Linux.

As operating systems have become intricate, the vectors for potential attacks have widened dramatically. Malware, rootkits, and other malicious tools can exploit kernel vulnerabilities to gain escalated privileges or disrupt normal operations. For this reason, developing a resilient security posture within the kernel is essential. It begins with ensuring that the kernel is designed and built with security in mind, employing the principle of least privilege at every stage to minimize the impact of any security breach.

One critical aspect of kernel security is the implementation of strong access controls. The kernel manages user permissions through User IDs (UIDs) and Group IDs (GIDs), and by leveraging additional layers of mandatory access control (MAC) systems like SELinux and AppArmor. These MAC systems enforce stringent policies that dictate what resources processes can access and under what conditions. For example, SELinux uses security policies to confine programs to specific resources, ensuring even if a process is compromised, it cannot easily escalate privileges or access sensitive data.

Another essential consideration is the management of kernel memory. Buffer overflows, improper input validation, and other vulnerabilities can lead to memory corruption, providing a pathway for attackers to manipulate kernel behavior. Implementing secure coding practices is imperative; developers must use functions that inherently limit the risk of such vulnerabilities, including proper bounds-checking and handling of user input. Furthermore, tools like Address Sanitizer (ASan) can help in detecting and preventing memory corruption issues.

Proactive patch management is vital for kernel security, as vulnerabilities are often discovered after a code release. The Linux community emphasizes the necessity of timely updates and applying security patches to address identified weaknesses. Organizations running Linux systems must have policies in place to quickly incorporate kernel updates and maintain communication with the kernel development community to stay informed about newly discovered vulnerabilities.

Real-time monitoring of security events elevates kernel security through continuous visibility into system behavior. Logging systems like the Linux Audit Framework (auditd) keep records of system calls and security-related events, allowing for analysis and detection of suspicious activities. Installing intrusion detection systems (IDS) provides another layer of protection by actively monitoring network and system behaviors, alerting administrators to potential incidents before they escalate.

The need for kernel security also extends into emerging technologies. The rise of cloud computing and containerization presents unique challenges; for instance, containers share the host kernel, creating potential vulnerabilities if not properly configured. Employing the principle of isolation through namespaces, along with stringent resource allocation using cgroups, mitigates this risk. Implementations that incorporate Security Contexts can further enforce stringent security measures within containerized environments.

Despite these robust security mechanisms, challenges remain. The dynamic nature of the threat landscape means security must be continually assessed and adapted. For example, new attack vectors may emerge with advancements in technology, necessitating a proactive stance in evaluating and implementing innovative defenses against potential infiltrations.

As the community surrounding Linux kernel development grows, the culture of security awareness must also evolve. Creating an environment that encourages developers to prioritize security by including security assessments in code reviews fosters a mindset that values the protection of the entire system architecture.

In conclusion, security considerations and challenges within the Linux kernel necessitate a multifaceted approach that includes robust access controls, continuous monitoring, proactive patch management, and the adoption of secure coding practices. The landscape continues to shift, and as technology evolves, kernel security measures must adapt to remain effective. Engaging the kernel development community in ongoing discussions around security will enhance resilience against emerging threats, ensuring that Linux remains a reliable and secure foundation for an ever-connected digital world. The challenges are significant, but the continued commitment to developing a secure kernel and fostering collaboration within the community can offer a pathway to success in maintaining a secure environment.

14. Performance Profiling: Analyzing Kernel Efficiency

14.1. Performance Monitoring Tools

The expansive interface of the Linux kernel is intrinsically tied to the performance monitoring tools available to its developers and users, which form the essential framework supporting the operational integrity of Linux systems. Throughout the Linux ecosystem, performance monitoring is critical not only to identify and address inefficiencies but also to thoroughly understand resource usage patterns and enhance overall system performance. This can be achieved by leveraging a suite of tools designed to monitor, analyze, and optimize various aspects of kernel performance.

To begin with, one of the most prominent performance monitoring tools in the Linux kernel is `top`. This interactive program offers real-time insights into system performance, displaying CPU usage, memory usage, and the processes consuming resources. By providing a dynamic view of what is actively running, `top` helps users gain immediate visibility into system behavior, enabling prompt adjustments or troubleshooting when necessary. Variants like `htop` extend this functionality, presenting data in a more user-friendly, visual format, allowing for easier navigation and management of processes.

Another powerful utility is `perf`, a flexible performance analysis tool directly integrated into the kernel. `perf` can capture a wide array of performance metrics, ranging from CPU cycles and cache misses to context switch counts and instruction durations. This granularity of data enables developers to conduct in-depth analyses of performance bottlenecks in kernel code or user applications. The output generated can inform optimization strategies, revealing hotspots—specific areas where performance issues are most pronounced—allowing developers to focus their efforts effectively.

I/O performance analysis further benefits from tools like `iostat`, which monitors system input/output device loading by observing disk and partition activity over time. This tool plays a vital role in diagnosing I/O-related bottlenecks, as it provides insight into read/write rates and how effectively devices manage queue lengths. Utilizing this information, administrators can adjust disk management practices and optimize workloads based on the hardware capabilities they observe.

Memory usage and efficiency are equally important when assessing kernel performance. Tools such as vmstat facilitate monitoring of memory, processes, and system I/O performance, presenting a snapshot of system activity and revealing potential issues related to memory pressure or paging. Further analysis tools like free and smem provide a breakdown of memory usage across processes, enabling administrators to diagnose memory leaks or mismanagement within the kernel or applications effectively.

Network performance monitoring is also an essential component of overall system health. Tools like netstat and ss provide statistics regarding network connections, while tcpdump allows for packet capture and analysis at a granular level. These tools enable both real-time monitoring and troubleshooting of network performance, assisting in diagnosing latency issues or identifying bottlenecks during peak load periods.

When it comes to system logging, the combination of syslog and journalctl in systemd-based distributions enables administrators to maintain comprehensive logs of system events and kernel messages. The detailed logging facilitated by these utilities allows for historical analysis and identification of trends or patterns that may indicate underlying issues affecting system performance.

Profiling tools, such as ftrace and oProfile, are employed to qualify performance at a deeper level within kernel operations. These tools allow engineers to trace function execution paths, gauge execution time, and analyze how code paths contribute to overall performance. The insights gained from profiling sessions can reveal potential inefficiencies or hotspots, serving as the foundation for optimization efforts in kernel code.

As the Linux kernel and its ecosystem evolve, monitoring tools will inevitably adapt to accommodate new hardware capabilities, software requirements, and user demands. Emerging technologies—such as artificial intelligence and machine learning—are likely to integrate into performance monitoring frameworks, potentially allowing for predictive analysis and adaptive optimizations based on performance trends. These advanced systems could detect anomalies and suggest dynamic adjustments in real time, resulting in self-optimizing kernels.

In conclusion, performance monitoring tools play a critical role in the ongoing development and optimization of the Linux kernel. By providing detailed insights into system activity, resource usage, and performance metrics, these tools empower users and developers to enhance system efficiency, identify bottlenecks, and cultivate an environment conducive to robust kernel performance. As technology advances and the demands on systems grow, the integration of innovative performance monitoring solutions will continue to shape the landscape of kernel development, ensuring that Linux remains capable of meeting contemporary and future computational challenges.

14.2. Benchmarking Techniques

Benchmarking techniques are vital for measuring and evaluating the performance and efficiency of the Linux kernel and the myriad systems reliant upon it. As technology evolves, understanding precisely how the kernel interacts with hardware and applications is essential for optimizing performance, resource management, and overall system reliability. This section will explore various benchmarking methods, their implementation within the Linux ecosystem, and best practices for ensuring accurate, actionable results.

At its core, benchmarking involves running a suite of tests designed to quantify specific performance metrics under predefined conditions. These metrics can vary widely, ranging from CPU load and memory usage to input/output operations per second (IOPS) and network throughput. The fundamental purpose of benchmarking is to provide insights that can inform development decisions and identify areas for optimization.

One of the primary benchmarking techniques used within the Linux kernel environment is micro-benchmarking. This approach focuses on measuring the performance of specific kernel functions or subsystems in isolation. By targeting performance at a granular level, developers can identify bottlenecks or inefficiencies in kernel code. For instance, tools such as bench or latencytop can be employed to assess latency or function call duration, aiding in the diagnosis of performance hiccups during kernel operation.

In addition to micro-benchmarking, macro-benchmarking evaluates the performance of the entire system under real-world workloads. This process involves running comprehensive tests that simulate actual usage scenarios—such as web serving, database querying, or heavy computational tasks. Tools like sysbench or fio provide frameworks for generating load and measuring performance over time, allowing developers to observe how their changes impact overall system functionality.

I/O benchmarking holds particular significance in the Linux kernel due to the critical role that storage devices play in system performance. Tools like iozone and bonnie++ can be leveraged to assess the speed and efficiency of read and write operations across various storage configurations. These tests help identify optimal configurations and reveal potential issues with disk IO that could lead to degraded performance.

Networking performance benchmarking is equally crucial, especially given the increasing reliance on networked applications. Tools such as iperf or netperf measure network throughput and latency, providing developers with key insights into how different configurations of the Linux kernel impact networking performance. By simulating various networking scenarios, developers can optimize the way the kernel handles network packets, improving responsiveness and data transmission speeds.

To ensure the validity of benchmarking results, several best practices should be adhered to during the benchmarking process. First, it is vital to establish a consistent and controlled testing environment. This includes ensuring that tests are conducted under stable conditions, such as limiting background processes and network activity that could introduce noise into the results. Variability in testing conditions can lead to inconsistent results, making it challenging to draw actionable conclusions from benchmark data.

Moreover, selecting appropriate metrics is essential for a meaningful analysis of performance. Depending on the objectives—whether measuring throughput or latency—tailoring the benchmark suite to the specific requirements of the testing scenario ensures relevant results.

When examining benchmarks, context matters. Understanding what workloads were tested, the hardware on which they ran, and how changes to the kernel may have influenced results provide invaluable context for interpreting data. Developers should analyze trends in performance over time and compare results against various configurations to quantify the effects of modifications accurately.

Finally, documenting and sharing benchmarking results with the broader community fosters collaboration and knowledge sharing. By discussing insights and findings in forums or mailing lists, kernel contributors can collectively engage with performance-related challenges, ultimately driving collaborative problem-solving and innovation.

In summary, benchmarking techniques provide critical insights into the performance and efficiency of the Linux kernel, informing decisions that can improve system reliability and responsiveness. By employing both micro- and macro-benchmarking methods, focusing on relevant metrics, controlling the testing environment, and leveraging community collaboration, developers can optimize the Linux kernel and enhance its capabilities in the complex ecosystem of modern computing. The ongoing development of benchmarking tools and processes will remain essential as technology continues to evolve and as new opportunities for optimization present themselves.

14.3. Interpreting Profiling Data

Interpreting profiling data is a vital aspect of understanding and optimizing the performance of the Linux kernel and the systems it supports. Kernel profiling enables developers to analyze the execution characteristics of various subsystems, identify bottlenecks, and enhance resource allocation strategies that lead to improved efficiency and system responsiveness. This process involves collecting data about how the kernel interacts with various processes, measuring execution time, and determining the resource consumption associated with specific tasks.

The first step in interpreting profiling data is to collect the necessary information, which is typically done using profiling tools integrated into the Linux kernel. Tools such as `perf`, `ftrace`, and `oprofile` are indispensable in this context, providing developers the ability to gather detailed insights about kernel performance during execution. For instance, `perf` allows users to measure CPU cycles, cache hits, and context switches, providing a comprehensive overview of how the system behaves under load.

Once the data has been collected, the next step is to analyze and visualize it effectively. Profiling tools often come with built-in reporting features that aggregate performance data and present it in a manner conducive to understanding. For instance, `perf report` provides a graphical representation of CPU usage patterns, helping developers to identify which functions are consuming the most resources. This data can be sorted and filtered to focus on specific areas of interest—be it a particular subsystem or process—enabling targeted optimization efforts.

Key performance metrics from profiling data include function execution time, call frequency, and context switch rates. By analyzing these metrics, developers can pinpoint which parts of the kernel or applications are leading to inefficient resource utilization. For example, if a particular function is identified as consuming an inordinate amount of CPU cycles, developers can investigate and optimize it to enhance overall system performance. Profiling data also enables developers to understand the interplay between different kernel subsystems and user-space applications, revealing how changes in one area can impact overall system efficacy.

An essential component of interpreting profiling data involves contextualization. Data should not merely be viewed in isolation; rather, it should be compared against established baselines or during different execution conditions. For instance, profiling data collected during heavy loads can reveal different bottlenecks than data collected during idle system states. By establishing context, developers gain a deeper understanding of how workload patterns can affect kernel performance and behavior.

Understanding specific kernel subsystems, such as memory management, I/O scheduling, and process scheduling, enhances the interpretation process further. Profiling tools can provide critical insights into how these subsystems operate during normal and stressed conditions. For instance, profiling data related to memory allocation patterns can reveal fragmentation issues, while I/O profiling may highlight inefficiencies that could benefit from improved load balancing across storage devices.

In the iterative development process, profiling data serves as a guide for optimizations. After adjustments are made to the kernel or associated applications, repeating the profiling process can confirm whether the optimization efforts have yielded the desired improvements. This feedback loop fosters a culture of continuous enhancement, allowing developers to refine their approaches over time and adapt to newly emerging data patterns.

Additionally, interpretation of profiling data can lead to explorations of advanced techniques, such as speculative optimization or adaptive scheduling. For instance, if profiling data indicates specific performance bottlenecks related to scheduling decisions, developers can investigate adaptive scheduling algorithms that respond dynamically to real-time workloads, optimizing task allocation based on profiling insights.

As the complexity of systems continues to increase, emerging technologies such as cloud computing, artificial intelligence, and machine learning play a significant role in enhancing profiling techniques. The integration of machine learning algorithms into profiling tools allows for predictive analysis—anticipating which resources may become bottlenecks based on historical data. This clever use of profiling data not only enhances the kernel's performance but also fosters systems that adapt intelligently to user demands and operational changes.

In conclusion, interpreting profiling data is a fundamental skill for developers looking to optimize Linux kernel performance and enhance overall system efficacy. By utilizing various profiling tools, contextualizing performance metrics, and continuously iterating on the data gathered, developers can identify bottlenecks and areas of improvement, leading to refined and efficient kernel operations. As the landscape of technology evolves, the ability to leverage profiling insights will remain a critical determinant of success in making the Linux kernel a more robust, responsive, and resource-efficient platform for modern computing environments.

14.4. Optimizing for Maximum Efficiency

The pursuit of maximum efficiency in the Linux kernel involves a multifaceted approach encompassing performance optimization strategies, resource management, and adaptive techniques tailored to the diverse environments in which the kernel operates. Achieving optimum performance not only enhances user experience but also ensures the stability and reliability of systems across various hardware architectures. This section elaborates on the principles, techniques, and best practices for optimizing the Linux kernel to attain maximum efficiency while addressing the unique requirements of modern computing environments.

One fundamental aspect of maximizing efficiency is understanding the intricacies of the kernel architecture and how it interacts with hardware resources. The kernel's design is inherently modular, allowing certain features and drivers to be loaded or unloaded dynamically based on the specific needs of the system. This modular structure minimizes memory usage by ensuring that only the necessary components for a particular workload are active, resulting in a leaner, more efficient kernel. Customizing the kernel by enabling only essential modules and drivers through configuration tools such as `make menuconfig` or kernel command-line options can significantly enhance performance tailored to user-specific scenarios.

Memory management plays a pivotal role in optimizing kernel efficiency. The mechanisms that govern how memory is allocated, reclaimed, and accessed can have substantial implications for performance. Implementing strategies such as page caching, where frequently accessed data is stored in memory, can drastically reduce latency for I/O operations. Employing monitoring tools to analyze memory usage patterns can help identify opportunities for further optimization, such as adjusting swappiness to balance RAM and swap usage and prevent excessive paging.

Caching not only improves memory access but also enhances performance across the entire system. By leveraging advanced caching strategies—such as hierarchical caching or write-back caching—developers can optimize disk I/O operations. Monitoring tools such as `iostat` and `vmstat` can provide valuable insights regarding cache hit ratios, enabling developers to fine-tune caching configurations that ensure optimal responsiveness and efficiency.

Furthermore, optimizing process scheduling within the kernel can yield substantial gains in efficiency. The choice of scheduling algorithm, particularly in environments with real-time requirements, has direct implications on resource distribution among processes. The Completely Fair Scheduler (CFS) is the default in modern Linux kernels; however, selecting the appropriate scheduler for specific use cases—such as real-time tasks or low-latency applications—can mitigate latency issues and improve responsiveness. For example, employing the Real-Time (RT) scheduler can benefit systems where time-sensitive tasks must take precedence.

Network performance is another critical area where kernel optimization leads to maximum efficiency. Optimizing parameters such as Maximum Transmission Unit (MTU) size, TCP window sizes, and congestion control algorithms can improve throughput and reduce latency for network applications. The kernel's network stack can be monitored using tools like `iperf` and `netstat` to analyze traffic and identify potential bottlenecks, enabling adjustments to kernel parameters through the sysctl interface.

In addition to performance optimization, improving energy efficiency is increasingly crucial, especially in mobile and embedded systems. Implementing effective power management strategies within the kernel, such as dynamic voltage scaling, CPU frequency scaling, and sleep states, can extend battery life while maintaining optimal performance. The Linux kernel provides interfaces that allow developers to monitor and control power usage, facilitating the design of applications that adapt based on power availability and usage patterns.

The integration of advanced profiling tools into the development process enhances developers' ability to identify performance bottlenecks. Building upon optimization methodologies, tools such as `perf`, `ftrace`, and `systemtap` allow developers to collect profiling data, analyze system behavior under load, and identify inefficiencies that warrant attention. By leveraging this data, developers can apply targeted optimizations, leading to cycles of continuous improvement.

In the context of the evolving cloud ecosystem, performance optimization must also consider orchestration of resources across distributed environments. The Linux kernel plays a central role in container orchestration tools like Kubernetes, which optimize application performance across clusters. By employing kernel features like namespaces and cgroups within containerized applications, developers can more efficiently allocate and manage resources, ensuring that applications remain responsive under varying loads.

As technology continues to evolve, emerging practices, such as the incorporation of machine learning to automate performance optimizations, are becoming standard. Algorithms that adaptively allocate resources based on observed usage patterns can lead to significant efficiency gains in kernel performance. The kernel's capacity to support these advancements will be critical in addressing the increasingly complex demands of modern applications and infrastructures.

In summary, optimizing for maximum efficiency in the Linux kernel is a multifaceted effort that encompasses memory management, process scheduling, caching, network performance, energy efficiency, and the utilization of performance profiling tools. By taking a holistic approach and embracing innovative strategies for kernel optimization, developers can ensure that the Linux kernel meets the demands of contemporary computing while providing users with a reliable, high-performance experience. The commitment to ongoing optimization will ultimately reinforce the Linux kernel's position as a versatile, resilient choice in the dynamic landscape of technology.

14.5. Forecasting Performance Trends

In the context of kernel development, forecasting performance trends encompasses an assessment of shifting demands, technological advancements, and anticipated changes in usage patterns that influence the Linux kernel's optimization landscape. As one of the most flexible and widely adopted operating systems, the Linux kernel's ability to adapt to evolving environments is critical for ensuring its continued relevance in various applications—from cloud computing to embedded systems.

One key aspect in forecasting performance trends is the rise of artificial intelligence (AI) and machine learning (ML) applications. With increasing reliance on AI-driven solutions, the demand for processing capabilities that can handle large datasets and computationally intensive tasks is skyrocketing. The Linux kernel must evolve to optimize resource allocation for these workloads effectively, integrating AI capabilities directly into its architecture. This may involve developing specialized scheduling algorithms that prioritize AI tasks, enhancing memory management for handling vast amounts of data, and leveraging hardware acceleration techniques through dedicated instruction sets found in modern processors.

Another trend indicative of the direction in which the kernel is headed is the continuing rise of containerization and microservices. As businesses and projects increasingly adopt container architectures like Kubernetes, performance tuning within these environments will take precedence. The kernel must refine its capabilities in managing containers, enhancing features such as cgroups and namespaces to facilitate efficient resource allocation, and ensuring network performance optimizations that cater to service discovery and inter-container communications. This trend signifies a broader move toward highly dynamic, scalable applications that require the kernel to adapt rapidly, providing seamless orchestration and resource management across clusters.

The evolving landscape of edge computing also bears implications for kernel performance forecasting. As computing moves closer to the data source—enabling faster processing and reduced latency—the Linux kernel must accommodate the unique demands of distributed systems and IoT devices. This involves optimizing the kernel for constrained environments, focusing on power management features that ensure efficient operation without sacrificing performance. The kernel should also extend its capabilities to process data locally while maintaining synchronization with cloud instances for broader data management tasks.

Performance trends will also reflect an increasing need for security within the kernel. As cyber threats become more sophisticated, the kernel must implement enhanced security mechanisms that not only protect data integrity but also maintain system performance. This dual emphasis on security and efficiency will lead to the integration of advanced security protocols, real-time monitoring tools, and proactive threat detection technologies. Such measures will ensure that while systems remain responsive and performant, they are also fortified against potential vulnerabilities.

As data privacy regulations become more stringent globally, kernel development will be influenced by the need to incorporate privacy-preserving technologies. The performance of the kernel must not only meet operational metrics but also comply with legal requirements concerning data handling and user privacy. Developing lightweight encryption methods that do not introduce significant overhead will be essential, as will ensuring that the kernel accommodates user consent mechanisms that align with privacy standards.

Moreover, integrating advanced power management mechanisms and optimizing kernel performance in battery-powered devices will continue to be a focal point. With the proliferation of mobile and edge devices, the ability to balance performance and energy efficiency will be pivotal. This will entail refining the kernel's sleep states, enhancing CPU frequency scaling, and optimizing memory usage—all while ensuring that performance does not suffer during peak demands.

In summary, forecasting performance trends for the Linux kernel involves a multifaceted assessment of emerging technologies and evolving societal demands. Attention to AI and ML integration, ongoing adaptation to containerization and microservices, responsiveness to edge computing requirements, heightened security protocols, and compliance with privacy standards will collectively inform the kernel's performance trajectory. As these trends unfold, kernel developers will be tasked with innovating solutions that balance performance, efficiency, security, and compliance—positioning the Linux kernel as a robust and adaptable foundation for future computing needs. The community's collaborative efforts will be essential in shaping these innovations, ensuring that the kernel continues to evolve and thrive in an ever-changing digital landscape.

15. Real-Time Enhancements: Achieving Precision and Dedication

15.1. Principles of Real-Time Systems

The principles of real-time systems serve as foundational concepts crucial for achieving the high levels of predictability, responsiveness, and resource management in real-time applications. These principles are particularly relevant in environments where precise timing and immediate responses are paramount, such as in embedded systems, automotive control systems, telecommunications, and robotics. The Linux kernel, with its ongoing adaptations, seeks to meet the needs of these real-time applications effectively.

At the core of real-time systems is the distinction between hard real-time and soft real-time requirements. Hard real-time systems require that critical tasks be completed within strict time constraints, where any delay could result in catastrophic failures. Examples include flight control systems and medical devices. Conversely, soft real-time systems aim to prioritize tasks to meet performance criteria but can tolerate some degree of latencies. Applications in multimedia processing or online gaming often fall into this category. Understanding these distinctions is vital for developers working in real-time environments as it influences system design and resource allocation strategies.

One central principle is task prioritization, which dictates that time-sensitive tasks are given precedence over standard tasks within the system. Real-time scheduling algorithms, such as Rate Monotonic Scheduling (RMS) and Earliest Deadline First (EDF), are employed to prioritize tasks effectively based on their urgency and deadlines. These algorithms enable the kernel to allocate CPU time to higher-priority tasks first, ensuring that time-critical processes can execute on time. Developers working on real-time applications must carefully design their task scheduling to align with these principles to allow smooth and efficient execution.

Latency is another critical consideration in the principles of real-time systems. Minimizing latency—the delay between a task being initiated and its completion—is essential to achieving desired performance levels. In real-time environments, this often means minimizing both interrupt latency and context-switching time. The Linux kernel includes features for optimizing scheduling and interrupts to cater to real-time needs. For instance, the introduction of the PREEMPT_RT patch set enhances the Linux kernel's capability to preempt standard tasks, allowing real-time tasks to gain access to CPU resources more quickly. Understanding how to configure the kernel for minimal latency disruption is crucial for developers working with time-sensitive applications.

Resource management also plays a significant role in real-time systems. The kernel must ensure that resources—such as CPU time, memory, and I/O bandwidth—are allocated dynamically and efficiently to maintain system performance. In addition, the use of control groups (cgroups) provides mechanisms for managing resources and prioritizing tasks based on their real-time requirements, enabling effective resource sharing and utilization between standard and real-time workloads. In Linux, understanding how to implement cgroups effectively allows for better separation and management of real-time tasks alongside other processes, ensuring predictability in performance.

Real-time systems often exhibit deterministic behavior, where responses to input events occur in predictable time frames. The Linux kernel supports deterministic behaviors by incorporating features such as real-time clock management and high-resolution timers. Leveraging high-resolution timers ensures that real-time tasks can be more accurately scheduled, allowing developers to create more responsive systems. The kernel offers interfaces to configure timers for precise control, an essential element when developing low-latency, time-sensitive applications.

Moreover, the increased integration of real-time systems within the burgeoning Internet of Things (IoT) landscape presents unique challenges and opportunities. The kernel must adapt to ensure that real-time processing capabilities are reliably supported in diverse,

interconnected environments. Real-time enhancements can be leveraged to ensure timely data processing and responsiveness, enabling devices to act on real-time data input while ensuring synchronization across distributed networks.

As technology advances, the principles of real-time systems will likely continue to evolve, with ongoing developments in the Linux kernel enhancing its ability to support real-time applications. Embracing trends such as machine learning, edge computing, and advanced networking will require kernel developers to remain sharply attuned to the needs of real-time systems, adapting kernel features to meet increasing demands for performance and adaptability.

In summary, the principles of real-time systems center around precise timing, task prioritization, latency minimization, resource management, and deterministic behavior. Understanding these principles is vital for developers working on real-time applications, as they dictate how the Linux kernel can be effectively leveraged to create responsive, high-performance systems. As the landscape of computing evolves, these principles will remain significant in guiding the adaptation and enhancement of the Linux kernel to meet the challenges of real-time processing and applications in dynamic environments.

15.2. Integrating Real-Time Enhancements

As technology progresses at an unprecedented pace, the Linux kernel remains a cornerstone of the operating system landscape, continuously evolving to meet the demands of modern computing. This subchapter, "Integrating Real-Time Enhancements," discusses the incorporation of real-time capabilities into the Linux kernel, detailing the principles, features, and implications of enhancing kernel performance for specific timing-sensitive applications.

Real-time enhancements are essential for systems that require timely processing and responses to inputs. These systems span various applications, including robotics, automotive control, telecommunications, and industrial automation. To meet the stringent demands of real-time application environments, the Linux kernel must offer mechanisms that ensure tasks are executed within predefined constraints, minimizing jitter and maximizing predictability.

The foundation of real-time enhancements begins with understanding real-time scheduling principles. Traditional Linux scheduling algorithms, designed for general-purpose computing, might not satisfy the timing guarantees required by real-time applications. Therefore, specific real-time scheduling policies, such as the Real-Time Scheduling (RT) policy, are incorporated into the kernel. Real-time tasks can be assigned higher priorities, allowing them to preempt non-real-time tasks, thus ensuring predictable execution times.

Two main scheduling algorithms—Earliest Deadline First (EDF) and Rate Monotonic Scheduling (RMS)—are often employed for real-time systems. EDF dynamically prioritizes tasks based on deadlines, ensuring that tasks closer to their deadlines have precedence, while RMS assigns static priorities based on the frequency of task execution. These algorithms enable the Linux kernel to adapt to time-critical applications, allowing developers to manage task execution effectively based on system requirements.

Latency optimization is another vital aspect of integrating real-time enhancements into the kernel. Linux offers mechanisms to reduce both interrupt latency and context-switching times—two critical factors influencing a system's responsiveness. The PREEMPT_RT patch set transforms the Linux kernel into a more preemptible environment, allowing real-time tasks to preempt ongoing non-real-time tasks, thereby reducing response times. Developers can tune kernel parameters to optimize scheduling behaviors and fine-tune the interrupt handling process for specific use cases.

Balancing real-time and standard workloads presents a unique challenge in integrating real-time enhancements. While certain applications demand strict timing constraints, others may operate within a less constrained performance spectrum. The kernel must strive to allocate resources intelligently, ensuring that real-time tasks receive priority without compromising overall system performance. The use of control groups allows administrators to enforce resource limits on standard workloads, preventing them from interfering with real-time processes and promoting efficiency across diverse workloads.

The integration of the real-time kernel within Internet of Things (IoT) frameworks stands as a significant opportunity for leveraging these enhancements. As IoT devices proliferate, each device's ability to perform tasks in real-time is paramount. The Linux kernel can accommodate real-time application requirements through careful consideration of the hardware resources available to each IoT device, ensuring timely responses to sensor inputs, actuations, and networking interactions.

As developments in technology continue to shape the future landscape, emerging strategies for real-time enhancements in the Linux kernel will need to evolve. With the integration of machine learning into applications, the kernel will need to support frameworks that facilitate resource allocation based on predictive analytics, close monitoring of workloads, and dynamic prioritization of tasks. These advancements highlight the kernel's adaptability and commitment to maintaining high performance across diverse applications.

In conclusion, integrating real-time enhancements into the Linux kernel is vital for accommodating the demands of timing-sensitive applications. From implementing real-time scheduling policies and optimizing latencies to balancing workloads and supporting IoT integrations, these enhancements are essential for ensuring that the kernel meets contemporary performance expectations. The continuous evolution of these capabilities reinforces the Linux kernel's position as a trusted backbone for a wide array of applications, setting the stage for future innovations in real-time computing.

As technology continues to advance, the commitment to integrating real-time enhancements will enable the Linux kernel to adapt and thrive in an increasingly complex digital landscape, attesting to the versatility and responsiveness that characterize its ongoing evolution.

15.3. Scheduling and Latency Optimization

In the landscape of modern computing, optimizing scheduling and latency is essential for enhancing the performance of the Linux kernel, especially in environments where timely responsiveness is paramount. This involves meticulous coordination of kernel processes and ensuring efficient resource utilization, particularly in real-time and performance-sensitive applications, such as telecommunications, audio processing, and industrial automation. By understanding and implementing advanced scheduling techniques and latency optimization strategies, developers can significantly enhance system performance and user experience.

The Linux kernel employs various scheduling algorithms to determine the order of executing processes or threads. The Completely Fair Scheduler (CFS) is widely utilized as the default scheduler in modern Linux kernels, balancing the time allocation among processes to achieve fairness. However, in contexts where real-time performance is critical, alternative scheduling algorithms can provide more favorable characteristics. Real-time scheduling policies such as First-In, First-Out (FIFO) and Earliest Deadline First (EDF) are adept at managing time-sensitive tasks by ensuring they receive immediate attention from the CPU.

FIFO scheduling allows real-time tasks to execute without being preempted by other processes, making it suitable for applications that require deterministic behavior. However, this approach can result in starvation for lower-priority processes. EDF, conversely, dynamically assigns priorities based on deadlines, allowing more responsive handling of tasks as they approach their execution limits. Understanding the nuances of these scheduling techniques, and selecting the appropriate one based on the workload characteristics, is crucial for achieving precise control over execution timing.

Latency, defined as the delay between the initiation of an action and its effect, must be minimized in real-time applications to ensure that they operate effectively. The kernel's response to interrupts is a key contributor to latency. Kernel developers can optimize interrupt handling by reducing the interrupt latency to guarantee high responsiveness. This involves minimizing the time taken to service interrupts and ensuring quick context switching between processes. Techniques such as utilizing high-resolution timers, implementing priority-based interrupt scheduling, and designing efficient interrupt service routines (ISRs) can significantly enhance kernel responsiveness.

Additionally, the kernel's approach to managing sleep states and wake-up events plays an essential role in optimizing latency. Processes that are waiting for resources should be efficiently transitioned into sleep states to conserve CPU resources while ensuring that they can be awakened promptly when the required resources become available. This careful management ensures that lower-priority tasks do not block higher-priority tasks and that performance remains responsive.

Furthermore, balancing real-time and standard workloads is essential in systems where both types of tasks coexist. This involves configuring the kernel to allocate resources effectively between real-time tasks that require immediate execution and standard tasks that may not have stringent timing demands. Utilizing control groups (cgroups) allows administrators to enforce strict limits on resource usage for specific groups of tasks, thereby preventing non-real-time tasks from degrading the performance of critical real-time tasks.

The kernel can also leverage techniques such as CPU affinity, where processes are bound to specific CPU cores to enhance locality and reduce the overhead associated with migrating tasks between cores. This can effectively lower the latency for time-critical applications by ensuring that they run on the same core, reducing context switch penalties and cache misses.

For systems specifically oriented towards real-time applications, the PREEMPT_RT patch set transforms the Linux kernel into a more preemptive environment, allowing for preemption of non-real-time tasks, engaging in real-time scheduling practices, and reducing latencies associated with standard Linux kernels. Integrating this patch can significantly improve responsiveness and is particularly advantageous in systems that require high precision and minimal jitter.

Finally, maintaining and optimizing for maximum throughput alongside latency considerations is vital. Employing performance profiling tools to analyze scheduling behavior provides insights into which tasks are consuming the most resources and how effectively the scheduler is prioritizing workload. Such optimization can lead to identifying bottlenecks in the scheduling process, guiding adjustments to the kernel's scheduling policies and resource allocation strategies.

In summary, optimizing scheduling and latency within the Linux kernel is a critical endeavor that directly influences system responsiveness and overall performance. By leveraging advanced scheduling algorithms, minimizing interrupt latencies, efficiently managing sleep states, balancing real-time and standard workloads, and adopting profiling techniques, developers can fine-tune the kernel to meet the needs of performance-critical applications. As demands for latency-sensitive tasks continue to grow, the kernel's evolution will undoubtedly reflect the ongoing commitment to optimizing performance for future technological landscapes.

15.4. Balancing Real-Time and Standard Workloads

In the landscape of modern computing, balancing real-time and standard workloads within the Linux kernel represents a critical challenge that transcends mere performance tuning; it requires an intricate understanding of scheduling, resource management, and system architecture. As the demand for real-time processing capabilities continues to rise—particularly in fields such as telecommunications, automotive systems, and industrial automation—kernel developers face the task of ensuring that time-sensitive tasks can coexist and function optimally alongside standard processes that do not have such stringent timing requirements.

The concepts of real-time and standard workloads encompass distinct priorities in terms of execution and responsiveness. Real-time workloads are characterized by their need for predictability, where tasks must be completed within constrained time frames to avoid failure or adverse outcomes. This is especially relevant in systems where safety is paramount, such as embedded systems that control machinery or respond to critical sensor inputs. Standard workloads, on the other hand, may be less time-sensitive, focusing more on throughput and efficient resource utilization without strict deadlines.

To achieve a harmonious balance between these two types of workloads, the Linux kernel employs several strategies centered around scheduling and resource allocation. Scheduler algorithms such as Completely Fair Scheduler (CFS) fulfill the needs of standard workloads by distributing CPU time equitably among processes. However, the kernel also incorporates real-time scheduling policies—like FIFO and Round Robin—that prioritize real-time tasks, allowing the kernel to respond to urgent requests with minimal latency.

Determining the appropriate balance requires a nuanced approach. Resources must be allocated intelligently to ensure that real-time tasks receive the necessary CPU time and responsiveness without starving standard tasks of their share. Control groups (cgroups) play a critical role in this context by enforcing limits on resource usage across different workload classes. By categorizing processes into specific groups, developers can ensure that real-time applications retain adequate resources while maintaining performance safety margins for standard workloads.

Moreover, the kernel can optimize scheduling through various techniques that involve understanding CPU affinities and load averages, allowing real-time processes to run on dedicated cores while reserving other cores for standard workloads. This separation minimizes context-switching penalties and optimizes CPU performance, ultimately enhancing responsiveness for both types of workloads.

Monitoring tools present developers with an opportunity to analyze performance metrics that inform their balancing strategies. Tools such as `perf` and `ftrace` facilitate the collection of data that reflects CPU utilization, scheduling delays, and resource consumption among processes. By analyzing this data, developers can identify bottlenecks, adapt resource allocation strategies, and refine their scheduling configurations to optimize performance across the entire system.

As technology continues to evolve, the integration of machine learning and predictive analytics into kernel scheduling offers a promising frontier for balancing real-time and standard workloads. By analyzing historical execution patterns and workload behaviors, the kernel could make dynamic adjustments to scheduling decisions, proactively prioritizing tasks based on current system conditions and predicted future demands.

Furthermore, the advent of cloud computing and virtualization introduces additional considerations for balancing these workloads. In environments where virtual machines (VMs) or containers manage both real-time and standard processes, the kernel must dynamically adjust resource allocations based on the workloads' real-time requirements while ensuring that all other processes are managed effectively. The deployment of sophisticated resource management techniques across distributed architectures signifies the need for adaptability at the kernel level.

In conclusion, achieving a balance between real-time and standard workloads within the Linux kernel involves a rich interplay of scheduling algorithms, resource management strategies, and ongoing monitoring of system performance metrics. By understanding these principles and leveraging tools like cgroups and profiling utilities, developers can create systems that respond predictably to real-time tasks while efficiently executing standard workloads. As technology progresses and the demands of diverse applications continue to evolve, the Linux kernel will remain poised to adapt, ensuring that it meets the requirements of modern computing environments while maintaining the necessary performance and reliability for all work-loads.

15.5. Leveraging Real-Time Kernel for IoT

In recent years, the Internet of Things (IoT) has become increasingly significant, bringing with it the need for reliable and responsive systems to handle numerous connected devices. One of the compelling advantages of using the Linux kernel in these channels is its capability to leverage real-time kernel enhancements, which can effectively manage the demands of time-sensitive applications inherent in IoT solutions. This integration allows developers to make full use of the kernel's functionalities while ensuring that devices operate efficiently and with minimal latency.

In the context of IoT, leveraging a real-time kernel is essential. Real-time capabilities provide strict timing guarantees, allowing devices to respond promptly to events, such as sensor readings or user inputs. This responsiveness is critical in applications where missed deadlines may lead to safety risks, operational inefficiencies, or diminished user experiences. By utilizing real-time enhancements, developers can define priorities for critical tasks, ensuring that they receive precedence during execution.

The Linux kernel supports real-time scheduling policies which, as mentioned previously, allow for prioritized task execution. For instance, the use of the PREEMPT_RT patch set transforms the standard kernel into a preemptive environment, enabling more effective handling of real-time tasks. By integrating these patches, IoT developers can benefit from lower latencies and enhanced predictability, ensuring timely event handling within their applications.

Moreover, the kernel's ability to dynamically load and manage modules is synergistic with IoT's evolving landscape, where different devices may necessitate unique functionalities. Whether adding support for new sensors or modifying device drivers to accommodate specific use cases, kernel module management allows developers to extend capabilities without compromising overall system stability.

This extensibility is vital in IoT applications that require adaptation to shifting deployment scenarios.

Resource management becomes a key consideration when operating within an IoT framework. As devices often function in environments where power efficiency is critical, the Linux kernel offers extensive power management strategies. Utilizing features such as control groups (cgroups) and other power-saving features, developers can tailor resource allocations, optimizing battery life without sacrificing performance. Moreover, these mechanisms enable the kernel to monitor CPU frequency scaling and sleep states dynamically, ensuring that devices can remain power-efficient during periods of inactivity.

In conjunction with real-time enhancements and power management, ensuring secure communication between IoT devices is vital. The Linux kernel accommodates various encryption protocols and security frameworks, allowing for secure data transmission between devices. Utilizing methods such as Transport Layer Security (TLS) and network isolation through namespaces enhances the security posture of IoT applications, protecting sensitive data from potential breaches and unauthorized access.

As innovations within the IoT space continue to flourish, the Linux kernel stands poised to exploit these technologies, affirming itself as a favored platform for robust, responsive, and efficient IoT solutions. Advancements in machine learning and AI exemplify this landscape, as the kernel can support deployments that harness CPU acceleration for advanced computation on data generated by IoT devices. These capabilities facilitate the growth of intelligent applications that can adapt in real-time to the surrounding environment, leading to more autonomous operation.

Additionally, the emergence of edge computing dovetails seamlessly with real-time enhancements within the kernel. Processing data locally at the device or edge level minimizes latency associated with cloud responses, significantly improving responsiveness in applications where immediate action is necessary. Here, the Linux kernel's adaptability in handling real-time tasks complements the goals of edge deployments, paving the way for increased performance and efficiency.

In summary, leveraging real-time enhancements in the Linux kernel for IoT applications is an asset that empowers developers to create time-sensitive, resource-efficient, and secure applications that operate at the forefront of modern technology. With real-time capabilities, the ability to manage kernel modules dynamically, and the integration of comprehensive power management strategies, the Linux kernel continues to provide an exceptional platform for the evolution of IoT solutions. These developments reaffirm the kernel's role as a cornerstone of responsive and adaptable systems, positioning it favorably to meet the demands of the continually expanding connected device landscape.

16. Embedded Systems Integration: Kernel at the Core

16.1. Embedded System Architecture

Embedded systems stand at the intersection of hardware and software, and their architecture plays a significant role in determining how efficiently these devices operate. As a subset of computing systems, embedded systems are designed for specific applications or functions within larger systems, often characterized by real-time computing constraints, limited resources, and a focus on reliability.

Unlike general-purpose computing devices, embedded systems have strict operational requirements. They frequently operate within predetermined parameters related to memory, processing power, and power consumption. As a result, the architecture of embedded systems must be designed meticulously to accommodate these limitations, ensuring that every component serves a specific function and contributes to the overall performance and reliability of the system.

The embedded system architecture typically comprises various key components: a microcontroller or microprocessor, memory (both volatile and non-volatile), input/output interfaces, and often a set of real-time operating systems (RTOS) or specialized software tailored to interact with the hardware effectively. The Linux kernel, with its modularity and flexibility, has found increasing application within embedded systems, offering a powerful foundation for developing robust, scalable applications.

When considering how to adapt the Linux kernel architecture for embedded use, several key modifications may be made to optimize performance for the unique constraints imposed by embedded systems. First, developers can customize the kernel's configuration by compiling only essential components necessary for the target application. The Linux kernel's rich configuration options allow developers to enable or disable various features, ensuring that the kernel can be tailored to fit the exact hardware configuration and application requirements. By removing unnecessary subsystems or drivers, developers can streamline the kernel, conserving memory and storage.

Power management strategies are particularly vital in embedded systems due to their dependence on battery power or energy efficiencies. The Linux kernel provides several mechanisms for managing power consumption, including CPU frequency scaling, which adjusts the processor's clock speed based on workload demands, and the use of sleep states to reduce power consumption during periods of inactivity. These features help extend battery life and minimize thermal output, crucial for many embedded applications where energy efficiency is paramount.

Cross-compiling is another critical skill for developers working with the Linux kernel in embedded systems. Unlike desktop or server environments, embedded devices often use a different architecture, necessitating a cross-compilation toolchain that allows developers to compile the kernel for the target architecture from a host system. This process requires setting up an appropriate toolchain that includes the necessary compilers, libraries, and build scripts tailored specifically for the target architecture, enabling seamless integration. Developers will typically utilize build systems like Yocto or Buildroot to manage dependencies, set build options, and automate the compilation process, streamlining the overall development workflow.

When it comes to tailoring the kernel for specific hardware, understanding the underlying architecture becomes critical. The Linux kernel's modularity allows developers to write custom device drivers or utilize existing ones to interact with hardware components effectively. Custom drivers can provide greater control over hardware interactions, ensuring optimized performance for specialized devices. This is particularly essential given the diversity of embedded hardware configurations encountered in applications ranging from automotive systems to home automation solutions.

Moreover, as the world shifts towards increasingly interconnected devices, integrating advanced technologies within embedded systems becomes salient. Many modern embedded applications now incorporate features such as artificial intelligence (AI), machine learning (ML), and even blockchain technology. The Linux kernel must evolve to support these functionalities, encompassing the integration of neural network frameworks, robust networking stacks, and ensuring secure data exchange protocols.

In summary, the embedded system architecture is designed to meet the specific needs of constrained applications, distinguished by a focus on functionality, power efficiency, and reliability. The integration of the Linux kernel within these systems underscores its flexibility and adaptability while providing essential features required to enhance performance. By customizing configurations, implementing power management strategies, engaging in cross-compilation techniques, and tailoring the kernel for specific hardware, developers can harness the full potential of embedded systems, paving the way for innovative applications in a growing digital landscape. As technology advances, the kernel's role in facilitating the development of advanced embedded systems will continue to expand, ensuring its relevance across a diverse array of applications.

16.2. Adapting Kernel for Embedded Use

Adapting the Linux kernel for embedded use is a complex but rewarding endeavor that allows developers to personalize the kernel according to the specifications and constraints of embedded systems. This subchapter explores the essential strategies, tools, and considerations necessary for effective adaptation, ensuring that the Linux kernel can meet the unique demands of embedded devices while maintaining optimal performance and reliability.

Embedded systems often operate in environments characterized by limited resources. Memory, processing power, and storage capacity are typically constrained, necessitating a tailored approach to kernel configuration. The first step in adapting the kernel involves selecting only the necessary features and modules that match the intended use case. By utilizing tools such as `make menuconfig`, developers can customize and compile the kernel with only essential drivers and subsystems—resulting in a leaner and more efficient build. This selective inclusion is crucial, as it directly conserves valuable resources that can be allocated to user applications.

The modular nature of the Linux kernel further facilitates adaptation for embedded systems. Kernel modules can be loaded and unloaded dynamically at runtime, allowing for greater flexibility and responsiveness to changing requirements. Developers can take advantage of this to design systems that only load the necessary modules during specific tasks or operations, enhancing overall system performance and resource management. Properly managing kernel modules also means that developers have to consider dependencies and potential conflicts, ensuring that the correct modules are present and configured appropriately for the target hardware.

Power management is a critical concern in embedded systems, as many devices operate on limited power sources, such as batteries. Therefore, integrating power management strategies into the adapted kernel is essential to conserving energy without compromising performance. The Linux kernel provides various methods to manage power consumption, including CPU frequency scaling and dynamic voltage scaling. Implementing these features allows the kernel to adjust processing power based on workload demands, leading to increased energy efficiency and extended battery life.

Another key aspect of adapting the kernel for embedded use is cross-compiling, which is necessary because embedded devices often utilize different architectures than the host development machine. Developers must set up a cross-compilation toolchain appropriate for the target architecture, allowing them to compile the kernel for the intended device from the host system. Establishing this toolchain involves the selection of a suitable compiler, libraries, and necessary tools tailored to the device's specifications. Utilizing build systems like Yocto or Buildroot can also simplify this process, providing the necessary infrastructure for managing dependencies and creating a complete build environment for embedded applications.

Tailoring the kernel to meet specific hardware requirements involves writing or modifying device drivers to communicate effectively with the intended peripherals. The Linux kernel has a rich array of existing drivers for popular hardware components, but custom device drivers may also be necessary for unique or proprietary hardware. To facilitate seamless operation in an embedded environment, developers need to understand the hardware architecture and the kernel's device management models intimately. This includes leveraging the kernel's APIs to ensure proper interaction with the hardware and maintaining high levels of efficiency during operation.

As embedded systems continue to evolve, so too must the Linux kernel adapt to support new technologies and standards. The kernel community actively analyzes and incorporates emerging trends such as the Internet of Things (IoT), real-time processing, and machine learning into its fabric. This elevated focus means that those adapting the kernel for embedded use need to stay informed about innovations and best practices in these domains, ensuring that their adaptations remain relevant and capable of leveraging new advancements.

In summary, adapting the Linux kernel for embedded use encompasses a multi-faceted approach that involves customizing configuration, optimizing power management, engaging in cross-compiling, tailoring drivers to specific hardware, and remaining flexible to incorporate emerging technologies. By understanding and implementing these strategies effectively, developers can create sophisticated embedded systems that fulfill the rigorous demands of performance and efficiency, while also capitalizing on the versatility and robustness that the Linux kernel provides. As time progresses, the kernel's adaptability will likely continue to solidify its role as the operating system of choice for a broad range of embedded applications.

16.3. Power Management Strategies

In the context of optimizing power management within the Linux kernel, several strategies and considerations are essential for enhancing the efficiency of embedded and general computing systems. Power management is a critical concern, especially in devices with limited power resources, as inadequate management can lead to reduced battery life and increased operating costs. This section will explore various power management strategies, their integration within the Linux kernel, and practices to maximize energy usage without compromising performance.

Power management encompasses a variety of techniques designed to minimize energy consumption associated with running and managing processes in the kernel. At its core, effective power management aims to dynamically adjust system behavior based on workload characteristics while balancing the trade-offs between performance and energy efficiency.

One of the fundamental aspects of power management is CPU frequency scaling, enabled by the CPU frequency scaling driver within the Linux kernel. This mechanism allows the kernel to adjust the CPU's clock speed based on the current workload, ramping up performance when demand increases and scaling down frequencies during idle periods. The kernel employs governors—implemented policies governing how frequency scaling should occur—such as 'ondemand' and 'conservative', which dynamically adjust CPU speeds based on usage patterns, or 'powersave,' which prioritizes energy conservation.

In parallel, integrating sleep states (known as CPU idle states) is crucial for power conservation during periods of inactivity. When the CPU is idle, it can enter low-power modes, effectively suspending operations and reducing energy consumption. The Linux kernel takes advantage of various idle states defined by the hardware architecture. The kernel's idle management mechanism enables efficient transitions between active and idle states, ensuring that the CPU only wakes up when necessary for processing, thus extending battery life in mobile and embedded devices.

Memory management also plays a significant role in power management strategies. The Linux kernel utilizes techniques like page reclamation and memory compression to operate efficiently while conserving power. By efficiently managing memory, the kernel can reduce RAM access frequency and consolidate active memory pages, reducing power draw on memory modules. Techniques such as zero-page sharing and dynamic memory allocation can be employed to optimize memory usage further, enhancing overall efficiency.

Another critical feature in power management is device power management. The kernel provides mechanisms for suspending and resuming devices based on usage patterns and demand. For instance, USB devices can be configured to enter low-power states when not in use, and the kernel can track and manage power states for various peripherals through the Power Management features in the kernel. This mechanism ensures that connected devices do not draw unnecessary power when not actively engaged in data transfer or processing.

In modern computing environments, the increasing importance of thermal management further influences power management strategies. Effective cooling strategies are essential for controlling system temperatures, especially in high-performance applications. The Linux kernel encompasses thermal frameworks that can monitor temperature sensors and execute adjustments to CPU speeds or fan activity based on real-time thermal readings, balancing performance with thermal efficiency.

As technology continues to advance, the integration of machine learning and artificial intelligence into power management systems holds significant promise. By utilizing predictive models that analyze historical data on workloads, kernel systems can preemptively adjust resource allocations and power management strategies, ensuring quick responsiveness and initiating energy-saving measures before overloads occur. The adaptability of machine learning algorithms offers new opportunities for optimizing power management in dynamic environments.

Additionally, with the rise of software-defined infrastructure and cloud computing, the Linux kernel's power management strategies must evolve alongside these changes. As cloud workloads become increasingly distributed, monitoring and managing power consumption across diverse environments presents new challenges. The kernel community must invest in developing solutions that provide efficient resource allocation and workload management, supporting data center infrastructure while emphasizing energy efficiency.

In summary, optimizing power management in the Linux kernel involves a comprehensive approach that encompasses CPU frequency scaling, idle state management, memory optimization, device power management, and effective thermal management strategies. These practices not only enhance application performance but also ensure that systems conserve energy, thereby extending battery life and minimizing operational costs. As technology continues to advance, ongoing innovations and integrations of intelligent systems will further refine power management within the Linux kernel, positioning it as a robust platform for a wide array of applications in an increasingly power-conscious world.

16.4. Cross-Compiling for Embedded Systems

In the world of embedded systems, cross-compiling for embedded platforms is a vital practice enabling developers to build kernel images tailored for specific hardware architectures. Unlike desktop and server environments, embedded systems often run on hardware with varying architecture specifications, necessitating the need for a specialized cross-compilation process. By understanding the principles of cross-compiling and using the right tools, developers can streamline the deployment and improve the functionality of embedded applications.

To begin, the primary goal of cross-compiling is to produce a binary executable on one architecture (the host) that can run on another architecture (the target). The Linux kernel, being highly modular, provides the necessary flexibility for developers to build kernels and modules that can work seamlessly with their target hardware. The cross-compilation toolchain consists of a cross-compiler, related libraries, and build scripts configured specifically for the target architecture. Common toolchains include GCC-based compilers adapted for ARM, MIPS, PowerPC, and other embedded architectures.

The initial step in the cross-compilation process involves setting up the appropriate cross-compilation toolchain. Developers can typically obtain pre-built toolchains from distribution repositories or compile their own. It's crucial to ensure that the toolchain matches the target architecture precisely, as binaries compiled incorrectly may fail to run on the intended hardware.

Once the toolchain is configured, developers can initiate the compilation of the kernel source code specifically for the target architecture. The process begins with downloading the kernel source files and navigating to the kernel's root directory. The next step is to configure the kernel for the target environment; users can either select an existing configuration file that matches their target or use tools like make menuconfig to customize options based on specific requirements.

To ensure that the kernel is built correctly for the target device, developers must set the appropriate environment variables that indicate which cross-compiler will be used. This is typically done by exporting the ARCH variable (the architecture) and CROSS_COMPILE variable (the cross-compiler prefix):

```
export ARCH=arm
export CROSS_COMPILE=arm-linux-gnueabi-
```

With these variables set, developers can proceed to compile the kernel using the standard make command. The cross-compiler specified will handle the architecture-specific requirements:

```
make
```

If modules are included in the kernel's configuration, the developer should also run:

```
make modules
```

Following compilation, the next step is to install the generated kernel and modules onto the target hardware. This often involves using tools like rsync, scp, or creating an image for flash storage. Once the kernel and modules are transferred, the necessary bootloader configurations must be updated to ensure the system recognizes and can boot from the newly compiled image.

As developers begin working with different embedded platforms, they must be prepared to address specific configurations and dependencies that may need adjustment based on the target hardware. Compiling drivers for peripherals like sensors, audio processors, and network interfaces will often require tailored handling, demanding attention to the specifics presented by those devices.

Troubleshooting cross-compilation errors also presents a common challenge. Developers may encounter issues related to missing dependencies or misconfigured paths, requiring them to meticulously check the configuration files, ensure all necessary libraries are available, and verify that the environment variables are correctly set.

In conclusion, cross-compiling for embedded systems is an essential practice, empowering developers to tailor the Linux kernel to meet specific hardware requirements. By harnessing the capabilities of cross-compilation toolchains, configuring kernel options appropriately, and addressing architecture-specific needs, developers can enable enhanced performance and functionality in embedded applications. As embedded systems continue to advance, mastering cross-compiling will remain a key component of effective kernel development and deployment.

16.5. Tailoring Kernel for Specific Hardware

Tailoring the Linux kernel for specific hardware involves a specialized understanding of both the hardware capabilities and the kernel's inherent flexibility. This process is critical for optimizing performance, ensuring compatibility, and achieving the best operational efficacy for a particular device or system. More than mere customization, tailoring the kernel means creating a kernel that maximizes hardware performance while minimizing resources and handling unique operational constraints. This subchapter will delve into the methods and strategies necessary for adapting the Linux kernel to fit specific hardware configurations, exploring considerations of both the development process and the operational implications.

At the outset, understanding the hardware itself is paramount. Each piece of hardware, whether it be a CPU, GPU, peripheral device, or custom-built circuit, has its own specifications, architecture, and requirements. The kernel must be configured to leverage the strengths of the hardware while mitigating any limitations. For example, the kernel needs to be aware of the specific processor architecture—such as ARM, x86, or RISC-V—and its associated instruction set to execute optimally. This knowledge informs numerous decisions, from the initial configuration of the kernel to the modules and drivers that need to be included or excluded.

The first phase in tailoring the kernel is configuration. The Linux kernel's configuration system is robust and flexible, allowing developers to enable or disable specific options through tools such as `make menuconfig`. This interactive menu allows developers to traverse an extensive list of kernel features, selecting only those that are relevant to their hardware. When targeting specific devices, it is crucial to select drivers specific to the target hardware, as well as options that optimize kernel functionalities—such as enabling power management features, specialized file systems, or specific network protocols.

Beyond merely enabling specific options, customization often involves writing or adapting device drivers that allow the kernel to communicate effectively with the hardware. Device drivers are critical for managing interactions between the kernel and peripherals, translating generic commands to device-specific operations. If existing drivers do not meet the needs of a particular hardware configuration, developing custom drivers is often necessary. This process entails coding and potentially utilizing kernel APIs, managing interrupts, and engaging with hardware registers to establish proper communication channels.

Additionally, kernel modules enhance the kernel's adaptability and extensibility. Modules are portions of code that can be loaded or unloaded from the kernel at runtime, allowing for dynamic adaptability to hardware changes without requiring a complete kernel recompilation. This modular approach is particularly useful when dealing with hardware that may change over time, such as USB devices or peripheral connections. Developers can create custom modules specific to their hardware and load them as needed, optimizing resource allocations without affecting the overall stability of the system.

When tailoring the kernel for specific hardware, managing dependencies becomes a critical aspect of the process. Each kernel module may depend on other modules, existing functionalities, or specific kernel configurations to function correctly. Understanding these dependencies allows developers to load modules in the correct order and ensures robust operational behavior. Tools within the kernel, like depmod, can help resolve these dependencies and ensure that modules are correctly linked to one another.

Security considerations are paramount when tailoring the kernel. Custom drivers and modules can introduce new vulnerabilities if security best practices are overlooked. Developing secure drivers and understanding the kernel's security models—such as MAC systems like SELinux—can mitigate the risks associated with kernel extensions. Additionally, ensuring that security patches and updates are applied to the kernel configuration can fortify systems against emerging threats while preserving the functionality tailored to specific hardware.

In the context of embedded systems, tailoring the kernel becomes even more nuanced due to specific operational requirements and constraints. For instance, in devices with limited power availability, optimizing power management strategies—such as sleep states and CPU scaling—becomes critical. Kernel features focused on enabling efficient power consumption ensure that adapted kernels can run effectively within the operational limits set by such devices.

As emerging technologies continue to reshape the landscape of computing, the Linux kernel must remain adaptable. The integration of capabilities for artificial intelligence, machine learning, and edge computing increasingly necessitates that the kernel be tailored to harness these advancements. By recognizing hardware relationships and integrating relevant functionalities into the kernel architecture, developers can prepare for a future where adaptability to new technologies will remain critical.

In conclusion, tailoring the Linux kernel for specific hardware is a comprehensive process that encompasses configuration, module management, driver development, and security considerations. By understanding the capabilities and limitations of the target hardware, developers can customize the kernel to maximize performance, security, and resource efficiency. The Linux kernel's inherent flexibility and extensibility empower developers to adapt the kernel for an array of operating environments, paving the way for innovative applications and efficient computing solutions tailored to meet an increasingly diverse spectrum of needs. As technological advancements continue to unfold, the kernel will play a central role in embracing these changes, ensuring continued relevance and facilitating new possibilities in the landscape of system architecture.

17. Kernel Modules and Extensibility: Beyond the Basics

17.1. Dynamic Module Loading and Unloading

Dynamic module loading and unloading in the Linux kernel is a powerful feature that allows for the flexible and efficient management of kernel functionality at runtime. This capability is not only foundational for ensuring that the kernel can adapt to different hardware environments and application needs, but it also fosters a modular approach to code management that enhances maintainability, performance, and scalability. This section will delve into the mechanics of dynamic module loading and unloading, examining its significance in the kernel architecture, the processes involved, and best practices for its implementation.

At its core, dynamic module loading refers to the ability to insert and remove kernel modules into and out of the running kernel without the need for a system reboot. This feature is crucial in various scenarios. For instance, when new hardware is added to a system, the appropriate drivers can be loaded without downtime, allowing immediate access to the newly connected devices. Similarly, if a feature becomes unnecessary or needs to be replaced, modules can be unloaded to free up system resources.

The mechanism underlying dynamic module loading is provided by the kernel's core infrastructure, which maintains a dynamic linking system that manages module dependencies, versions, and states. Each module in the Linux kernel is essentially a collection of object files that contain executable code and is associated with a specific functionality, such as device drivers or filesystems. The kernel maintains a central namespace for these modules, enabling efficient management and avoidance of conflicts.

To load a module dynamically, developers typically utilize the `insmod` command, followed by the name of the module. For example:

```
sudo insmod my_module.ko
```

This command will insert the specified kernel module into the running kernel, at which point the kernel initializes the module and executes its initialization code. This initialization process may involve setting up data structures, registering device drivers, and requesting resources (such as interrupt lines or DMAs) from the kernel.

In addition to insmod, the more nuanced modprobe command can be employed. modprobe handles dependency resolution, ensuring that any modules that are required for the successful operation of the loaded module are also loaded automatically. This approach simplifies the process for developers by abstracting the complexities related to module interdependencies.

The unloading of modules follows a similar process. Using the rmmod command, developers can remove a module from the running kernel:

```
sudo rmmod my_module
```

When a module is unloaded, the kernel calls the module's cleanup code, allowing the module to release resources, de-register device drivers, and perform any necessary cleanup operations. If the module is actively in use by other processes, the kernel will prevent its removal until those dependencies are resolved, highlighting the importance of managing module dependencies effectively.

Proper error handling during both loading and unloading is essential for maintaining system stability. Developers should incorporate return codes and logging within module code to capture any issues that could arise when a module is loaded or unloaded. Using functions like printk allows for logging messages that help diagnose errors when loading modules, enhancing the ease of troubleshooting.

Best practices for dynamic module loading and unloading within the Linux kernel include ensuring that code is consistently tested for correct initialization and cleanup routines, leveraging existing kernel APIs for managing device states, and avoiding module conflicts through explicit dependency declarations. Moreover, extensive documentation about the module's functionalities and expected behaviors can benefit users interacting with the modules, and it enhances the maintainability of the kernel code.

As we explore the future of dynamic module loading in the Linux kernel, we are likely to see enhancements centered around improved automation and integration with emerging technologies. Features that allow more intelligent dependency resolution, automated versioning, and compatibility checking will support the dynamic nature of modern computing environments.

In conclusion, dynamic module loading and unloading is a vital feature within the Linux kernel that significantly enhances flexibility and efficiency. By facilitating the runtime addition and removal of kernel functionality, it allows for responsive adaptation to hardware changes and application demands while ensuring system stability. Proper error handling, adherence to best practices, and the ongoing optimization of kernel module management will contribute to the continued success of dynamic module loading in maintaining the kernel's integral role in modern computing. As technology advances, the principles governing dynamic module management will evolve as new challenges and opportunities emerge, ensuring that the Linux kernel remains adaptable and optimized for future developments.

17.2. Cash: Handling and Safety Measures

Cash handling and safety measures are critical components of developing a sound financial operational strategy in any environment, including technology ecosystems that revolve around open-source projects like the Linux kernel. While the subject of cash management can appear distant from kernel development, the principles governing this domain touch upon various aspects of operational integrity, risk management, and resource allocation that are equally applicable in collaborative environments like kernel development.

Cash management begins with the understanding of the financial ecosystem in which an organization operates. Organizations reliant on open-source systems often fund their initiatives through grants, donations, sponsorships, or revenue generated from services, support contracts, and other business ventures. Adopting a strong financial framework ensures that these organizations can effectively allocate resources toward development efforts, maintenance, community engagement, and infrastructure improvements—all crucial for the sustained success and evolution of the Linux kernel.

In terms of handling cash and expenses, the key principles include thorough tracking and recording of all transactions. This is mirrored in the Linux kernel development process where meticulous documentation of changes, contributions, and patches is vital for maintaining project integrity and ensuring transparency. Utilizing financial management software ensures accurate bookkeeping and can provide insights into spending patterns, funding sources, and profitability. Similarly, using version control systems to track contributions allows kernel developers to maintain a clear and accessible history of changes made to the codebase.

Safety measures related to cash management involve a multi-layered approach geared toward minimizing risk. In organizations, establishing clear protocols governing cash handling practices, such as dual-control systems for cash transactions, regular audits, and implementing electronic banking solutions can mitigate risks associated with theft or fraud. This principle resonates in the realm of coding and kernel contributions as well, where maintaining security protocols around code submission, integration, and review processes can prevent vulnerabilities that may compromise the kernel.

Awareness and training in financial literacy among developers and contributors are equally crucial. Many organizations often fail to recognize the importance of developing a culture of fiscal responsibility. A similar analogy can be drawn to the need for developers to be aware of security practices and the potential ramifications of their code changes. Both financial and technical literacy drive a culture of transparency and accountability, enabling participants to take ownership of their contributions and responsibilities.

Moreover, fostering a community that emphasizes ethical practices, whether in financial dealings or software contributions, is vital for long-term success. Transparency in funding sources, expenditure, and resource allocation builds trust within a community. Similarly, transparency in kernel project management and decision-making processes fosters an environment where contributors can freely and actively engage, significantly strengthening the collaborative model of kernel development.

Reporting and accountability mechanisms are essential for assessing the financial health of an organization engaged in kernel development. Regular reporting on cash flow, budgeting, and forecasting should mirror the practice of maintaining documentation regarding kernel changes, feature requests, and community feedback. Such reports enable organizations to track financial performance and understand funding availability, ultimately influencing resource allocation toward kernel enhancements, community events, and ongoing support initiatives.

In the context of open-source kernel development, the successful integration of cash handling and safety measures can inspire organizations to adopt similar structures in their operational practices. Creating a robust financial framework that aligns with the collaborative and transparent ethos of Linux kernel development enhances the overall sustainability and adaptability of the project while safeguarding against financial vulnerabilities.

In conclusion, cash handling and safety measures, while seemingly divergent from the technical intricacies of kernel development, share many principles related to accountability, transparency, and resource management. Leveraging these principles ensures that organizations can effectively allocate resources toward development efforts, soundly manage finances, and cultivate a responsible and vibrant community that supports the evolution of the Linux kernel. As technology continues to evolve and the demands for innovative solutions increase, the importance of cash handling and safety will remain integral to maintaining operational integrity and sustainable growth within the Linux landscape.

17.3. Creating Your Own Kernel Extensions

Creating your own kernel extensions is an empowering process that allows developers to tailor the Linux kernel to meet specific needs, enhance system performance, and experiment with new functionalities. Kernel extensions, often implemented as loadable kernel modules (LKMs), offer the flexibility to add or modify features without the need for a complete recompilation of the kernel. This accessibility makes it significantly easier for developers to iterate on changes and enhance their systems dynamically. This section explores the necessary steps and considerations for creating kernel extensions, highlighting best practices and potential challenges.

Before embarking on the journey of developing kernel extensions, it is crucial to understand the overall architecture of the Linux kernel and the role that modules play within it. LKMs allow developers to implement new device drivers, file systems, networking protocols, or other functionalities that integrate seamlessly into the existing kernel structure. Understanding the kernel's modular approach is essential to ensure that the extensions interact appropriately with both user-level applications and kernel subsystems.

The initial step in creating your kernel extension is setting up the development environment. This process includes configuring the necessary tools and libraries required for kernel programming, such as the kernel source code, the GNU Compiler Collection (GCC), and the appropriate headers for your kernel version. Developers typically retrieve the kernel source from an official repository, and it is recommended to work with the version that corresponds to the currently running kernel to ensure compatibility with the underlying architecture.

Once the development environment is ready, the next step is to write the kernel module code. Kernel modules are written in C, and closely resemble user-space programs but must adhere to specific guidelines and conventions due to their operation in kernel space. Developers should start by including the necessary header files—most notably `linux/module.h`, `linux/kernel.h`, and any relevant subsystem-specific headers. The code must define initialization and cleanup functions, typically labeled `module_init()` and `module_exit()`, respectively. The initialization function is executed when the module is loaded into the kernel, while the cleanup function is responsible for releasing resources and de-registering the module upon unloading.

Building the kernel module involves crafting a Makefile that specifies how the module is compiled. The Makefile should link to the kernel build system, ensuring that all compilation options correspond with the currently running kernel. A typical Makefile might include:

```
obj-m += my_module.o

all:
  make -C /lib/modules/$(shell uname -r)/build M=$(PWD) modules

clean:
  make -C /lib/modules/$(shell uname -r)/build M=$(PWD) clean
```

With the Makefile in place, developers can compile the kernel module using the `make` command. Upon successful compilation, developers can use commands like `insmod` to dynamically load the module into the running kernel, followed by `rmmod` to unload it when necessary.

Testing is a critical component of module development. Unlike user-space programs, kernel modules can lead to system crashes or instability if there are flaws in the code, making rigorous testing and debugging essential. Utilizing kernel debugging mechanisms such as `printk()` for logging kernel messages is vital for diagnosing issues and improving the quality of the module. Effective logging practices will allow developers to track execution flow and pinpoint any problematic behaviors within the module.

In addition to testing, developers must also consider the implications of concurrency within their kernel extensions. The kernel is inherently multi-threaded, and proper synchronization mechanisms, like mutexes or spinlocks, must be employed to prevent data races. Integrity and stability depend on a thorough understanding of kernel concurrency, as improper handling can lead to kernel panics or loss of data.

As kernel extensions often interact with various subsystems, careful management of dependencies and potential conflicts is paramount. If a foundation of the kernel's architecture is altered through an extension, it is crucial to assess how that change will affect existing functionality. Reviewing documentation, engaging with community discussions, and utilizing kernel tracing tools like `ftrace` can support effective debugging and conflict resolution.

Furthermore, it is beneficial to engage with the broader Linux kernel community. Contributions to forums, mailing lists, and collaborative projects can provide invaluable feedback and assistance, as they foster an environment where developers can share their challenges and triumphs.

In conclusion, creating your own kernel extensions is a rewarding endeavor that necessitates a thorough understanding of kernel architecture, adherence to best practices, and a commitment to testing and optimization. By leveraging the capabilities of loadable kernel modules, developers can enhance their systems, streamline processes, and contribute to the ever-evolving landscape of the Linux kernel. As technology continues to advance, the ability to create tailored solutions through kernel extensions will remain an indispensable tool for developers across various fields, ensuring continued innovation in open-source environments.

17.4. Managing Dependencies and Conflicts

In the landscape of software development, particularly within the context of the Linux kernel, managing dependencies and conflicts is a pivotal aspect that ensures stability, performance, and coherence throughout the kernel's vast ecosystem. The intricacies of the Linux kernel, coupled with the continual influx of contributions, necessitate robust strategies to maintain the quality and functionality of the system while accommodating new features and enhancements. This subchapter will explore the processes, challenges, and approaches involved in effectively managing dependencies and conflicts in kernel development.

At the heart of dependency management lies the understanding of how various components and modules within the kernel interact with one another. Each kernel module or feature often relies on a specific set of functions and data structures, creating a web of interdependencies that must be navigated during the development and integration processes. Understanding these dependencies is crucial for developers, as failure to acknowledge them can lead to issues such as module loading failures, system crashes, or unpredictable behavior.

One of the first steps in managing dependencies involves thorough documentation and clarity in coding practices. The Linux kernel community places a premium on documenting how modules and features are constructed, including specifying their relationships and any specific configurations necessary for successful integration. Utilizing clear commit messages and descriptive comments within the code can provide insights into the purpose of dependencies and the rationale behind particular implementations. Documenting the expected behavior of modules during the review phase aids maintainers in fully understanding potential impacts before merging changes.

The kernel's build system, predominantly orchestrated through the `Makefile`, plays a crucial role in dependency management. The `kbuild` system ensures that modules are compiled only when their dependencies are satisfied. This process automates the tracking of file modifications, triggering recompilation as necessary, thus streamlining development and minimizing the likelihood of conflicts arising from outdated modules. Ensuring that the build system accurately reflects the relationships between different components is essential in mitigating risks associated with module conflicts and mismatches.

During the submission and review process, maintaining a dialogue with other contributors is instrumental in addressing dependencies and conflicts. The Linux kernel mailing list serves as a vibrant forum for discussions related to new patches, features, and issues. Developers should actively engage in conversations surrounding their contributions to ensure that any dependencies are clearly communicated to maintainers and fellow developers. This open approach fosters collaborative problem-solving and allows for collective identification of potential conflicts that may arise from overlapping changes.

Nested in this collaborative environment is the importance of utilizing automated testing frameworks. Tools such as KernelCI facilitate continuous integration by automatically running tests against newly submitted patches or modifications. By employing a comprehensive suite of tests that assess the kernel's performance, these frameworks help identify dependency-related issues before they can negatively impact the mainline kernel. Engaging in thorough testing practices not only improves the submitter's changes but also protects the overall integrity of the kernel.

Common conflicts that arise in kernel development often stem from overlapping changes to specific features, functions, or APIs. As developers evolve existing functionalities or introduce new features, conflicts may occur if two contributions modify the same code path or interface. To mitigate such conflicts, the kernel community encourages adherence to coding standards and collaboration, allowing for thorough discussions focused on reconciling competing changes. By fostering an environment that prioritizes cooperation, conflicting contributions can be harmonized rather than competing for dominance.

An additional challenge in managing dependencies involves maintaining backward compatibility. When developers introduce new features or modifications, they must consider how these changes may impact existing users or modules that depend on legacy functionality. Striving for backward compatibility ensures that users can transition to newer versions of the kernel without breaking existing functionalities, ultimately leading to better user experience and satisfaction.

Monitoring tools and audit frameworks can assist in identifying and addressing dependency-related issues post-integration. By analyzing system logs and performance metrics, developers can detect when modules are failing to load or when unexpected behaviors occur due to broken dependencies. Taking a proactive approach to monitoring fosters a culture of early detection and mitigates the risk of prolonged unresolved dependency issues.

In conclusion, managing dependencies and conflicts in the Linux kernel development process is a multifaceted effort driven by collaboration, documentation, clear communication, and testing. By embracing these best practices, developers can enhance their contributions and ensure that changes harmoniously integrate into the broader kernel landscape. The Linux kernel community's commitment to maintaining high standards for contributions is augmented by these strategies, contributing to its reputation as a resilient and high-quality operating system foundation. As technology continues to evolve and new contributors engage with the kernel, the principles of managing dependencies and conflicts will remain vital in sustaining the dynamism and health of the Linux kernel ecosystem.

17.5. Extensible Future of Kernel Modules

In the ever-evolving landscape of technology, the Linux kernel has shown remarkable adaptability and resilience, positioning itself not only as a fundamental component of countless systems but also as a beacon of innovation in the realm of operating systems. The future of kernel modules and their extensibility is a critical aspect of this ongoing journey, paving the way for novel features, improved performance, and seamless integration with new technologies that arise in an increasingly interconnected world.

The extensible future of kernel modules lies in their ability to dynamically adapt and evolve in response to the demands of emerging technologies. One primary avenue for this adaptability is through the ongoing refinement of the module loading and unloading mechanisms within the kernel. Developers are continuously improving the methods by which modules can be dynamically inserted or removed during runtime, allowing systems to reconfigure themselves based on current requirements without the need for a reboot. This flexibility not only enhances performance but also leads to greater resource efficiency, as modules can be tailored to specific workloads as needed.

As we move into a future where artificial intelligence (AI) and machine learning (ML) play increasingly prevalent roles, the extensibility of kernel modules will be pivotal for integrating advanced capabilities directly into the kernel. The kernel must be equipped to manage workflows that require AI processing, such as real-time data analysis or autonomous decision-making systems. By extending the kernel's capabilities through specialized modules that optimize how AI and ML models are executed and managed, developers can leverage the kernel as a powerful engine for processing vast amounts of data efficiently and effectively.

With the rise of blockchain and decentralized technologies, the Linux kernel's extensibility will also prove valuable in creating modules that support new decentralized protocols and frameworks. These modules could facilitate communication with distributed ledger systems, enabling the kernel to handle transactions, manage identity verification, and integrate with decentralized applications (DApps). As these technologies continue to gain momentum in various sectors, developing kernel modules that interact seamlessly with blockchains will solidify the Linux kernel's relevance in the emerging decentralized digital economy.

Moreover, the continued evolution of cloud computing and virtualization paradigms dictates that the Linux kernel be adaptable and extensible to support the unique characteristics of cloud environments. New kernel modules can be developed to streamline resource management, enhance virtual machine performance, and improve networking efficiency for cloud-native applications. The ability to deploy modules that optimize cloud interactions will enable the kernel to support various cloud providers' infrastructure, ensure seamless integration, and facilitate decentralized storage solutions.

Anticipating technological shifts remains an essential aspect of the kernel's extensibility. The Linux kernel is characterized by its commitment to forward compatibility, often incorporating new features that cater to emerging trends such as high-performance computing, quantum computing, and edge computing. Developing kernel modules that leverage next-generation hardware will be critical in harnessing the full potential of these advancements while retaining backward compatibility.

Collaboration within the kernel community will continue to play a central role in shaping the future of kernel modules. The Linux community thrives on shared knowledge and cooperative development, allowing contributions from developers worldwide to drive innovation in kernel extensibility. Engaging with educational programs, outreach initiatives, and workshops will help promote the growth of new contributors who are passionate about advancing the kernel and exploring novel ideas for enhancing kernel modules.

Furthermore, the culture of inclusivity within the Linux kernel community strengthens its resilience, fostering diversity in problem-solving perspectives that can lead to innovative kernel interactions with future technologies. By empowering individuals from various backgrounds, the community can tackle challenges uniquely, promoting a dynamic environment for discovering new kernel functionalities.

In summary, the extensible future of kernel modules is marked by their ability to evolve and adapt alongside emerging technologies such as AI, blockchain, cloud computing, and others. By refining dynamic loading mechanisms, creating specialized modules for new workloads, and promoting a culture of open collaboration, the Linux kernel is well-positioned to meet the challenges of the future with agility and innovation. As developers continue to engage with the kernel's evolution, they pave the way for an adaptable, efficient, and powerful operating system that remains at the forefront of technological advancement. Embracing extensibility not only ensures the kernel's sustained relevance but also reinforces its role as a catalyst for innovation within the broader technology landscape.

18. Integration with Emerging Technologies: A Future-Proof Kernel

18.1. Interfacing with Artificial Intelligence

In the ever-evolving landscape of technology, the Linux kernel stands as a robust foundation that integrates underlying hardware functionalities with the software applications that rely upon them. One of the most exciting areas of development lies in the intersection of the kernel and artificial intelligence, a field that is rapidly gaining prominence across various sectors. The integration of artificial intelligence into the Linux kernel offers a path toward enhancing system performance, optimizing resource management, and enabling intelligent decision-making capabilities.

Interfacing with artificial intelligence within the kernel revolves around the use of AI algorithms and models to analyze data and optimize system operations based on real-time inputs. By embedding machine learning models directly into kernel modules or utilizing them in user-space applications linked to the kernel, developers can leverage the kernel's robust resource management capabilities to enhance the efficiency and adaptability of applications. This integration enables the kernel to make intelligent decisions, such as dynamically adjusting resource allocations based on workload patterns or optimizing scheduling based on predicted future demands.

One of the primary areas where artificial intelligence can significantly enhance kernel performance is in resource management. Implementing machine learning models that analyze historical data on CPU, memory, and I/O usage can help identify patterns in how applications utilize resources. By predicting future resource requirements based on historical behavior, the kernel can proactively allocate resources, ensuring that critical applications receive the necessary processing power at the right time. This predictive resource allocation fosters a more responsive computing environment, mitigating the risk of latency and bottlenecks.

Furthermore, AI-driven optimizations can extend beyond resource allocation into various kernel subsystems. In IoT applications, for instance, machine learning models can be leveraged to monitor sensor data in real time, allowing the kernel to dynamically adjust processing priorities based on the urgency and importance of incoming data. This integration empowers the kernel to excel in environments where decisions must be made swiftly, enhancing both operational efficiency and user experiences.

Another compelling application of artificial intelligence pertains to security within the kernel. By integrating anomaly detection models, the kernel could analyze access patterns and system behaviors to identify potential security threats. These models can flag unusual activities that deviate from normal operating patterns, enabling the kernel to enact preemptive measures before breaches occur. This proactive approach to security can be vital in protecting the kernel and the systems built upon it, particularly as cybersecurity threats continue to evolve and increase in sophistication.

As artificial intelligence integrates with the kernel, considerations around training and implementing AI models will arise. Developers must ensure that the models used are lightweight and efficient enough to run within the constraints of the kernel environment. Additionally, maintaining user data privacy and ensuring ethical AI practices should be paramount, particularly when analyzing sensitive data. The kernel community must remain vigilant about the implications of integrating AI within the kernel, establishing guidelines and best practices focused on responsible usage.

The Linux kernel's adaptability extends to various other emerging technologies as well, one being blockchain. Adapting for blockchains and decentralized technologies presents challenges and opportunities alike, necessitating the kernel's evolution to support these innovations. As enterprises and developers increasingly recognize the potential of blockchain technology for secure, decentralized transactions, the kernel must incorporate support for blockchain protocols and integrate with existing cryptocurrencies.

The kernel can serve as a robust platform for managing distributed ledger functionalities, where data immutability and security are essential. By supporting the necessary cryptographic protocols and functions required for blockchain interactions, the kernel can provide the groundwork for reliable and efficient blockchain applications. Additionally, maintaining secure communication channels within the kernel remains paramount to safeguard against potential exploits that could undermine the decentralized principles of blockchain technology.

Incorporating machine learning models into the Linux kernel architecture presents captivating prospects. This integration involves not just the deployment of pre-trained models but also ensuring that the kernel can effectively manage the data pipelines that feed training datasets, optimize model execution, and monitor performance. The kernel must be adaptable enough to accept various AI/ML frameworks and easily integrate with hardware acceleration capabilities, such as GPUs or TPUs, to improve computational efficiency.

Further, enhanced cloud integration features will remain a topic of considerable focus in kernel development. As organizations increasingly rely on cloud-based infrastructures, the Linux kernel must support seamless interactions with cloud services, including efficient resource management, dynamic load balancing, and secure communication protocols. Incorporating features that streamline the deployment of containerized cloud applications will also be crucial to maximizing the potential of cloud computing technologies within the Linux kernel.

By anticipating technological shifts, the Linux kernel can position itself as a leader in innovation, ensuring ongoing relevance in the face of emerging trends. Understanding how transformations in technology—from quantum computing to distributed systems—affect kernel architecture can guide future enhancements, securing its status in the realm of operating systems while fostering a community of continuous improvement and adaptation.

In summary, the integration of artificial intelligence into the Linux kernel represents a significant leap toward intelligent, responsive, and efficient systems. By interfacing directly with emerging technologies, adapting for blockchains, supporting machine learning models, enhancing cloud integrations, and anticipating future technological shifts, the Linux kernel stands to capitalize on novel advancements while reinforcing its role as a premier platform for innovative applications. The kernel community's commitment to collaboration and innovation positions it well for addressing the evolving landscape of modern computing.

18.2. Adapting for Blockchains and Decentralized Tech

In the rapidly evolving landscape of technology, particularly with the rise of blockchain and decentralized systems, adapting the Linux kernel to effectively interface with these advancements represents a crucial step forward. The Linux kernel, as a robust and versatile foundation for countless operating systems, must continuously evolve to accommodate the requirements posed by these innovative technologies, ensuring compatibility and performance in a decentralized world.

Blockchain technology introduces a paradigm shift in how data transactions are recorded and verified, emphasizing cryptographic security, immutability, and decentralization. The Linux kernel's adaptability will allow it to support the implementation of distributed ledger technologies, enabling businesses and developers to leverage the power of blockchain for secure and efficient data management. To accomplish this, specific kernel extensions may be necessary to facilitate interactions with blockchain nodes, cryptography, and consensus algorithms, thereby extending the kernel's capabilities in ways that align with emerging technologies.

The integration of decentralized technologies into the Linux kernel will also require the implementation of enhanced security measures. Given that the dynamic nature of decentralized networks poses unique challenges, it is essential that the kernel can natively support cryptographic protocols fundamental to blockchain operations. This includes handling transactions safely, validating blocks securely, and ensuring that the data stored is resistant to tampering. The Linux kernel's existing support for cryptography can be further enhanced to provide robust functionalities catering to the requirements of blockchain operations.

Moreover, as IoT proliferates and connects with blockchain architectures, it will become increasingly important to manage the security of these interconnected devices. The integration of decentralization principles with the Linux kernel must consider resource management and security for IoT devices that may interact with blockchain networks. This might involve real-time monitoring and dynamic scaling of resources to accommodate the distinct demands of decentralized IoT applications.

Furthermore, to extend kernel capabilities for blockchain integration, it will be important to develop interfaces that facilitate cross-communication between blockchain networks and local kernel resources. These interfaces will help promote seamless interactions between distributed applications and the kernel, ultimately facilitating the storage, retrieval, and processing of data securely and efficiently.

Simultaneously, the anticipation of technological shifts, including emerging trends such as cloud-native solutions, machine learning, and edge computing, will play a significant role in shaping kernel development. The kernel must adapt to increasingly diverse workloads and integrate seamlessly within various processing environments to remain competitive. Continuous integration of AI-driven optimizations into the kernel can bolster its effectiveness, enabling intelligent resource allocation based on real-time analysis of workload patterns.

Engaging with the developer community is paramount to embracing these shifts. Open communication channels that foster collaboration among kernel developers, IoT engineers, security experts, and blockchain advocates will drive innovation in kernel adaptations.

Participating in conferences and workshops and creating platforms for knowledge sharing can empower contributors to disseminate insights and refine strategies for kernel and blockchain integration.

In summary, adapting the Linux kernel for effective integration with blockchain and decentralized technologies involves a comprehensive approach encompassing security enhancements, resource management considerations, and the development of interfaces for seamless communication. By anticipating technological shifts and fostering collaborative community engagement, the Linux kernel can position itself not only as a leading platform for traditional applications but also as a bedrock for the future of decentralized computing. As the landscape continues to evolve, the kernel must embrace these innovations and remain dynamic in its capabilities, ensuring its central role in modern, interconnected systems.

18.3. Incorporating Machine Learning Models

In the Linux kernel ecosystem, the integration of machine learning models represents a transformative evolution in how the kernel interacts with emerging technologies. As artificial intelligence becomes increasingly prevalent across various domains, the kernel's ability to support machine learning directly influences its adaptability, performance, and utility. This section explores how kernel integration with machine learning models can enhance system efficiency, optimize resource management, and drive intelligent decision-making capabilities.

Machine learning requires substantial computational resources to analyze vast datasets and build predictive models. The Linux kernel must adapt to manage these workloads effectively, harnessing the capabilities of modern hardware, including GPUs and TPUs, that are designed for high-performance computations. Integrating optimized drivers for these hardware accelerators allows the kernel to streamline data processing and maximize throughput, thereby improving the efficiency of machine learning tasks.

One key area where machine learning can be leveraged within the kernel is in predictive resource allocation. By employing machine learning algorithms that analyze historical usage patterns of CPU, memory, and I/O, the kernel can anticipate future demands, adjusting resources dynamically to suit workloads as they change in real time. This predictive capability minimizes latency and maximizes responsiveness, particularly in scenarios involving high transaction volumes or fluctuating resource needs. Developers can implement frameworks within the kernel to facilitate the handling of this predictive resource allocation, ensuring that machine learning models contribute effectively to performance enhancements.

In addition to resource management, machine learning can be harnessed to improve security measures within the kernel. By utilizing anomaly detection techniques, the kernel can monitor system behaviors and flag suspicious activities or deviations from expected patterns, which may indicate security threats. This proactive approach not only enhances the security posture of the kernel but also allows system administrators to respond swiftly to potential breaches before they escalate into critical issues.

The kernel's inherent modularity and extensibility also facilitate the integration of machine learning capabilities. Developers can create extensions that leverage existing machine learning frameworks, such as TensorFlow or PyTorch, within kernel modules. These extensions can enable real-time data analysis and processing directly within the kernel, allowing for intelligent adaptations and optimizations that enhance application performance. This seamless interaction between machine learning models and kernel modules promotes the efficiency of various applications, from real-time analytics to responsive IoT devices.

As the landscape of machine learning continues to evolve, the kernel must also account for the growing importance of data privacy and ethical considerations. Implementing features that support secure data handling practices, ensuring that sensitive information used in machine learning models is protected, will be paramount. The kernel community must remain vigilant about upholding principled practices while leveraging machine learning technologies, prioritizing responsible development and deployment that align with ethical guidelines.

In summary, incorporating machine learning models into the Linux kernel provides an exciting avenue for enhancing system performance, improving resource management, and enabling intelligent behaviors. By effectively integrating these models within the kernel architecture, developers can harness the power of machine learning to optimize various aspects of computing, from security to resource allocation. As technology advances and the demands for intelligent systems continue to grow, the ongoing integration of machine learning capabilities within the Linux kernel will play a pivotal role in shaping its future, ensuring that it remains a leading platform for a wide array of applications in an increasingly interconnected world.

18.4. Enhanced Cloud Integration Features

In today's rapidly evolving technological landscape, enhanced cloud integration features are becoming increasingly critical as the Linux kernel adapts to support modern computing needs. Cloud computing has transformed how businesses and individual users manage their IT resources, allowing for scalability, flexibility, and dynamic resource allocation. Understanding how the Linux kernel integrates with cloud environments is essential for developers and system administrators who aim to build efficient, robust cloud-based solutions.

One of the defining aspects of cloud computing is virtualization —the ability to run multiple virtual machines and containers on a single physical server. The Linux kernel excels in this regard, providing strong support for various virtualization technologies, including KVM (Kernel-based Virtual Machine) and containerization solutions like Docker and Kubernetes. These technologies enable the efficient management of workloads, allowing multiple tenants to share resources while isolating their environments for security and efficiency.

Within the context of cloud integration, the kernel's extensibility through loadable kernel modules (LKMs) allows for the dynamic addition of features tailored for cloud deployments. For example, specific drivers can be integrated to enhance the handling of network operations or storage functionalities, ensuring that cloud services maintain optimal performance regardless of the volume of data being processed. The ability to load and unload kernel modules based on current demands provides cloud administrators with the flexibility needed to adapt to changing workloads efficiently.

Another noteworthy feature that enhances the cloud integration of the Linux kernel is the support for high-performance networking protocols, such as RDMA (Remote Direct Memory Access) and various overlay networks. RDMA allows for efficient data transfer between servers, bypassing traditional protocols to reduce latency. This capability is vital in cloud environments, where quick data retrieval and processing are essential for maintaining user satisfaction and service quality.

Optimizing the kernel's I/O handling is equally important for cloud integration. The Linux kernel has various configurations that can fine-tune I/O scheduling algorithms, enabling administrators to tailor the kernel to specific cloud workloads better. For instance, configuring storage queues and optimizing read/write operations based on the patterns of use can lead to significant performance improvements in cloud storage solutions, ensuring that data is delivered quickly and reliably.

As cloud infrastructure grows, multi-cloud and hybrid cloud strategies are becoming more prevalent. The Linux kernel's adaptability to different environments allows organizations to take advantage of resource efficiencies across various cloud providers or private data centers. Moreover, features such as cgroups help manage resource allocation and enforcement across diverse environments, enhancing operational flexibility and cost-effectiveness.

Security is another critical consideration in cloud integration. The Linux kernel includes built-in security frameworks like SELinux and AppArmor that help enforce permissions and protect containerized applications from potential attacks. Providing proper support for encryption protocols and monitoring for intrusion detection fosters a secure environment in which cloud resources can operate safely, ensuring regulatory compliance and protecting sensitive data.

Integration with orchestration tools, such as Kubernetes, presents additional challenges and opportunities for the Linux kernel. As workloads in the cloud become more dynamic, the ability to integrate seamlessly with orchestration frameworks is crucial. The kernel must continue evolving to accommodate the needs of containerized applications, ensuring smooth interactions between the kernel, container runtimes, and orchestration platforms.

While the kernel has strong foundations for cloud integration, there are ongoing developments to enhance its capabilities further. The integration of machine learning and AI can be valuable, enabling the kernel to adaptively allocate resources based on predicted workloads. This intelligent approach ensures that the system is optimized for performance while considering the unique demands of cloud environments.

In summary, enhanced cloud integration features signify an evolution in the capabilities provided by the Linux kernel, ensuring it remains relevant in an era increasingly dominated by cloud computing. By providing robust virtualization support, optimizing I/O processing, securing interactions, and continuing to evolve with emerging technologies, the Linux kernel is well-positioned to meet the demands of modern cloud-based applications. As cloud computing techniques evolve and new challenges arise, the kernel's commitment to flexibility, performance, and security will ensure its critical role in the future of cloud infrastructure. The continual enhancements and integrations with cloud technologies will reinforce the Linux kernel's status as a foundational platform for a vast array of applications across various sectors.

18.5. Anticipating Technological Shifts

In the dynamic and ever-evolving landscape of technology, anticipating technological shifts is crucial for the continued success and relevance of the Linux kernel. As a foundational component of countless systems, the kernel must evolve in response to emerging trends and innovations to ensure it remains effective and efficient. This subchapter will explore the key technological shifts on the horizon that are likely to impact the Linux kernel profoundly, from advancements in hardware to the changing nature of software development and deployment methods.

One significant shift to anticipate is the increasing use of artificial intelligence (AI) and machine learning (ML) across various applications. The demand for more intelligent, efficient systems calls for enhancements in the kernel that facilitate the seamless integration of AI workloads. Future iterations of the Linux kernel may see the incorporation of specialized modules specifically designed to handle machine learning tasks more effectively. For instance, optimizing memory management for AI models and providing rapid APIs for accessing hardware accelerators (like GPUs and TPUs) will be essential for enabling high-performance AI processing. This integration will not only improve the performance of AI applications running on the Linux kernel but will also solidify its position as a platform for data-intensive workloads.

Another anticipated technological shift is the continued growth of the Internet of Things (IoT). As IoT devices proliferate, the need for Linux to provide robust support for a vast array of connected devices becomes critical. The kernel must evolve to manage the resource constraints typical of embedded environments while maintaining security and reliability. Future developments may include enhancements to power management strategies, improving how the kernel operates in low-power modes, and ensuring efficient communication in environments with numerous interconnected devices. By adopting these enhancements, the Linux kernel can better serve the growing number of IoT applications that demand quick response times and minimal latency.

The rise of cloud computing also necessitates a shift in the Linux kernel's architecture and capabilities. As organizations increasingly adopt hybrid and multi-cloud strategies, the kernel must adapt to ensure that it can effectively manage resources and workloads across various cloud environments. This could mean integrating features that allow for dynamic resource allocation, enhancing scheduler algorithms to improve workload distribution, and ensuring compatibility with cloud-native technologies such as container orchestration platforms. Continuous improvements in the kernel's ability to support cloud infrastructures will bolster its relevance in enterprise computing, enabling organizations to achieve greater scalability and flexibility.

In addition to cloud computing, the kernel will likely need to incorporate advancements in security technologies. As cyber threats become more sophisticated and pervasive, the Linux kernel must evolve to adapt to newly identified vulnerabilities and attacks. This may involve implementing enhanced cryptographic protocols, improving intrusion detection and prevention capabilities, and ensuring rigorous access controls are enforced at multiple levels. By actively prioritizing security, the kernel can protect itself from potential exploits and maintain trust within its community of users.

Furthermore, the shifting landscape of software development practices, such as the rise of DevOps and continuous integration/deployment (CI/CD), will influence how the Linux kernel is developed and maintained. As these practices gain traction, the kernel must adapt to support faster and more efficient development cycles—integrating with emerging tools and methodologies to streamline the contribution and review process. This can include enhanced testing frameworks that automate the validation of patches, enabling developers to focus on innovation while ensuring the continued quality of the kernel.

As the kernel embarks on this evolution, maintaining an inclusive and collaborative community remains essential. The Linux kernel community has long embraced diversity and inclusion, and this ethos must continue to be cultivated as new contributors join. By creating an open and welcoming environment for contributors from all backgrounds, the Linux kernel will benefit from a broader range of perspectives, bolstering innovation and creative problem-solving.

In summary, anticipating technological shifts is fundamental to the future of the Linux kernel. By embracing advancements in artificial intelligence, preparing for the demands of IoT, adapting to cloud computing trends, enhancing security protocols, and leveraging evolving software development practices, the Linux kernel can ensure its continued relevance and authority in the technological landscape. The collaborative efforts of the kernel community will play a significant role in navigating these changes, fostering an inclusive environment where innovation thrives and bolstering the Linux kernel's status as a cornerstone of modern computing. As we look forward, the kernel's journey continues, driven by adaptability and resilience in the face of change.

19. Community and Culture: The Human Side of Kernel Development

19.1. Diversity and Inclusion in Kernel Development

Diversity and inclusion are critical components in the development of the Linux kernel, significantly influencing its culture, community dynamics, and overall progress. The kernel's evolution over the years has underscored the necessity of welcoming diverse perspectives and experiences from contributors, as these differences bolster creativity, problem-solving, and ultimately, technological innovation.

For the Linux kernel to thrive in an increasingly complex technological landscape, it must engage with a broad range of contributors from various backgrounds, including gender, ethnicity, nationality, and socioeconomic status. Achieving diversity in kernel development ensures that the varied needs of users and enterprises are reflected in the features, performance, and functionality of the kernel itself. These diverse contributions enrich the development process, leading to resilient solutions that cater to a wider audience.

To foster diversity and inclusion effectively, the Linux kernel community has implemented several initiatives aimed at engaging underrepresented groups in technology. Outreach efforts, mentorship programs, and targeted training opportunities have become integral to the kernel community's endeavors. Programs such as the Outreachy internship, which offers opportunities for underrepresented groups to contribute to open-source projects, provide a pathway for newcomers to enter the kernel development space. By connecting aspiring developers with experienced mentors, the community not only builds talent but also cultivates an environment that values diverse experiences.

Moreover, conferences and workshops play a significant role in enhancing diversity within the kernel development ecosystem. Events such as the Linux Kernel Summit and other open-source conferences serve as platforms for knowledge exchange, networking, and collaboration among developers from around the world. Organizing sessions that focus on diversity and inclusion can help raise awareness, share best practices, and inspire community-led initiatives that improve engagement. Encouraging the participation of speakers and contributors from diverse backgrounds enriches discourse and promotes the notion that a broad array of perspectives enhances the kernel community.

Open communication channels are essential in establishing an inclusive community in kernel development. The kernel mailing list acts as a central hub for discussion, feedback, and collaboration. By fostering respectful and constructive dialogue, the community can cultivate an atmosphere that empowers contributors to voice their observations and engage with others. Respectful communication encourages collaboration, strengthens relationships, and builds trust across developers, ultimately benefitting everyone involved.

Additionally, the leadership and mentorship roles within the Linux kernel community are crucial for guiding new contributors and fostering inclusivity. Experienced developers who engage in mentoring can help newcomers navigate the complexities of kernel development, offering guidance on coding standards, community dynamics, and technical challenges. By empowering mentors to take on these roles, the community fosters a culture of sharing knowledge that can inspire and encourage underrepresented groups to persist in their development journeys.

The evolution of developer communities lies at the heart of diversity and inclusion efforts. Traditional notions of community are shifting, with increased connectivity facilitated by online platforms and communication tools. These platforms enable individuals to form bonds based on shared interests, ideas, and passion for technology, rather than being constrained by geographical limitations. This shift creates opportunities for inclusive dialogue where developers can collaborate on projects regardless of their locations or backgrounds, providing even more insights and approaches to kernel development.

Despite the progress made thus far, the Linux kernel community acknowledges that diversity and inclusion initiatives are ongoing commitments rather than one-off endeavors. Continued engagement, assessment of community practices, and adaptation to emerging challenges will help ensure that diversity remains integral to kernel development. This commitment will lead to innovative solutions, increased participation, and a kernel community that truly represents the richness of its user base.

In summary, diversity and inclusion in kernel development are essential elements that shape the community, culture, and progress of the Linux kernel. Emphasizing a broad engagement approach through outreach initiatives, mentorship programs, community-led events, and open communication channels fosters a space where developers from various backgrounds can thrive. By continuing to prioritize diversity, the Linux kernel will evolve into a more resilient, innovative, and inclusive foundation, capable of meeting the challenges of an increasingly interconnected and diverse technological landscape. As the kernel community continually adapts to these dynamics, it reaffirms its commitment to inclusivity and, thereby, strengthens its role as a leader within the open-source ecosystem.

19.2. The Role of Conferences and Workshops

The role of conferences and workshops in the Linux kernel ecosystem is paramount, serving as a vital nexus for knowledge exchange, collaboration, and community building. These gatherings provide developers, maintainers, and users with opportunities to share insights, discuss ongoing projects, and explore innovations in kernel development. Emphasizing the importance of face-to-face interactions, conferences and workshops contribute significantly to the vibrancy and dynamism of the Linux kernel community.

Conferences such as the Linux Plumbers Conference and the Linux Kernel Summit bring together key contributors and experts in various kernel subsystems, fostering in-depth discussions that shape the future of the kernel. These events allow attendees to delve deep into technical topics, whether they concern performance optimizations, security enhancements, or advances in virtualization and container technology. Participants can present their work, garner feedback from peers, and engage in collaborative problem-solving, leading to tangible improvements in kernel development practices.

In addition to formal presentations, conferences provide workshops as conduits for hands-on experience and learning. These interactive sessions enable attendees to engage directly with the kernel, offering practical experience in tasks such as patch submission, debugging techniques, and code reviews. Workshops create an environment of mentorship, whereby experienced developers can guide newcomers and encourage their active participation in the kernel community. This apprenticeship model is particularly valuable in cultivating the next generation of kernel developers, ensuring knowledge continuity and fostering inclusivity.

Open communication channels are a cornerstone of effective collaboration within the Linux kernel community. Mailing lists, forums, and real-time chat platforms facilitate discussions that extend beyond coding practices. These channels allow developers to voice concerns, seek guidance, and share achievements, ultimately enhancing community engagement and solidarity. The Linux kernel mailing list, in particular, serves as a dynamic forum for discussing patches, soliciting feedback, and addressing technical challenges.

Maintainers play an integral role in these communication channels, guiding discussions and ensuring that correspondence remains productive and focused on kernel advancement. By fostering a culture of respect and constructive dialogue, maintainers empower contributors —both new and experienced—to participate meaningfully in discussions surrounding kernel features and development processes.

As kernel development evolves, embracing leadership and mentorship roles within the community becomes increasingly crucial. Experienced developers are encouraged to take on mentorship roles, guiding newcomers through the complexities of kernel contributions, improving collaboration and knowledge sharing. Mentorship fosters a culture of inclusivity and support, allowing underrepresented groups to gain confidence and contribute to kernel development actively.

Another notable pattern within the Linux kernel community is the continual evolution of developer communities. The rise of online collaboration tools has transformed the landscape, connecting developers across geographical barriers. This connectivity promotes diversity, allowing individuals from various backgrounds to engage with the kernel community. Open-source development fosters collaboration not only on a technical level but also in establishing a shared culture of knowledge exchange and innovation.

In conclusion, the role of conferences and workshops, alongside open communication channels, mentorship initiatives, and adaptive community engagement, shapes the future trajectory of Linux kernel development. By fostering a collaborative spirit, these gatherings ensure that the community remains vibrant, innovative, and inclusive, laying the groundwork for ongoing success in navigating the complexities of kernel development. The road ahead is bright, driven by a commitment to advancing the Linux kernel through shared knowledge, creativity, and cooperative problem-solving.

Upcoming features and enhancements are anticipated to shape the future of the Linux kernel, ensuring its continued relevance and performance as technology evolves. With contributions from a diverse community of developers, the kernel is poised to integrate myriad advancements aimed at improving functionality and expanding its capabilities. As we look ahead, several key areas of focus stand out, reflecting the community's commitment to innovation and responsiveness to emerging trends.

One area expected to see significant enhancements is the integration of machine learning into the kernel ecosystem. As AI applications become increasingly prevalent, kernel developers will explore ways to leverage machine learning frameworks, enabling intelligent decision-making in resource allocation, predictive analysis for workload management, and enhanced security mechanisms. This integration aims to optimize performance across various workloads, ultimately elevating the kernel's capabilities in supporting complex applications that require real-time reactions to changing conditions.

Another focal point for upcoming enhancements is the ongoing refinement of security measures within the kernel. As cyber threats become more sophisticated, there is a pressing need for evolved security protocols that safeguard system integrity. Anticipated enhancements may involve implementing advanced cryptographic algorithms and enabling hardware-based security features, ensuring that the kernel can proactively defend against vulnerabilities and attacks.

As the landscape of cloud computing and containerization continues to grow, the kernel will also reflect these advancements through enhanced integration features. Upcoming improvements are expected to optimize container performance, provide seamless orchestration capabilities, and support new containerization technologies as they emerge in response to industry demand. The kernel will foster efficient resource management practices tailored to cloud-native computing, ensuring that organizations can leverage the full power of distributed infrastructures.

Long-Term Support (LTS) versions of the Linux kernel will continue to receive focus, ensuring stability and reliability for enterprise environments. The community's commitment to maintaining LTS releases will be crucial in ensuring consistent updates, security patches, and feature enhancements for organizations that depend on the stability of the kernel. This sustained support aligns with the growing demand for dependable, production-ready environments within various sectors.

Exploration of uncharted territories in kernel development may encompass innovative approaches to hardware interfaces, novel programming paradigms, and advanced resource management techniques. Developers will likely seek ways to refine system calls, improve interoperability between hardware and software implementations, and enhance kernel architecture to support the growing complexities of modern applications.

Sustainability in development practices will take precedence as the kernel grows, particularly in adhering to open-source principles and promoting collaborative contributions. The Linux community is committed to inclusivity, ensuring that diverse voices are engaged in the development process. Addressing potential challenges related to resource constraints, knowledge sharing, and community cohesion will be vital for maintaining the kernel's adaptability and relevance.

Finally, the vision for the next decade of kernel innovation rests on the community's ability to navigate and embrace these changes. By emphasizing collaboration, harnessing advancements in technology, and remaining responsive to user needs, the Linux kernel will secure its position as a leading platform for a wide array of applications. This vision encompasses a commitment to ongoing growth, ensuring that the kernel continues to evolve and thrive in an ever-changing technological landscape.

In conclusion, the Linux kernel stands poised for a bright future, driven by a commitment to innovation, collaboration, and adaptability. The anticipated features, enhancements, and community engagement efforts will shape its trajectory, ensuring that it remains a robust framework capable of meeting the demands of modern computing environments. As the kernel community unites around these shared goals, the roadmap to future success will reflect an ongoing dedication to excellence, inclusivity, and technological advancement.

19.3. Open Communication Channels

Open communication channels play a pivotal role in the Linux kernel ecosystem, facilitating collaboration, knowledge sharing, and continuous improvement among contributors, maintainers, and users. These channels create a dynamic environment where developers can discuss ideas, resolve issues, and drive the kernel forward. Understanding the mechanisms of effective communication within the

Linux kernel community is crucial for anyone interested in participating in this vibrant collective effort.

At the heart of the communication process is the Linux Kernel Mailing List (LKML), one of the most critical platforms for discussions among kernel developers. The LKML serves as a centralized forum where developers can submit patches, share insights, and engage in discussions about kernel features and changes. It is a place for collaboration and criticism, where contributors are encouraged to provide and receive feedback on proposed changes. The mailing list culture emphasizes clarity and conciseness—devotees should articulate their ideas clearly and present their contributions in a respectful manner, recognizing the expertise and perspectives of others.

Using the LKML effectively requires familiarity with the mailing list's etiquette. Best practices for communication include providing comprehensive patch descriptions, stating clear objectives, summarizing the rationale behind contributions, and engaging with new ideas in an open-minded manner. This supportive environment fosters constructive dialogue, encouraging contributors to refine their work based on peer feedback and ensuring the continuous evolution of the kernel.

In addition to LKML, the Linux kernel community employs other communication platforms to enhance collaboration. Online forums, chat applications like IRC or Discord, and dedicated platforms for hosting discussions (such as GitHub) are utilized to facilitate real-time interaction and knowledge sharing. These tools enable developers to engage in prompt discussions, explore troubleshooting methods, and collectively solve challenges, enriching the sense of community among contributors.

Documentation serves as another critical open communication channel within the kernel ecosystem. The Linux kernel emphasizes detailed documentation practices, which outline coding standards, development processes, and features to guide contributors. Maintaining comprehensive and up-to-date documentation is vital for enhancing overall understanding and accessibility of kernel internals for newcomers, facilitating their contributions and experiences efficiently.

Moreover, the kernel community actively engages with conferences and workshops, which provide valuable opportunities for face-to-face interactions among developers. Events like the Linux Kernel Summit and Linux Plumbers Conference allow contributors to present their work, share insights, and foster collaboration in a more personal setting. These gatherings strengthen relationships within the kernel community, leading to improved cooperation, mentorship opportunities, and the potential for long-term collaborations.

Community outreach initiatives also contribute to open communication channels within the Linux kernel ecosystem. These initiatives aim to attract developers from diverse backgrounds, encouraging contributions and participation from underrepresented groups within the tech community. Programs such as internships and mentorships facilitate different individuals to engage with kernel development, expanding the pool of knowledge and experience within the community.

To ensure effective communication channels, the kernel community must also consider the implications of different cultural contexts and language diversity. As the community expands globally, facilitators must be observed to encourage respectful and inclusive interactions. Providing resources that accommodate language barriers, inviting participation from various cultures, and maintaining an open-minded approach to different perspectives enhance the kernel's collaborative spirit.

In conclusion, open communication channels are vital to the success and dynamism of the Linux kernel ecosystem. By utilizing mailing lists, forums, conferences, and mentorship initiatives, contributors continue to foster collaboration and knowledge exchange, driving kernel development forward. Understanding and adhering to the best practices of communication within this community not only enhances individual contributions but also enriches the collaborative culture, ensuring robust and effective kernel operations in the ever-evolving landscape of technology.

19.4. Leadership and Mentorship Roles

Leadership and mentorship roles play a pivotal part in the success and evolution of the Linux kernel community. As a collaborative open-source project, the Linux kernel depends not only on the technical contributions of its developers but also on the ability of leaders to facilitate communication, provide guidance, and foster an inclusive environment that encourages knowledge sharing and growth. This section delves into the critical aspects of leadership and mentorship roles within the kernel community, highlighting how these dynamics shape the ongoing development and sustainability of this vital open-source project.

At the heart of effective leadership in the Linux kernel community lies the ability to inspire and mobilize contributors around a shared vision. Kernel maintainers are often seen as authoritative figures within their respective subsystems, responsible for guiding the development and integration of patches. These maintainers play a crucial role in setting priorities, reviewing contributions, and ensuring that the codebase adheres to established quality and functionality standards. As such, they are tasked with not only making technical decisions but also nurturing a collaborative culture wherein contributors feel valued and encouraged to participate.

Mentoring is a fundamental responsibility of leaders within the kernel community. As new developers join the project, they often encounter a steep learning curve, grappling with the complexities of kernel code, development practices, and community dynamics. Experienced contributors have a unique opportunity to guide newcomers through this journey, offering insights into best practices, coding standards, and the intricacies of kernel internals. By establishing a mentorship framework, leaders can empower newer contributors to develop their skills, facilitating their transition into active contributors who contribute meaningfully to the kernel's evolution.

Effective leadership within the Linux kernel community also emphasizes fostering diversity and inclusivity. As the community expands, attracting participants from various backgrounds is essential for driving innovation and ensuring the kernel remains relevant for a diverse user base. Leaders are encouraged to create welcoming environments that promote engagement from underrepresented groups in technology, establishing outreach programs and initiatives aimed at connecting with a broader audience. By championing diversity, leaders can help cultivate a culture of respect and understanding, enhancing the kernel's capacity for growth and adaptation.

Furthermore, leaders within the community must be strategic in navigating the complexities of collaboration. The Linux kernel's breadth means that contributions may come from various organizations, companies, and independent developers. Maintaining open communication channels is vital in managing these relationships effectively. Leaders can facilitate discussions through mailing lists, forums, and conferences, ensuring that contributors feel comfortable sharing their ideas. Creating an atmosphere of transparency encourages constructive feedback and fosters collaborative problem-solving, which ultimately strengthens the community.

As technology evolves, the role of leadership must also adapt to accommodate emerging trends. Leaders within the kernel community should remain abreast of innovations in fields like cloud computing, IoT, artificial intelligence, and containerization. Anticipating these trends allows them to guide the community toward focusing on necessary skill sets and areas of investment, ensuring that the Linux kernel remains a robust and adaptable foundation for future technologies.

The impact of mentorship extends beyond individual contributors to the kernel community as a whole. Cultivating mentors within the community can create a ripple effect, where mentees become mentors in turn, perpetuating a cycle of knowledge transfer and skill development. This succession planning helps ensure that the Linux kernel remains resilient and continues to attract new talent while nurturing the next generation of kernel developers.

In summary, leadership and mentorship roles within the Linux kernel community are instrumental in fostering a collaborative, inclusive, and innovative environment. By guiding new contributors, promoting diversity, establishing effective communication channels, and adapting to emerging technological trends, leaders play a critical role in the kernel's growth and sustainability. The commitment to mentorship not only elevates the skills of individual contributors but also strengthens the collective resilience of the Linux kernel community, ensuring it thrives in the ever-evolving landscape of technology. The future of the Linux kernel relies on these robust leadership dynamics, which will continue to shape its trajectory and impact on the computing world.

19.5. Evolution of Developer Communities

In the rapidly advancing field of computing, the Linux kernel stands at the forefront, constantly evolving to meet the needs of modern technology. Its journey has been characterized by collaboration, innovation, and a steadfast commitment to quality. As we look to the future, the kernel is set to embrace a myriad of upcoming features and enhancements, ensuring its relevance and adaptability in the face of change.

One of the most significant areas of focus is the continued integration of artificial intelligence (AI) and machine learning (ML) capabilities within the kernel. The demand for intelligent processing will likely drive the kernel to incorporate dedicated modules and support for AI algorithms, facilitating efficient execution of ML models. By enabling predictive resource allocation and optimized scheduling, the kernel can elevate application performance while responding to emerging demands in real time.

Another critical enhancement expected in the kernel is the evolution of security features. As cyber threats continue to escalate, the importance of proactive security measures cannot be overstated. The Linux

kernel will likely see significant advancements in its security protocols, including enhanced support for encryption, more sophisticated
intrusion detection mechanisms, and improved frameworks such as
SELinux and AppArmor to enforce robust security boundaries. This
focus on security will be essential for protecting sensitive data,
particularly as industries increasingly rely on cloud computing and
containerization.

Long-term support (LTS) for kernel versions remains a cornerstone
of the Linux kernel's sustainability. The commitment to ensuring that
specific kernel versions receive timely updates, bug fixes, and security
patches is vital for organizations relying on stable environments.
The LTS framework will continue to address the evolving needs and
expectations of enterprise users, ensuring they maintain reliable and
secure systems powered by the Linux kernel.

The exploration of uncharted territories in kernel development will
also be a key driver for future innovation. With advancements in
quantum computing, blockchain technology, and decentralized architectures promising to redefine the landscape, the Linux kernel will
need to adapt to support these emerging paradigms. Integrating features that facilitate interaction with distributed systems or optimize
performance for quantum applications will encourage the kernel to
remain relevant and resilient in these new technological frontiers.

Sustainability in development practices will play an increasingly vital
role in shaping the future trajectory of the Linux kernel. As the demands for environmentally friendly technology intensify, the kernel
community must prioritize resource optimization, including energy-
efficient operations. This adaptation will require kernel developers to
embrace strategies that minimize resource consumption and promote
energy-conscious computing.

As we anticipate the next decade of kernel innovation, a collaborative community emerges as the driving force behind ongoing
advancements. Encouraging inclusivity and diversity in developer
engagement will foster a rich ecosystem that nurtures creativity and

supports the continuous growth of the kernel. Initiatives designed to mentor new contributors and bolster their involvement in the community will ensure a sustainable pipeline of innovation.

In conclusion, the road ahead for the Linux kernel is filled with exciting upcoming features and enhancements. By integrating artificial intelligence, advancing security measures, ensuring long-term support, exploring uncharted territories, committing to sustainable practices, and fostering a collaborative community, the kernel is poised to remain a foundational technology in the ever-changing landscape of computing. The collective effort of the Linux community will shape the future of the kernel, ensuring that it continues to thrive as a versatile and innovative operating system for years to come.

20. The Road Ahead: Expected Milestones and Future of the Linux Kernel

20.1. Upcoming Features and Enhancements

In the Linux kernel ecosystem, the road ahead is marked by an exciting trajectory of anticipated milestones and emerging enhancements that are set to redefine its capabilities. As the technology landscape evolves, the Linux kernel must adapt to meet these changing demands, ensuring it remains a robust and versatile platform for an array of applications. This section explores the expected milestones and the future trajectory of the Linux kernel, highlighting key areas of focus and the community's commitment to innovation.

One of the most significant upcoming features is the integration of advanced artificial intelligence and machine learning capabilities within the kernel. As AI technologies gain traction across various industries, the kernel is expected to incorporate dedicated modules that optimize the execution of machine learning models. These integrations would involve the kernel intelligently managing computational resources, allowing for effective predictive analytics and real-time data processing. The aim is to enhance system responsiveness while making efficient use of available hardware.

Security is another focal point in the kernel's future enhancements. As cyber threats grow in sophistication, the kernel community recognizes the urgency of bolstering security protocols. Upcoming features may include more robust implementations of encryption, improved intrusion detection mechanisms, and advanced frameworks such as SELinux and AppArmor to enforce stringent security measures. With a heightened focus on data privacy and protection, the Linux kernel is set to stay ahead of potential vulnerabilities, ensuring that it remains a trusted environment for users and enterprises.

Long-term support (LTS) continues to form a crucial part of the Linux kernel's sustainability, with expected milestones focused on ensuring that certain kernel versions receive timely updates and security patches. This framework caters to enterprises relying on stable systems for continuous operations and underscores the community's commitment to maintaining long-term health and reliability for critical infrastructure.

The kernel is also poised to explore uncharted territories marked by emerging technologies, including quantum computing and decentralized systems like blockchain. As these areas evolve, the kernel's ability to support new paradigms will be essential. Upcoming enhancements might include tools for managing decentralized applications, compatibility with new hardware architectures, and performance optimizations that leverage advancements in quantum processing. Adapting to these novel domains will require a forward-thinking approach and a willingness to embrace transformative technologies.

Sustainability in development practices will be paramount as the Linux kernel community seeks to lead by example in environmental stewardship. As concerns regarding energy consumption and carbon footprints increase, the kernel must adapt its operational strategies to minimize resource usage. Focusing on energy-efficient operations, optimizing the use of hardware resources, and implementing power management strategies are all avenues expected to gain traction. The commitment to sustainability underscores the kernel's role not only as a technological leader but as a responsible steward of resources in an increasingly eco-conscious world.

Moreover, the vision for the next decade of kernel innovation emphasizes community engagement and collaboration. As the landscape of contributors evolves, ensuring a diverse and inclusive environment will be vital for fostering creativity and driving progress. Initiatives aimed at mentorship, community outreach, and shared knowledge will continue to promote the growth of the Linux ecosystem, facilitating the entry of new developers and enhancing the sustainability of the project.

In many ways, the Linux kernel exemplifies the spirit of open-source development—one built on collaboration, shared knowledge, and continuous improvement. The anticipated features, long-term support, exploration of new frontiers, sustainable practices, and the commitment to fostering a diverse community collectively herald a promising future for the Linux kernel. As it navigates the challenges and opportunities that lie ahead, the kernel will continue to evolve as an indispensable foundation for modern computing, ensuring its place as a vital technology in the lives of users around the world.

20.2. Long-Term Support and Maintenance

In the rapidly evolving field of technology, the principles of long-term support and maintenance for the Linux kernel are pivotal in ensuring its continued functionality, reliability, and performance over time. The Linux kernel serves as the backbone for a multitude of systems— ranging from personal computers and servers to embedded systems —and its long-term viability is critical for managing the complexities of modern computing environments. This section will explore the significance of long-term support (LTS), the maintenance mechanisms involved, and the impact these practices have on the broader Linux ecosystem.

Long-term support primarily focuses on delivering a stable and secure version of the Linux kernel that receives continuous updates, including security patches, bug fixes, and feature enhancements over an extended period. The concept of LTS is particularly important for organizations and users who rely on the kernel for mission-critical applications, as these environments demand stability without the disruptive overhead of frequent updates or version migrations. An LTS kernel can provide the assurance that it will operate securely and reliably, allowing users to plan effectively and allocate resources carefully.

The Linux kernel community has established several versions designated as LTS, with maintainers committed to providing support for those versions for years after their initial release. This commitment includes actively monitoring the LTS kernels, addressing reported issues, and responding to vulnerabilities that may emerge over time. A dedicated team of maintainers is tasked with overseeing LTS releases, ensuring that users receive timely updates and maintaining the overall integrity of the kernel.

Maintenance mechanisms associated with long-term support encompass various activities, including comprehensive testing, quality assurance, and regression testing. Each update or patch released for the LTS kernel undergoes rigorous testing processes to validate that it does not introduce new issues or negatively impact existing functionality. The community employs automated testing frameworks, such as KernelCI and continuous integration tools, to streamline this process and enhance confidence in the reliability of kernel updates. These testing routines will verify that new patches function correctly across myriad hardware configurations and scenarios, further ensuring long-term stability.

The focus on security in long-term support is of paramount importance. LTS kernels receive prompt attention to vulnerabilities, with security advisories released as soon as possible after a vulnerability is identified. This proactive approach is essential for maintaining system integrity, especially given the growing emphasis on security in modern computing. Regular security monitoring, patch releases, and engagement with the community ensure that the LTS kernel remains secure and resilient against emerging threats.

Documentation plays an essential role in the success of long-term support projects. Clear and comprehensive documentation for LTS kernels helps users navigate updates, understand new features and adjustments, and ensures that system administrators are well-informed about any changes that could impact their environments. Maintaining up-to-date documentation fosters a culture of transparency, enabling users to adapt quickly while reducing the likelihood of issues arising from misconfigurations.

As the landscape of technology continues to evolve, sustainability in development practices has become a critical area of focus within the kernel community. Adopting sustainable practices ensures that the kernel remains viable in an ever-changing environment that increasingly emphasizes environmental stewardship and resource management. Sustainability extends beyond energy efficiency; it encompasses a commitment to maintaining code quality, enhancing performance, and fostering community engagement to ensure that future developers can continue building on the established foundation.

Exploring uncharted territories is another exciting aspect of long-term support in the Linux kernel, particularly as new technologies and paradigms emerge. The kernel community must remain agile and open to adopting new features and optimizing existing functionalities to ensure that the kernel can adapt to developments in areas like cloud computing, AI, and IoT. This exploration involves collaboration across various disciplines, encouraging contributions from developers with diverse backgrounds and expertise, ultimately enriching the kernel's capabilities.

Finally, as advancements proliferate across the technological spectrum, the vision for the next decade of kernel innovation must remain forward-looking and proactive. By prioritizing long-term support and maintenance, fostering sustainable practices, and engaging with emerging trends, the Linux kernel will continue to secure its position as a leading choice for both traditional applications and new, innovative solutions. The commitment to excellence, collaboration, and a strong community ethos will shape the future of the kernel, empowering it to meet the ever-increasing demands of modern computing.

In conclusion, long-term support and maintenance for the Linux kernel are essential elements that ensure its ongoing viability and reliability over time. By embracing testing, security measures, collaborations, and sustainability practices, the kernel community reinforces its commitment to delivering a robust platform that meets users' evolving needs. As technology continues to advance, the principles of long-term support and maintenance will remain paramount in shaping the trajectory of the Linux kernel, ensuring its continued relevance in an increasingly complex and interconnected world.

20.3. Exploration of Uncharted Territories

In the rapidly evolving world of technology, the Linux kernel has become a fundamental component that supports a diverse range of systems—from personal computers to critical embedded devices. The path forward is filled with opportunities and challenges, requiring ongoing exploration and refinement. The exploration of uncharted territories in kernel development is crucial for unlocking the full potential of this powerful platform. This section will delve into various aspects of this exploration, focusing on emerging trends, innovative practices, and the continuous journey toward enhancing kernel capabilities.

One area of significant exploration is the continued integration of artificial intelligence (AI) and machine learning (ML) technologies within the kernel. As these technologies permeate more industries, they're leading to a demand for kernels capable of supporting AI-driven applications. Developers are actively investigating methods for integrating machine learning frameworks with kernel functionalities, aiming to optimize workflows and processing efficiencies. By enabling the kernel to manage AI workloads, developers can leverage its robust resource management capabilities to enhance the efficiency of data processing and decision-making.

Furthermore, the kernel community is committed to exploring enhancements in security measures. As the landscape of cyber threats evolves, so too must the approaches used to safeguard the kernel and its applications. This exploration involves adopting innovative practices, including real-time monitoring of system behaviors to detect anomalies or threats, as well as integrating advanced cryptographic solutions to protect data integrity and confidentiality.

The rapid rise of Internet of Things (IoT) technology presents another exciting frontier for exploration. Integrating real-time capabilities into the Linux kernel allows it to efficiently manage the constraints posed by numerous low-power, resource-constrained devices. The community is working to ensure the kernel not only can support the massive influx of IoT devices but also intelligently allocate resources and optimize performance, demonstrating the kernel's adaptability to meet the demands of modern applications.

Addressing the challenges posed by containerization is also an area of ongoing exploration. As organizations increasingly leverage containerized applications for their agility, the need for the kernel to integrate seamlessly with container orchestration platforms—such as Kubernetes—becomes more pronounced. Kernel developers are focused on enhancing system calls, resource management, and networking configurations, to ensure that containerized applications run optimally in various environments.

Sustainability isn't just a trend; it's becoming a core principle in kernel development practices. The commitment to reducing environmental impact drives the exploration of energy-efficient technologies and coding practices. By developing kernels that minimize power consumption and resource usage, the community addresses the growing concerns regarding the ecological footprint of computing. This sustainability effort emphasizes optimizing power management techniques and exploring advancements in low-power computing for embedded devices.

As technology continues to advance, the vision for the next decade of kernel innovation is critical for ensuring that the Linux kernel remains at the forefront of open-source development. The kernel community recognizes the importance of welcoming contributions from diverse developers, including those from underrepresented groups, to enrich the development process and broaden perspectives. By cultivating a culture of inclusivity and shared responsibility, the kernel community fosters an environment conducive to innovation and growth.

Moreover, ongoing education and mentorship initiatives play a key role in shaping the future of kernel development. By engaging newcomers and providing resources for skill development, the community can ensure a sustainable pipeline of talent. These efforts help to build a diverse ecosystem of contributors who can continue the legacy of the Linux kernel, adapting to new challenges and opportunities as they arise.

In conclusion, the exploration of uncharted territories in kernel development promises continued innovation and advancement. By embracing emerging technologies, enhancing security measures, supporting IoT expansion, optimizing performance for containerization, committing to sustainability, and fostering inclusivity within the community, the Linux kernel stands firmly poised for a vibrant future. As developers embark on this journey of exploration, the ongoing collaboration and shared vision will undoubtedly shape the landscape of Linux kernel development, paving the way for new applications and solutions that meet the demands of modern computing.

20.4. Sustainability in Development Practices

In today's technologically driven world, where the Linux kernel serves as the backbone for millions of systems globally, sustainability in development practices is crucial for the long-term viability and health of both the kernel itself and the ecosystem surrounding it. As the community behind the Linux kernel continues to expand and diversify, it becomes imperative to focus on sustainable practices that prioritize resource efficiency, collaborative efforts, and the responsible management of human and technological resources. This section will illuminate the principles and practices associated with sustainability in kernel development, emphasizing their importance in ensuring that the Linux kernel remains a relevant and adaptable platform for future innovations.

Sustainability in development practices begins with the understanding of resource management across various dimensions—be it computational resources, human talent, or environmental considerations. One of the foundational elements of sustainability is optimizing the kernel's codebase to reduce its resource footprint. By adopting efficient coding practices, developers can minimize the use of CPU cycles, memory, and storage, ensuring that the kernel performs optimally across diverse hardware configurations. This is particularly vital for embedded systems and mobile devices, where resource constraints necessitate careful coding and profiling to deliver the best possible performance while conserving energy.

In addition to optimizing code, sustainability also involves the lifecycle management of contributions to the kernel. Maintaining a clear pattern of version control, documentation, and patching practices ensures that the kernel remains manageable and comprehensible over time. Implementing processes for continuous integration ensures that new contributions are tested rigorously and integrated smoothly, reducing the risk of introducing regressions or undesirable consequences.

Moreover, fostering a culture of collaboration within the Linux kernel community is essential for building a sustainable ecosystem. The kernel thrives on diverse contributions from individuals and organizations alike, reinforcing the notion that a collaborative spirit drives innovation. By actively engaging in mentoring programs and outreach initiatives, the community can guide new contributors, creating an inclusive atmosphere where shared knowledge leads to better development practices. This continued emphasis on diversity and inclusivity not only enhances the pool of talent within the kernel community but also encourages fresh perspectives on problem-solving and innovation.

Sustainability extends into community engagement, where discussions surrounding the future of the kernel must also encompass the principles of ethical technology adoption. As the demand for innovative solutions rises—particularly in areas such as cloud computing, artificial intelligence, and the Internet of Things—an ethical approach is necessary to ensure that the kernel serves the greater good without compromising user privacy or safety. Engaging in transparent discussions around the impact of technology, its implications for society, and the kernel's role in promoting responsible computing will solidify the kernel's standing as a leader in ethical technology development.

The Linux kernel's community must be proactive in addressing environmental sustainability as well. With significant attention on minimizing the carbon footprint and energy consumption of computing systems, the kernel can play an influential role by driving resource-efficient practices within the wider ecosystem. Optimizing power management strategies, implementing energy-efficient protocols, and contributing to green technologies can significantly reduce the environmental impact of systems relying on the Linux kernel. As developers embrace this responsibility, they can work collaboratively to ensure that sustainability becomes an integral aspect of kernel development.

Finally, the vision for the next decade of kernel innovation hinges on the community's ability to remain agile and responsive to emerging trends and challenges. The ongoing exploration of uncharted territories, such as quantum computing, blockchain, and machine learning applications, should be pursued with sustainability principles in mind. Aligning research and development efforts with sustainable practices will not only ensure the kernel's adaptability to new technologies but also solidify its role as the foundation for resilient, high-performance applications poised for future success.

In conclusion, the integration of sustainability into development practices within the Linux kernel ecosystem is crucial for fostering long-term viability and adaptability. From optimizing resource management and maintaining clear documentation to promoting inclusivity and addressing environmental considerations, the community's commitment to sustainability enhances the kernel's resilience in the face of evolving challenges. As technology continues to advance, the focus on sustainability principles will pave the way for innovative solutions, positioning the Linux kernel as a leader in responsibly advancing modern computing.

The Linux kernel community is committed to fostering a vision for the next decade that emphasizes innovation, inclusivity, and adaptability to meet emerging technology demands while ensuring that sustainability becomes a core principle of its ongoing development efforts. The dedication to these principles will continue to shape the

Linux kernel's future, securing its role as a vital technology in the ever-changing landscape of computing.

20.5. Vision for the Next Decade of Kernel Innovation

As we stand at the precipice of the next decade of kernel innovation, the Linux kernel community is poised to embrace a vision that not only anticipates the demands of emerging technologies but also reinforces a commitment to collaboration, inclusivity, and sustainability. The dynamic nature of technology continues to evolve, presenting both challenges and opportunities that will undoubtedly shape the trajectory of the Linux kernel. This vision for the future encompasses several key focal points, outlining how the community plans to navigate the complexities of an interconnected world while empowering innovation and advancing the kernel's capabilities.

One of the foundational elements of this vision is the integration and enhancement of artificial intelligence (AI) and machine learning (ML) capabilities within the kernel. As AI technologies gain traction across various industries, the integration of machine learning algorithms into kernel functions will become increasingly vital. By embedding AI-driven resource management within the kernel, we can enable intelligent decision-making that optimizes performance based on real-time analysis of workload patterns. The kernel's ability to predict resource demands, automate scaling processes, and adapt to changing conditions will be instrumental in catering to the high-performance applications of the future.

Furthermore, as the Internet of Things (IoT) continues to proliferate, the kernel must adapt to support the diverse hardware configurations and operational constraints inherent to this ecosystem. Enhancements are expected in real-time capabilities, power management strategies, and efficient resource allocation mechanisms to ensure that the Linux kernel can respond promptly to the data generated by connected devices. As IoT applications demand close-to-real-time processing, the kernel's integration with edge computing will be pivotal, shifting compute power closer to the data source and reducing latency.

The importance of security within the Linux kernel will only amplify as technological threats become more sophisticated. The community envisions a future where state-of-the-art security mechanisms are embedded within the kernel architecture itself. The integration of advanced threat detection systems utilizing machine learning will enable the kernel to monitor for anomalies and potential breaches, implementing proactive measures to maintain system integrity. Continual collaboration with security experts and researchers will drive the development of rigorous security protocols that adapt to evolving challenges, ensuring that the kernel remains a reliable foundation for secure computing.

Cloud-native technologies and containerization will continue to influence the kernel's development practices. As organizations increasingly adopt hybrid and multi-cloud strategies, the kernel must support seamless interoperability with various cloud platforms and container orchestration tools. The community envisions the design of specific kernel features that cater to the unique needs of cloud-based applications, enabling efficient resource management, service discovery, and load balancing, which will be crucial in optimizing performance in distributed environments.

Sustainability will remain a core principle guiding kernel innovation in the coming decade. As the global focus on environmental responsibility intensifies, the Linux kernel must embody practices that prioritize energy efficiency and resource conservation. This entails refining power management strategies, optimizing system performance for lower energy consumption, and reducing the kernel's overall carbon footprint. Emphasizing sustainable practices will not only contribute to the environmental goals of the community but will also enhance the kernel's appeal to organizations seeking to adopt greener technologies.

The vision for the next decade also emphasizes the importance of diversity and inclusivity within the Linux kernel community. By fostering an environment that welcomes contributors from various backgrounds, the kernel can harness the collective creativity and diverse perspectives that drive innovation. Community-led initiatives aimed at mentorship, outreach, and supporting underrepresented groups will be critical in building a sustainable pipeline of talent, ensuring that the Linux kernel attracts and nurtures future contributors.

In addition, the exploration of uncharted territories will remain paramount. The kernel community must be proactive in investigating nascent technologies such as quantum computing, decentralized systems, and advanced networking protocols. By continually pushing the boundaries of what is possible, the Linux kernel can establish itself as a leading platform for future innovations, ensuring that it meets the demands posed by emerging scientific and technological advancements.

In conclusion, the vision for the next decade of kernel innovation is characterized by a commitment to integrating AI capabilities, adapting to IoT and edge computing demands, enhancing security measures, optimizing for cloud-native environments, embracing sustainability, fostering inclusivity, and exploring new technologies. The Linux kernel community's dedication to collaboration and innovation positions it for success, paving the way for a resilient, adaptable kernel that rises to meet the challenges of modern and future computing. As we enter this transformative era, the Linux kernel stands ready to evolve, ensuring its continued significance in the ever-changing digital landscape.

www.ingramcontent.com/pod-product-compliance
Lightning Source LLC
LaVergne TN
LVHW022338060326
832902LV00022B/4101